R E A D I N G
L E S S O N S

ALSO BY GERALD COLES

The Learning Mystique: A Critical Look at "Learning Disabilities"

READING

LESSONS

The Debate over Literacy

GERALD COLES

HILL AND WANG

A division of Farrar, Straus and Giroux / New York

Hill and Wang
A division of Farrar, Straus and Giroux
19 Union Square West, New York 10003

Copyright © 1998 by Gerald Coles
All rights reserved

Printed in the United States of America
Designed by Abby Kagan
First published in 1998 by Hill and Wang
First paperback edition, 1999

Library of Congress Cataloging-in-Publication Data
Coles, Gerald.
    Reading lessons : the debate over literacy / Gerald Coles. — 1st ed.
    p. cm.
    Includes bibliographical references and index
    ISBN 0-8090-8038-9 (pbk)
    1. Reading—United States. 2. Reading, Psychology of. 3. Reading—
Social aspects—United States. 4. Literacy—United States. I. Title.
LB1050.C574   1998
428'.4—dc21   97-35066

Grateful acknowledgment is made for permission to reprint the poetry
on page x. Denise Levertov: *Poems 1960–1967*. Copyright © 1966 by
Denise Levertov. Reprinted by permission of New Directions Publishing
Corporation

TO THE MOTHERS:

Lee Altfeder Coles
"Que sera, sera"

Giuseppina Iannacome
"Quando ti vuoi mozzicare il gomito, sarà troppo tardi"

CONTENTS

ACKNOWLEDGMENTS

My first job as a reading teacher was in Watts, Los Angeles, in 1967. My supervisor, a strong advocate of phonics instruction, insisted that I use an intensive phonics program, some of which required class recitation of consonant and vowel sounds. I complied, the students complied, but not long after beginning the program, the students would groan each time we started a lesson, and jokingly refer to the work as the "ab-dab-blab stuff." Fortunately, the supervisor's supervision was lax, and I was able to take cues from the students and change to a more participatory way of teaching and learning, related more to their interests and lives. We still used the "ab-dab-blab stuff," but only when it was directly pertinent to the students' reading problems—and for that purpose they came to appreciate knowing about ab, dab, and blab. Their interest and motivation increased, as did their learning—and as did my pleasure in teaching them. It is to these students I first want to express my gratitude because they first inspired me to teach—and learn how to teach—reading. These days I often think about them and wonder how they feel seeing that the direct, systematic, intensive instruction of the "ab-dab-blab stuff" they detested is now legally mandated in California and other states as the "scientifically" verified teaching necessary for learning to read.

The other students I want to thank are those with whom I worked at Robert Wood Johnson Medical School in a program I directed for adult and young adult poor readers. It is they who repeatedly ingrained in me the awareness that the first question I always had to ask was not "How should I help this person learn?" but "Who is this person who wants to learn?" By finding answers to the second question, I usually was able to get answers to the first. I am also in debt to them because they helped keep in the forefront of my mind the question of how their literacy problems should have been prevented in the first place.

The book itself owes a debt to Wendy Wolf, Sara Bershtel, and Elisabeth Sifton for its sequence of homes. Lauren Osborne has been an exceptional editor, particularly in helping me discard scaffolding, ladders, and planks. What I wrote about Jonathan Cobb in another book, I want to repeat here: "His comments combined intelligence and caring, and were consistently correct." The manuscript also benefited greatly from Jenna Dolan's exceptional writing skills. Sheila Cohen, an outstanding professor of literacy education, offered valuable advice as the first reader of the manuscript. Appreciation goes to my dear friend, John Marciano, both for his help with the manuscript and for being a model partisan of social justice. Among the many colleagues who helped me formulate my ideas I especially want to thank Patricia Irvine and Joanne Larson.

To Katia Iannacome, a very special "thank you." My gratitude for their support goes to the Three Tregos, Walter Iannacome, Kim Curtis, Michael Coles, Elaine Reinhardt, Donna Coles, and John Reinhardt.

Denise Levertov wrote:

> . . . a Bard
> claims from me "on whose land they grow,"
> seeds of the forget-me-not.
> "I ask you
> to gather them for me . . ."

These words come to mind when I think of Maria, a poet, my love.

READING
LESSONS

INTRODUCTION

In February 1997, newspapers across North America trumpeted the findings of a study on the best way to teach reading.[1] The Toronto *Globe & Mail* praised the study for providing an answer to "the battle between the old tried-and-true method of teaching children to read and write against the revolutionary technique that swept North American schools 30 years ago,"[2] while *The Arizona Republic* informed its readers, "Sound it out: Phonics works better."[3] Shortly thereafter, *Education Week*, the major education newspaper in the United States, published my critique of the research.[4]

This report and the criticism surrounding it are typical of an impassioned debate over why millions of children do not learn to read and write well, and why millions more who have achieved a degree of literacy success still have substantial problems with reading. For example, a week before the 1996 United States presidential elections *The Wall Street Journal* led with an article highlighting the reach of the debate: "ABCeething: How Whole Language Became a Hot Potato in and out of Academia; Reading Method Ditched Phonics, Won Adherents But Test Scores Tanked." The article began: "To touch a nerve this election year, don't bring up abortion or taxes. Just talk about reading methods."[5]

Invariably, the arguments center on identifying the most effective instruction. Newspaper articles and letters to the editor attack one instructional approach or another—most often, whole language—for producing poor reading and writing test scores. State legislatures succumbing to lobbying, petitions, Mailgrams, and similar forms of pressure pass bills encouraging or mandating particular kinds of reading instruction. These literacy "wars" extend to the federal level. In 1992, a Republican Party policy paper, "Illiteracy: An Incurable Disease or Education Malpractice?," offered recommendations for teaching reading. In 1997, a Republican-led congressional panel held hearings purportedly aimed at basing reading instruction on "scientifically based research" and offering a "product recall" of instruction not "scientifically validated."

Statistics suggest some of the basis for this controversy. A national survey found that twenty-three million American adults are totally or functionally illiterate, with the number increasing annually. Among high school students, rudimentary reading ability seems to be improving, but many students cannot comprehend complicated texts. The same holds for writing ability: most eleventh graders can write a simple, straightforward explication, but few can communicate a reasoned point of view. These and similar appraisals are often criticized as inflated or misrepresentative, but literacy experts generally agree that the appraisals—however problematic—do reflect substantial, extensive problems that can affect people lifelong, in every part of their lives.

The dominant debate over which instruction can best solve these pervasive problems has focused on beginning reading, in the belief that children who are successful in the early grades build literacy achievement on a strong foundation. Although there are numerous aspects to helping a child begin to read, the central issue in the "Great Debate" has been the relative priorities of "skills" and "meaning." Those in favor of skills maintain that literacy learning should proceed from small to increasingly larger units of language parts and meanings imparted through intensive, systematic, teacher-directed instruction, with a preplanned sequence of reading books and materials. "Meaning" instruction has changed over the years. Until about twenty-five years ago, it meant teaching whole words (or "look-say"). More recently, "meaning" instruction has fallen within the umbrella term "whole language," an approach that emphasizes meaning and engages children's interest and motivation through the use of a variety of books and writing activities. Skills are learned and taught as they become relevant to accomplishing these meaningful endeavors. Skills-first proponents criticize whole language for not providing a sufficient foundation. In turn, whole-language advocates criticize the skills-first approach for breaking language into abstract, unnatural little pieces.

In arguing about teaching practices, educators have addressed myriad questions: What mental processes are involved in learning to read and how can instruction accord with those processes? Should reading textbooks or children's literature be used alone or in combination? Should children be grouped according to reading ability? How much emphasis should be placed on meaning and skills, and how can they be combined? How should writing be integrated with reading? Should children be allowed to "invent" spelling in their early writing or should they be taught correct spelling from the start? Is there particular knowledge about manipulating the sounds of written language that is necessary for learning to read? What kind of teaching works best for children who have difficulty learning to read and write? Such questions have tended to fall within the ever pressing practical concerns of how best to teach, concerns contained in the wry and anxious educator's question "What to do on Monday morning?"

The prevailing controversy does not mean there are not other, less prominent disputes over literacy instruction. For example, there is the more marginal debate around "critical literacy"—whether and how to teach children to appraise the assumptions and viewpoints in written material instead of simply accepting them. Other controversies, such as that around the cause of "reading disabilities," affect a smaller number of children than does the Great Debate, and are thus considered less consequential.

On the face of it, the central premise of the dominant debate seems to make sense: Children will learn to read and write only through effective instruction. Teachers struggling daily to make all their students literate and teacher education programs that emphasize instructional methods share this premise. More effective instruction is usually the chief demand of parents dissatisfied with their children's progress. And praise of one instructional approach and condemnation of another is typically the conviction around which advocacy groups coalesce.

I will argue in the pages ahead that if all children are to become literate, most of the assumptions and goals of the dominant debate need to be replaced with those of a very different debate. Without doubt, how teachers teach and children learn must be central in any discussion of improving literacy, but a focus on instructional approaches narrowly and insufficiently frames an understanding of literacy education and, ironically—despite its singular aim—will never be the course for finding the "best way" to teach and learn literacy.

Most educators and psychologists believe that before we can create the most effective teaching, we must understand the mental process involved in learning written language. Many on the skills side believe that the key to this "reading process" is the ability to differentiate and synthesize the sounds in written language, an ability called "phonological awareness." Whether it does play a causal role in beginning reading is a leading issue in today's debate, partly because those who believe in the causal importance of phonological awareness employ a comprehensive (and questionable) set of instructional assumptions and practices. I will argue that phonological awareness is an important element in beginning reading, but does not play the causal role its advocates claim. Rather, phonological awareness is a marker of social and literacy experiences that promote a whole array of written language abilities—of which phonological awareness is but one—and availability of these experiences to children is strongly determined by political-economic inequities in class, race, and gender. I will explain why more attention must be given to eliminating these inequities than to classroom training programs in phonological awareness or any other language ability.

Although there are sharp differences regarding phonological awareness and other specific issues pertaining to the reading process, all can agree on the importance of understanding this process. It is clear that new readers have some cognitive flexibility. There seem to be, however, certain mental processes necessarily involved, and instruction devised in accordance with them should work. So it would seem. I believe there is no single "reading process" waiting to be activated through the right instruction. There are inherent constraints and requirements in mental functioning (one cannot read by holding a book up to one's ear), but the mental processes involved are always considerably shaped by personal interactions and social influences both before and during formal schooling. In other words, the very learning and teaching that educators feel is necessary in response to the reading process actually contributes to determining that process.

Concern with the "reading process" is indicative of another of the dominant debate's assumptions about "cognition"—that is, that cognition is made up of mental processes, images, and concepts. Unquestionably this is true, but cognition—especially in learning to read—is always intertwined with other mental and bodily processes, especially emotions. Ironically, the emotion-filled dominant debate barely considers the role of emotions in learning to read, and no attempt has been made to determine how or which particular emotions might be allowed into or excluded from learning and teaching.

The dominant debate also fails to define literacy "success." At face value, the meaning of "successful" literacy seems readily evident—as Boston University president and politician John Silber has said, although this "may seem to be a truism: the most important duty of our schools is to teach all students to read and write."[6] There may be disagreement over how to measure the results: with standardized tests, by grade-level groupings, through assignments that test various kinds of written language (such as word lists and word skill tasks). But these important questions aside—and regardless of the animosity some have for Silber's views—Silber's observation is likely to elicit for all a common image of "success." A successful student would do well in classroom measures of reading comprehension and on achievement tests. A successfully literate adult would be able to read a newspaper or book, fill out an application, write a lengthy letter, do the reading and writing necessary for a job, read storybooks to children, read a bus or train schedule, and follow a cooking recipe.

Because we can all agree on such basic definitions, work toward literacy success appears to cross not only pedagogical divisions but political ones too. Barbara Bush, who in 1990 made literacy her chief personal project, and Fidel Castro, a leader of the national Cuban Year of Literacy in 1961, are worlds apart in many ways but not, it seems, when promoting successful literacy. Yet a close examination of the meaning of "successful" literacy reveals that this camaraderie is more in appearance than in reality. Like the concepts "democracy," "equality," "equity," and "power," "successful literacy" has embedded in it many assumptions around which everyone cannot join in common cause.

The failure of the dominant debate to address possible sharp, irreconcilable differences in defining literacy "success" reflects its failure to consider a major problem: namely, as promoted by many educators—and certainly by dominant political and economic groups—"successful literacy" can impair development of the intellectual tools the majority of Americans require for accurately comprehending and evaluating written material. For example, "successful literacy" can discourage looking beyond surface meanings, making sufficient connections among events, understanding phenomena historically, and exploring the meaning of facts. Stated another way: a huge part of the literacy problems in the United States and elsewhere is "successful literacy."

The dominant debate also assumes that we can identify the best instructional approach by comparing groups of children taught by contending approaches. Although this kind of experimental assessment is theoretically possible, I will argue that it has been (and will continue to be) fruitless, for at least two reasons. First, empirical studies on "which approach is best" have ignored fundamental assumptions about how children should think, feel, and act, criteria that are embedded in the success of an approach. As such, an empirically tested method judged "successful" by some educators and parents may be an abomination in the eyes of others. Second, the desired outcomes of the different instructional approaches may require very different financial, school, and classroom supports in order to achieve them. Thus, past instructional approaches considered outstanding in theory have been ineffective because they lacked the necessary supports to promote them. Although some teachers have implemented reforms even without supportive conditions, doing so requires arduous effort and thus happens rarely. As I shall discuss, if the issues of assumptions about children and supportive conditions were addressed in assessing instructional approaches, participants in the debate over literacy would see that the debate over "best instruction" is never separate from implicit or explicit choices about children's development.

Running through this book is the argument that the dominant debate disregards the myriad societal influences that affect teaching and learning, influences that are not readily visible in the classroom. No debate can adequately understand how literacy is taught and learned, what causes literacy achievement and underachievement, or how literacy "success" is defined unless it accounts for these "macro" influences. If the debate over literacy were more about the politics, economics, and power in society and less about the "best" way to teach literacy, we would better understand how to rear literate children.

Changing the terms of the literacy debate is crucial because the debate influences decisions about resources and types of instruction, which in turn affect how children learn to read and write and how they think, feel, and act—powerful determinants of their futures. I write at a time of many crises for America's children—crises of health, housing, homelessness, emotional stress, infant mortality, job loss, and insufficient income. These crises are integrally connected, and together they will have a dramatic impact on the nation. As we attempt to solve these crises, we must ensure that the debates about them are the right debates.

1

THE DEBATE OVER READING

A major book on reading published in 1990 observed that "the question of how best to teach beginning reading may be the most politicized topic in the field of education."[1] Marilyn Jager Adams meant that the debate over reading instruction was rife with professional partisanship that went far beyond a "passionate concern" for identifying the best kind of reading instruction. Passion was understandable. After all, reading specialists should be fervently committed to promoting literacy among children. But partisanship—"fierce" partisanship—had damaged efforts at coolheaded argumentation based on unclouded appraisals of research and evidence. Zealous advocacy prevailed, strong in desire and weak in reason.

Others observing the debate, particularly those in the media, have described its spirit in even stronger terms: as a "full-scale war,"[2] "the reading wars,"[3] and a "bicoastal uprising" and "revolt."[4] These martial terms may seem excessive even for arguments first called the "Great Debate" in 1967. In her influential book using that subtitle, Jeanne Chall[5] defined the essential difference between the phonics (sound-symbol relationships) and skills approach, which, Chall maintained, transports the learner from small to increasingly larger units of language, directly teaching each unit as reading advances, and the meaning approach, which expects the learner to intuit the smaller units through ample reading of written language.

But is the divergence between these views really the stuff of which wars are made? A casual observer may legitimately question just how perturbed anyone can get over phonics—over whether, how, and when to teach it. The same may be said of the ardor with which the meaning approach is defended: Don't all reading experts agree that reading is fundamentally about obtaining meaning from written language? Mustn't meaning be part of all reading instruction? Are the differences of opinion in the Great Debate sufficiently fierce to cause uprisings and revolts? Or, one may wonder, is this Great Debate a professional tempest in a teapot concocted by inflated feelings of self-importance?

It is not! No blood has been shed, but from local to national levels arguments have been heated. The Great Debate has affected state and federal legislation and legislative controversies. Letters to the editor hold one or the other side responsible for prodigious literacy problems. Parents and teachers grapple over the effect of teaching methods on how children learn in the wake of the Great Debate.

Before describing some of these quarrels, more must be said about the nature and history of the debate. In the early nineteenth century, skills instruction meant first recognizing and naming the letters of the alphabet, but repeated criticism of the excessive and unproductive time children spent on this task before relating sounds to symbols led to its elimination. Thereafter, children began by learning phonics and gradually advancing to more complex skills and text. The guiding theory of the skills approach was and is that children must acquire certain essential abilities—chief among them breaking the language "code" that connects sounds and symbols—and that they can best do this by tackling a coherent progression of intensive but systematic, manageable tasks.

Meaning instruction for most of the nineteenth and twentieth centuries meant the "word" or "look-say" method, in which children learned individual words separately and in sentences and stories, and eventually mastered—either intuitively or explicitly—specific skills for identifying parts of words. The graded reading series ("basal" readers) used to teach this approach never fully lacked phonics instruction, but used it less than did other texts. The meaning emphasis here can only be considered meaning in comparison to the emphasis in the skills texts. With few exceptions, the meaning stories were superficial and unimaginative, filled with stereotypical characters, artificial language, and lackluster plots. Meaning, in other words, was scant.

With the advent of "whole language" in the late 1960s, the meaning of meaning instruction changed. Whole language bears little resemblance to its historical antecedents; it uses written language that is "whole" rather than an aggregate of individual words. Children help choose interesting storybooks, rather than reading assigned textbooks (basal readers) filled with vapid stories. Students are more involved in decisions about what to read than they were in the days of the old meaning instruction, certainly more than students in skills-oriented classrooms, which call for more direct, structured, and managed teaching. For whole language, writing and reading are essential interactive processes. As for teaching word skills, here leaders of whole language differ. Most counsel teachers to teach skills as needed by each child. A minority of whole-language authorities, however, eschew skills altogether, insisting that if children work with stories and other materials with strong and useful significance to them, they will eventually deduce the skills required for deciphering the parts of the whole.

The National Quarrel

In December 1994, *The Atlantic Monthly* "revisited" the Great Debate and contended that the ascendancy in recent years of "meaning first" instruction "should be a cause of concern."[6] The article declared whole language to be a "fad" with "little hard evidence" to back up claims of success, and asserted that research had offered "a persuasive case for the importance of phonics." The whole-language fad was most insidious, said the author, in damaging the potential reading progress of "low-income and other disadvantaged students" by depriving them of the "intensive instruction in phonics that they need to master reading." The author decried the lamentable "intransigent" fervor of whole-language advocates who have disregarded "conventional standards of proof" in contrast to the reasonableness and rationality displayed by those partial to phonics. This article reflected a growing nationwide backlash against whole language, a backlash that soon showed up in legislatures and school boards throughout the country.

In Houston, Texas, after using a whole-language approach, teachers and principals at eight of 162 elementary schools persuaded local school officials to allow them to return to a phonics-based program. The request was made after the schools—all in the city's poorer, African-American neighborhoods—experienced a decline in reading test scores after having abandoned the heavily structured phonics program. Particularly compelling evidence for the request seemed to have been the test scores of the one school of poor, African-American students that had continued to use the phonics program; its scores were in the top third or quarter of all schools with similar youngsters. The educators who requested the change back to the phonics program argued that students did poorly with the whole-language method partly because the students' parents were not providing the at-home support needed to make the method work. One principal explained that without sufficient parental help in giving children more experience with written language and learning sound-symbols connections, the schools were required to teach fundamental skills.[7]

Around the nation, state legislatures have been mandating particular forms of instruction. After each member of the Wisconsin Senate in 1995 received a petition with 8,000 signatures requesting the return of intensive, systematic phonics to the schools, the Senate passed a bill authorizing the Department of Education to refuse to grant teaching licenses to applicants for any grade in which reading was taught (kindergarten through sixth grade) unless the applicants' training included instruction in teaching phonics.[8]

In 1993 Ohio became the first state to mandate phonics teaching and provided $500,000 to train already licensed teachers who lacked the skill.[9] North Carolina soon followed, requiring teachers (in the words of the bill's sponsor) "to use phonics first, and then if the child fails to read, they may try some other methods."[10]

In 1994 California achievement tests showed a decline in reading scores, tying Louisiana for the worst readers among thirty-nine states tested. Many blamed whole language, first sanctioned there in 1987. The example of San Diego was held up repeatedly: a year after whole language supplanted phonics there, the percentage of students scoring above the national median dropped from 51 percent to 25 percent. In response, the State Board of Education in 1996 approved a new reading program that stressed "systematic, explicit" phonics in the early grades. As an incentive, Governor Pete Wilson offered schools $127 million for new textbooks and teacher training.[11]

Ken Goodman, a major figure in whole-language education, replied that the blame was misplaced. In classrooms where teachers said they used a whole-language approach, Goodman reported, children scored better than average on reading tests. Conversely, classrooms using intensive phonics had worse scores. Goodman instead blamed California's class size, tied for the largest in the nation, and low per-pupil expenditure.[12]

Another voice raised against whole language was that of Texas governor George W. Bush (President Bush's son). The Texas literacy crisis was "obvious in the numbers," Bush told the Texas Education Agency: "Last year, one in four Texas school children who took the state reading test failed. That's 350,000 children who do not have the basic skill to learn. 90,000 of them were third and fourth graders—an at-risk population in the making." Bush's proposed solution was voiced in the political right's synonym code in which "trendy" means whole language and "basics" and "building blocks" connote phonics and word skills. Schools must get "back to the basics," he advised, "the building blocks of knowledge that were the same yesterday and will be the same tomorrow. We do not need trendy new theories or fancy experiments or feel-good curriculums. The basics work." He was not interested in "means," but in "results." "If drill gets the job done, then rote is right."[13]

One reading specialist observed that the move toward taking decision-making power out of the hands of educators and giving it to legislatures has stemmed in part from a "seeming inability of educators to make up their minds": "Mom and dad, who have children in school, look at articles in the newspaper and think if the reading people don't know what they're doing, maybe somebody else ought to make the decisions."[14]

The Republican Party jumped into the fray at a national level with a policy paper that urged phonics instruction as the remedy for the nation's deteriorating literacy skills.[15] Taking the long view, the Republicans saw the problem as a recent creation: "historically, all American school children were taught to read" with intensive, systematic phonics that enabled them to master the skills and logic of the English spelling system. This tried-and-true method was abandoned by the 1980s, and proof of the resulting degeneration in teaching methods was a survey of 1,609 professors of reading in 300 graduate schools. Asked to select the most significant studies in the field, the professors' top choices, the Republicans grumbled, showed they were "vociferous, dedicated, dogmatic enemies of early, intensive teaching of phonics."

Following circulation of the policy paper, the Republicans successfully orchestrated a new provision in the 1990 Adult Literacy Act that included phonics in a list of instructional methods eligible for federal funds. Senator William L. Armstrong, chair of the Republican Policy Committee, hailed the provision as a great victory: "Research shows phonics is the most effective way to teach people to read. It's the way most of us learned to read. But it fell out of use in the last 20 years, with disastrous consequences."[16] Republicans made an additional argument: phonics instruction was cheaper. One educator put the cost of phonics instruction at 80 percent less than competing programs—a claim that disregards the problem of how children can learn to read when 80 percent budget reductions slash the number of books a school can buy.

Chief among conservative groups seeking to influence state and federal legislation is the National Right to Read Foundation, whose president, Robert Sweet, is the major author of the aforementioned Republican policy paper. Prior to his work on the Republican Policy Committee, Sweet led the Moral Majority in New Hampshire. His contribution to Ronald Reagan's successful primary victory in New Hampshire "was rewarded by Reagan with powerful federal jobs in education and social policy, where he pursued the goals of the educational New Right—Christian private schools, public school prayer and fundamentalist values."[17] In 1997 Sweet was appointed to the staff of the Republican-led U.S. House of Representatives Committee on Education and the Workforce that has been promoting a skills-based reading curriculum. Besides being a strong champion of phonics, Sweet is an advocate of creationism. Sweet's self-description, found in each edition of the foundation's *Newsletter*, reads: "White House domestic policy adviser to President Reagan and head of the Office of Juvenile Justice under President Bush." The Right to Read Foundation concentrates on phonics, but also favors abolishing the U.S. Department of Education and reducing spending on education.

The legislative achievements of the skills approach have not come without opposition by, and even victories for, whole language. For example, the 1994 House and Senate bills reauthorizing all federal elementary and secondary education laws contained the following language: "The disproven theory that children must first learn basic skills before engaging in more complex tasks continues to dominate strategies for classroom instruction, resulting in emphasis on repetitive drill and practice at the expense of content-rich instruction, accelerated curricula, and effective teaching to high standards."[18]

This pleased whole-language proponents, but the National Right to Read Foundation and other conservative groups read the bills as an attempt to banish phonics in the public schools. After Republican Texas Congressman Dick Armey failed to eliminate the language from the bill, lobbying became more intensive. A "legislative alert" was mailed to members of organizations supportive of phonics, and a Western Union Pro-Phonics Hotline was established for facilitating Mailgrams to Congress. The model Mailgram read, in part:

Education reform is taking place all over the country. Many states and communities are beginning to restore phonics instruction in their local schools. Ohio recently passed legislation which will require phonics to be taught, and many states are following their example. With phonics, an individual becomes a reader by learning the alphabet, its 44 sounds, and how to blend these sounds together to form words.[19]

The Mailgram's conclusion urged deletion of the "anti-phonics" language and support for phonics instruction to "help our nation's children."

The campaign succeeded; the language was dropped from the final version of the bill. Its success appeared to lie in orchestrating constituent pressure. Conservative Congressman Armey and conservative organizations may have initiated the drive, but it was liberal Massachusetts Senator Ted Kennedy who joined them and affirmed: "Phonics plays a fundamental role in the education of young children. I do not believe that this role should be eliminated."[20]

State legislators, local educators, and national politicians were joined in their calls for phonics by prominent figures in academia. John Silber, president of Boston University, explained the cause of the problem this way: "The teaching of reading, which had once been the province of elementary school teachers, was delivered into the hands of so-called 'experts' in the schools of education." And what, according to Silber, did these "experts" do? "Inflamed by their dogmatism, they rejected the traditional use of phonetics in teaching reading, and replaced it with word recognition, often called 'look-see' [sic]." Blaming the International Reading Association, the major professional organization of teachers of reading and professors of reading education, for holding "the position that phonics and look-see [sic] are equally satisfactory methods of teaching reading," Silber likened the comparison to saying that "radar and astrology are equally satisfactory techniques for predicting the weather."[21]

The potency of the Great Debate was also unmistakable among public school educators. A 1995 issue of *American Educator*—"Learning to Read: Schooling's First Mission"—offered in every article an unmistakable articulation of a policy position. While giving a tepid tip of the hat to whole language—recognizing, for example, "many [of its] elements have brought new life to classrooms"—the issue unequivocally endorsed substantial phonics in the early grades. The editor admonished: "To the extent that [whole-language proponents] minimize the role of skilled decoding in reading comprehension they are wrong." By minimizing "decoding," the whole-language movement "has done a terrible disservice to the children whose lives depend on mastery of that skill."[22]

Similarly, Louisa Cook Moats, a reading researcher, to use one example, explained that "the scientific community has reached consensus" that the foundation for successful reading was knowledge of the linguistic "code," particularly phonological knowledge (the explicit awareness of the sound structure of words) and phonics.[23] Countless studies, said Moats, had demonstrated that a lack of phonological knowledge was the key deficit in the reading disabled. These findings established that teachers of beginning reading must "incorporate direct instruction" for learning these and similar code-emphasis units of language. This requirement naturally raised a question about teacher education: Was knowledge of this foundation, and of how to teach this foundation, a primary requisite for graduate school training?[24]

Moats's research showed that the answer was an incontrovertible "No." Few teachers and graduate students knew that researchers had documented the foundational knowledge beginning readers required and few faculty knew how to teach mastery of the code. "Lower level language mastery," Moats concluded, "is as essential for the literacy teacher as anatomy is for the physician. It is our obligation to enable teachers to acquire it."

Moats's article (and those that accompanied it) sent clear signals about the views of the American Federation of Teachers (sponsors of the journal). The AFT had come down on the side of basic language skills and was trying to influence graduate school curricula to support its agenda, unambiguously communicating a policy position to graduate schools of education about the "foundational" knowledge they had to teach!

Another example of the Great Debate played out in professional literature is a series of articles in *Phi Delta Kappan*, a major education journal. The series began from the whole-language side, with Marie Carbo arguing that "American students do not read as well as they should" because a "wide spectrum of potentially effective and practical instructional approaches" better than explicit phonics teaching have been precluded from the classroom.[25] Responses to Carbo found fault with both phonics and whole language: Richard L. Turner urged a search for "more powerful instructional treatments for beginning reading" and Denny Taylor pointed out that children learned in diverse ways and, therefore, required individually crafted instruction.[26] The next participant, Frank Smith, a prominent figure in the whole-language movement, thought children would learn to read on their own if provided with engaging reading materials.[27] Smith was in turn reproached by supporters of phonics, "structured methodologies," and direct teaching: If learning were so natural, they argued, adult illiteracy would not be a major problem in the United States.[28] And so the "never-ending debate"—or, in Smith's words, the "never-ending confrontation"—driven by ideology, not evidence, continued.[29]

Recent theoretical and practical attempts have been made to bridge these ideological differences by amalgamating the whole-language and skills approaches. Why, as Marilyn Jager Adams has implored, can't teachers use the best of both? Why can't both sides stop "bickering" and formulate a single system of reading instruction?[30] Similar amalgamation recommendations have appeared in professional journals, but these efforts have not reduced the intensity of the debate. Critics insist that each side's conception of literacy education is incompatible with the other's. Some sense of this incompatibility is evident in the language: the skills side insists that theirs is a "method," while the whole-language side insists theirs is an "approach" or "philosophy." What Yeats said of politics applies to attempted middle-ground resolutions of the Great Debate: "the center will not hold."

The Facts

Before looking more closely at the debate, it is important to emphasize that opponents do share several areas of common ground. Foremost is a concern about the many students who have difficulty learning to read and write and a desire to ensure that all students become literate. Although national tests are not the only or best indicator of our children's literacy (and some educators are sharply critical of them), there is no question that test results paint a troubling picture. Here are some of the figures:

- About one-third of fourth graders have difficulty understanding specific information in simple passages. (Of course, this also means that the majority of fourth graders *can* obtain this information.) Writing performance is even worse: less than a third can write well-developed stories.[31]
- Most eighth graders have mastered the specific information, but more than 40 percent have difficulty understanding main ideas in, or making inferences from, complex material. And most eighth graders cannot write an "explanation of why something happened as it did."[32]
- 60 percent of eleventh graders have serious problems with reasoning and problem solving in "relatively complicated" passages and few can compose an essay containing a reasoned point of view.
- The surveys that come up with these depressing findings do not include the millions of students who drop out before eleventh grade. The real extent of literacy problems in teenagers is much worse.
- African-American and Latino students fall behind their white peers by fourth grade, and the gap continues through high school.[33]
- Literacy problems unresolved by high school continue into adulthood.[34] A 1993 survey found that tens of millions of adults could do little more than comprehend brief and uncomplicated texts and documents.[35] (These numbers remained substantial even after subtracting immigrants just learning English or

adults over age sixty-five whose cognitive faculties might have declined.)

All sides in the Great Debate agree that these facts mean that many youngsters need better instruction in learning to read and write. There are several other areas of common ground as well. First, all sides agree that improved instruction should be the chief solution for eliminating literacy problems. Second, all agree that understanding the thinking processes in learning to read and write is the key to creating better instruction. Finally, many (though not all) adversaries in the Great Debate believe that they can resolve their differences through careful empirical comparisons of the effectiveness of instructional approaches.

A Closer Look at the Debate

These assumptions about the primacy of instruction and the thinking processes underpinning literacy learning run through professional discussions, teacher education, policy recommendations, and reform measures. But these assumptions—almost self-evident and seldom questioned—actually prevent a resolution to the Great Debate. Moreover, they contribute to the perpetuation of the very literacy problems the disputants want to eliminate. In short, the Great Debate is the wrong debate.

I do not mean to say that instruction is unimportant; obviously it is critical. But tackling narrow questions about types of instruction does nothing to address the deeper causes of literacy problems. Only by reformulating the debate can we understand and address literacy problems in all their political, empirical, professional, and instructional permutations.

I will also argue that the debate is wrong because it is grounded in a narrow meaning of literacy success—the comprehension considered proficient in standardized tests and classroom reading assessments and discussions and in adult comprehension of books, magazines, newspapers, etc. The problem of unsuccessful literacy achievement is obvious, but even if every student learned to read and write the nation would still have a literacy problem stemming from "successful" literacy. The omission of this issue from the current debate contributes mightily to conflicts over the reading process and the "best" instructional approach.

Since the participants in the Great Debate all agree that an understanding of the "reading process" is fundamental to resolving their differences, it will be useful to pause here and elaborate on what educators mean by the term "reading process."

The "Reading Process" and Instruction

The reading process refers to the thinking that is said to occur when a person reads. A reader sees an array of written symbols, associates them with sounds, syntax, and meanings (not necessarily in that order), and comprehends the symbols as facts, information, descriptions, or arguments. A reader may also make judgments about the truth of the meanings.

Many (though not all) reading experts generally believe that the reading process is composed of two chief tasks: decoding and comprehension.[36] Decoding means translating printed symbols into sound representations. Comprehension is "deriving meaning from the material we have decoded." These two work interactively and together influence higher levels of written language processing (such as comprehending main ideas). Or, if a beginning reader remembers words by their meaning (semantic memory), this memory will in turn facilitate the memory of the visual features and sound segments for decoding other words. Experts see this interactive model as a sophisticated advance over earlier, simpler, more linear models that saw reading beginning either with decoding or meaning.

Another mental process key to successful decoding and comprehension is that of attention. The amount of attention a reader has to devote to decoding depends (no great surprise) "upon the reader's skill as well as the reader's familiarity with the words in the text." The attention devoted to comprehension, in turn, "depends upon the degree to which the ideas presented by a writer are matched by the knowledge contained in the reader's head": a quick match means fast comprehension. Attention, therefore, is a crucial but shifting element in the reading process.[37]

According to the interactive model, the beginning reader faces the problem of having insufficient attentional capacity for meeting the dual tasks of decoding and comprehension. There are numerous strategies for solving this problem, such as devoting attention to one task more than the other, or alternating attention between the two tasks. A more skilled reader faces no such problem allocating attention because as decoding becomes "automatic" a reader can devote attention primarily to comprehension. A very highly skilled reader has even more flexibility in allocating attention: The reader might, at one time, attend to spelling and ignore meaning when proofreading a paper, for example. At another time that reader might scan a paper for an overview. And at still another time the reader might pay attention only to portions of a text that discuss a particular topic.

The interactive model will have a familiar ring to anyone who has seen a beginner struggling to read. The reader might first identify the middle portion of a word at the beginning of a sentence, after which he or she might shift attention by reading ahead, then, recognizing some subsequent words, might go back to the initial word, correctly identifying the initial sounds of the formerly perplexing letters and correctly identifying the word itself. Eventually, the beginning reader appears to orchestrate attention to the overall sentence by combining the accurate decoding and identification of the first word with the correct identification of the rest of the words in the sentence.

Those who subscribe to the interactive model believe that an equal emphasis on decoding and comprehension for those learning to read would excessively divide and ultimately encumber a reader's attention. The model instead favors more attention to decoding.

Of course, the interactive model, though widely adopted by educational theorists, is not the only one at the base of the Great Debate. Whole-language models, for example, have their own interactive versions. In one, a beginning reader uses certain knowledge (called "cues") to construct meaning from written language. These cues include letter patterns, letter-sound relationships, recurrent spelling patterns, function words (the, a, that), syntax patterns, whole known words, personal information, and similar language and experiential knowledge. Motivated by a desire to make sense out of print, a reader uses this array of knowledge in various strategies to obtain meaning. Both in learning to read and in proficient reading, a reader uses all of these cues. The proficient reader, however, does so more efficiently by using minimal cues and effective strategies.

In this model, reading involves the interrelationship and use of all language information. Obtaining meaning from print is, in whole-language proponent Ken Goodman's words, a "psycholinguistic guessing game," with the reader always actively using one cue or another in the reading process: "As readers make use of their knowledge of all the language cues, they predict, make inferences, select significant features, confirm, and constantly work toward constructing a meaningful text."[38]

Learning to do so efficiently requires reading "whole" written language, not focusing on one language cue (such as learning sound-symbol relationships in isolation from the whole). When instruction focuses on a single cue, the reading process is short-circuited because the reader's engagement in the whole process is no longer at work. Moreover, a single cue should not be isolated and emphasized because the reading process will vary with each individual as she or he learns to use cues on the way to becoming a proficient reader.[39]

Theoretical models cannot, of course, be proven by comparing one model with another. But many believe that models gain credibility if the forms of instruction based on them can be proved to be superior. Some educators are satisfied with simpler comparisons based on behaviorism and pragmatism. That is, if children are taught in a particular way, and that way seems to work better, regardless of why, one method can be said to be superior to another. But most claims for the superiority of an instructional approach are linked to paradigms of the reading process.

A good example of the belief in comparing reading process theories is Marilyn Jager Adams's extensive review that proposes that readers would learn best if instruction were based upon the reading process (or "reading system," as she calls it) and empirical comparisons of "which [instructional] approaches were most effective." Of comparisons already completed, Adams is quite clear about her conclusions: the most successful teaching of beginning reading emphasizes "explicit phonics, or the provision of systematic instruction on the relation of letter-sounds to words."[40]

I will not evaluate this and similar conclusions now. I wish only to establish that Adams's assessment—"widely regarded as the most thorough and ambitious analysis yet undertaken of the research regarding early reading"—like most of the debate over literacy, focuses narrowly on the "psychology and pedagogy of reading."[41] She makes no attempt to explore the other aspects of a child's thinking, life, and learning conditions that might shape his or her "reading system."

Another example of the widespread emphasis on this focus is *Theoretical Models and Processes of Reading*, a book published by the International Reading Association. Most of the twenty-nine of the third edition's (1985) chapters discuss language development, visual perception, word recognition, attention, comprehension, and metacognition (self-awareness of one's comprehension strategies).[42] Of the chapters that depart from these confines, two delve into emotion and reading, three consider cultural factors shaping reading.[43]

The editors do acknowledge that "Reader Environment," meaning a student's cultural and family background, and the characteristics of classrooms and schools, can influence the reading process, but only three features of this environment—textual, conversational, and instructional—are considered essential.[44] Textual features are words, pictures, and graphs of a student's reading materials. Conversational features are communication with others while the student learns to read. Instructional features are those "related to the act of teaching," including a teacher's plans and the student's learning activities.[45]

The Debate over Reading in National Reports

Assumptions about instruction and the reading process have not been limited to professional articles and books. They have also affected discussions of literacy policies at the national level. For instance, *Becoming a Nation of Readers (BNR)*,[46] a major report published in 1985 by the Commission on Reading of the National Academy of Education, began by defining reading as a "process of constructing meaning from written texts, a complex skill requiring the coordination of a number of interrelated sources." Fortunately, said *BNR*, many of the "practices of the best teachers" had been "verified." To produce a nation of readers, therefore, educators needed only to disseminate and implement these practices, rather than create new knowledge.

For beginning reading, the centerpiece of "verified practices" was phonics instruction: "The issue is no longer, as it was several decades ago, whether children should be taught phonics. The issues now are specific ones of just how it should be done." Other "verified practices" were also proposed for grouping children for reading instruction, teaching comprehension, minimizing discipline problems, and managing the "literacy environment." The commission did at least note a few other influences on learning to read. "Parents play roles of inestimable importance in laying the foundation for learning to read" and therefore "have an obligation to support their children's continued growth as readers." But beyond this chiding, and a call for better libraries and a few other improvements, the commission had nothing to say about any other influences on instruction.[47]

BNR was soon followed by the first national report on literacy since 1953. Written by Secretary of Education William J. Bennett with a study group "of twenty-one distinguished Americans," *First Lessons* echoed common assumptions: The elementary school could meet its "sublime and most solemn responsibility, the task of teaching every child in it to read," by drawing on the "unprecedented advances" in "knowledge about the basic processes involved in reading, teaching and learning." Bennett, like the authors of *BNR*, asserted that educators knew "how to achieve universal literacy among our young people" and should disseminate this knowledge to generate proper instruction. "With all we know," Bennett proclaimed, "we must not accept failure."[48]

And what do "we know"? We know, said Bennett, that the instructional method that fits "knowledge about the basic processes" is explicit phonics. We also know, Bennett continued, that the often stultifying content of reading primers and (basal) reading series must be improved (though these reading series should continue to be the foundation of instruction); that children should increase the amount of time they spend reading; that better use should be made of workbooks; and that elementary school libraries should be stocked with good literature. In other words, the recommendations were overwhelmingly aimed at strengthening conventional instruction.

A reply to *BNR*, published by the National Council of Teachers of English (1988), demonstrated that even sharp reproofs from an opposing viewpoint were likely to share the dominant assumption that instruction should be based on a firm understanding of the reading process. *Counterpoint and Beyond*[49] criticized the commission's narrow focus on phonics. It advocated "child-centered" whole-language instruction, and urged teachers to become facilitators, not managers, of learning to enable children to grasp the "meaningful nature of the reading act."[50]

Some authors in *Counterpoint and Beyond* did venture beyond the dominant terms of the debate by pointing to the effects of racism, poverty, politics, and school funding on learning. David Bloome and his colleagues maintained that "explicit and implicit discrimination against children" from low-income families and ethnic minorities lay at the heart of their literacy failures.[51] Rudine Sims Bishop pointed out that *BNR* had disregarded the political climate that would not only inadequately fund many of the recommendations of *BNR*—such as maintaining well-stocked school libraries—but more likely would cut funds for these recommended improvements.[52] As for *BNR*'s admonition that parents should work hard to support their children's literacy growth, Bishop underscored the economic and other stresses on many poor parents that would fetter these efforts.

The inclusion of these perspectives might appear to contradict my characterization of the debate. But the proportion of alternative ideas like those expressed by David Bloome and Rudine Sims Bishop is relatively small. Even in *Counterpoint and Beyond*, a response with socially progressive contributors who were uniformly critical of conventional education and largely in favor of whole language, most of the text was devoted to commentaries that used the dominant assumptions. For the debate overall, the proportions are much starker. Educational activists strive to change the nature of the debate—and strive and strive.

A Brief Look Backward and Elsewhere

An alternative to the dominant debate must replace the key assumptions in several ways. First, we must reject the "reading process" as the exclusive foundation for the best instruction and understand that it is both a determinant of and determined by instruction. Second, we must reject and replace the assumption that the solution to literacy problems lies principally in using the "best" instruction. And third, we must explicitly identify the assumptions about children's thinking, feeling, and acting that are always integral to learning and teaching but, for the most part, implicit in that process.

In the next chapter I will begin to amplify these alternative assumptions and what they mean for contemporary literacy issues. Here, I will begin to discuss the inadequacies of the present debate by exploring two examples of literacy, one historical, another cross-cultural, far removed from literacy in the United States. I do so to illustrate that even in these relatively uncomplex societal and economic contexts, the narrow terms of the present debate are insufficient for understanding literacy and solutions to literacy problems.

Western Asia

At the end of the fourth millennium B.C., the rise in trade in western Asia spawned a writing and reading system to keep accounts in long-distance commercial transactions.[53] Clay bullae, or envelopes (about the size of a tennis ball), were devised to accompany the goods. Clay tokens, incised with characters representing the kind and quantity of merchandise (e.g., wool, perfume, oil) were placed inside a bulla; on the outside were the personal seals of the merchants. The recipient of the shipment could verify its contents by breaking the bullae. In turn, the need to deliver intact bullae inhibited the transporters from stealing any of the merchandise in transit. In order to preserve a record of the transaction, the originating merchants soon began to mark the surface of each bulla with images of all the enclosed tokens. Eventually, two-dimensional portrayals of the tokens substituted for the tokens themselves and the bullae were replaced by clay tablets.

The relevance of this example to the current debate lies in whether or not we ask the same questions about this early "reading process" as we ask in today's debate. What merchandise information did the reader bring to reading the bullae? What perceptual and linguistic skills were correlated with learning to read the tokens and symbols? What kind of formal and informal instruction worked best? Did readers perceive and comprehend the symbols segmentally, sequentially, or as a whole? Were the symbols perceived as a composite of parts or as whole meanings? How did the organization and clarity of the symbols facilitate or impede comprehension?

No doubt questions such as these, about psychology and learning, could provide useful information, but by themselves provide only insufficient information. Imagine that this early form of reading had been created for uses that were other than commercial. Imagine too that writing and reading originated not because of the merchants' needs, but because of those of the transporters, who were maltreated by both buyers and sellers. Suppose buyers paid sellers for an order, but were short-ordered by the sellers, who blamed the shortage on the transporters. Even worse, imagine that buyers who received the correct order would sometimes claim it was short and blame the transporters. In either instance, the falsely accused transporters would be imprisoned. In response to this abuse, suppose transporters devised a method of written communication that not only documented the merchandise sent and delivered but also told the story of their mistreatment.

In other words, an understanding of any "reading process" would be impossible without accounting for the social relations in which reading occurs and for the ideas about social relationships and conditions that are allowed and disallowed. The thinking in the merchants' literacy would be starkly different in organization, content, and processing from that in the transporters' literacy. And these differences would in turn shape learning and comprehension.

To know even more about the respective literacies in this scenario, we would need to know about the uses of literacy—whose interests did literacy serve, why were ideas included or omitted? Merchants' literacy was used to organize the thinking of readers around quantities and kinds of merchandise within commercial transactions, but the written material was nevertheless more than symbols—it also embodied social relationships and conditions.

In contrast, the transporters' literacy would have conveyed a different conception of social relationships and conditions and transcended the commercial transaction upon which the merchants' literacy was wholly concentrated. The transporters' literacy would have been used to organize the thinking of readers in a particular way: to apprise them of the plight of the transporters and convince them of its injustice. The text would have conveyed ideas about individual and group motives and actions in a story line. All this would have orchestrated thinking differently than in the merchants' literacy. By comparing the particular thinking in each, we can see that literacy is not an abstract mode of using language—not a tool or technology. Rather, it embodies particular thoughts and practices and is used in a particular social context. In each literacy, the ideas would contain different conceptions of how readers should think, feel, and act. The uses and goals of reading would shape the "reading process," not the reverse.

What about teaching and learning these rudimentary literacies? Here, the most crucial influences would not be knowledge of the reading process and arguments for or against skills or meaning. Rather, the major influences would come from the thinking, feeling, and acting of the merchants and transporters. For example, pedagogy from the merchants' viewpoint need not—and should not—foster alternative interpretations of the material. Merchants needed literacy only for commercial transactions. These uses and assumptions would mean that instruction of merchants' literacy would be on skills, narrow in meaning and narrowly goal-directed. Again, the uses of reading helped shape the reading process. The transporters, on the other hand, would need more from their literacy—they would want to tell about their lives, achieve social change rather than social stability. A transporters' pedagogy would still be concerned about skills and symbol identification, but within overall meaning. Such a pedagogy would encourage more active participation of students and more individual and group creative expression. No "reading process" would inexorably produce the respective pedagogies.

Literacy in Liberia

A cross-cultural example of literacy is that of the Vai people in Liberia.[54] The Vai learn their own written language informally, through family and friends, rather than in schools. Psychologists Sylvia Scribner and Michael Cole compared a group who had acquired only this non-school literacy with the following groups: one that had learned English literacy (the official literacy of Liberia), which is learned in schools; another that knew Arabic, which is learned in religious classes; a group of nonliterates; and groups that had various combinations of these literacies. The central purpose of the research was to determine if learning to read and write produced singular psychological outcomes independent of school experiences.

Scribner and Cole concluded that literacy by itself—that is, literacy like Vai and Arabic learned outside of schools—was not "associated with what are considered the higher-order intellectual skills," such as categorization, abstraction, or syllogistic reasoning: cognition associated solely with literacy did not differ from nonliterate cognition.[55]

Those who had attended school did much better, however, than both nonliterates and unschooled literates—for example, in explaining problem-solving tasks:

> Justifications given by schooled individuals were more task-oriented and informative than those given by others; they more often made use of class and attributive names. Schooling affects verbal explanations over and above any influences it may exert on successful execution of the task itself. School—not English reading scores—was the best predictor. Thus, neither Vai script nor Qur'anic-learning-and-Arabic script act as surrogates for schooling. They do not produce the range of cognitive effects that schooling does. Men literate in Vai script qualify as having a written

language but they do not (behaviorally or verbally in the experimental tasks) "look like" their peers with schooling.[56]

These conclusions appear to say that schooling, not literacy, affects cognition. But whether or not this is accurate requires further examination (not provided by Scribner and Cole) of the comparative literacies. One of the inadequacies in this study is the conception of literacy that narrowly defines cognitive effects. In this study, cognitive effects were defined in terms of abstraction, memory, logic, metalinguistic knowledge (awareness of the language knowledge one has), and so forth. Knowing written language, however, means more than having the kinds of mental abilities that are usually the subject of psychological testing. To talk about learning to read as though it produced only these mental abilities independent of the thinking and practices generated by the social interactions greatly delimits the meaning of literacy.

To explain this—and to understand its bearing on the terms of the current debate over literacy—we need to examine Vai literacy within Liberian society at the time of the study, as the study's authors did not do. The living conditions of the tribal communities were abominable. More than 75 percent of Liberians were illiterate and "only 50 percent of school-age children were enrolled in school."[57] Most Vai were non-literate and only 12 percent could read and write English. The rate for all literacies—Vai script, Arabic, and English—was under 20 percent for the total population. Most women and 72 percent of men were nonliterate in any language.

The tribes lived under the control of the Americo-Liberian minority. These descendants of former American slaves had occupied "a position of political, economic, social, and religious superiority" since they arrived in Liberia in the early nineteenth century. From the time of the early settlements, "the settlers' arrogance in their relations with the indigenous inhabitants created a climate of hostility" that persisted at the time of the Scribner and Cole study, when "4 percent of the population owned more than 60 percent of the wealth."[58]

Within these political-economic relationships, the ruling Americo-Liberian elite was very aware of the "cognitive effects" certain kinds of reading could have among nonelite Liberians. Before and during the time of the study, newspaper editors were imprisoned for publishing articles critical of the government or the rule of the elite. Where censorship was lifted, nongovernmental newspapers still remained cautious and restrained in their criticism:

> The printed word was not the critical source of revolutionary change in Liberia that it had been in Asia or even in Nigeria and Ghana. The history of the opposition press in Liberia was a checkered one at best, with editions of a dissident publication seldom going on beyond a year, a month, or even a single issue. Lack of funding, or outright government suppression and harassment of journalists and editors, frequently brought the antiestablishment critics "into line."[59]

Clearly, reading publications the government quelled, or tried to quell, had the potential to produce changes in thinking, and is a strong instance of literacy's cognitive effects—effects quite evident when the ideas "in" written material are viewed within their connection with the actual world, and not as abstract categories of mental processing.

Other cognitive effects are evident in Vai literacy. Occurring at the local village level, this literacy, for the most part, included only the ideas and practices of the personal and narrow governmental affairs of the Vai. In other words, within Liberian political and social conditions, the absence in Vai literacy of concepts about those oppressive conditions, and therefore the preclusion of opportunities to think about those conditions, meant Vai literacy had its own cognitive effects. Implicitly, the cognition in this literacy helped perpetuate the powerlessness and poverty of the Vai.

Examination of Liberian literacy raises another issue about cognitive effects. When we broaden the definition of literate thinking to include more than general mental operations, we can see how literacy "success" through schooling could have negative psychological effects. English literacy in Liberia embodied ideas and practices that reinforced power and powerlessness. Hence, being literate in English could mean having one's thinking organized from the view of those who controlled Liberia. Such a cognitive effect might enable one to do well on formal psychological tests of "higher-order mental processes" but be deficient in understanding actual life in Liberia.

For instance, former students literate in English had higher scores on test questions measuring an understanding of "modernity" than did people literate only in Vai. By an understanding of modernity Scribner and Cole meant understanding acting and thinking in "modern" society, not defined as understanding actually existing modern conditions. The differences between these two kinds of understanding, and their implications for test results and conclusions about cognition, can be demonstrated by placing the questions about modernity used in the study within the context of actual political life in Liberia. One question asked, "Have you ever been so concerned about some public problem that you really wanted to help do something?" Another inquired, "Have you ever talked with a government official to tell him your opinion about some public issue such as what the government should do about building schools or carrying the road to your town?" The answer "Never" was considered a sign of a deficient modern thinking.

Was this true for Liberia, where public participation in bringing about social change was not welcomed by those in power? There, expressions of interest in public issues could be considered a sign of subversiveness and "smart" people knew how to think and act in order to survive. So "Never" in this context might well have demonstrated a very accurate understanding of Liberian "modernity." Those schooled Liberians who answered positively might either have been ignorant of the reality of conditions that governed the country or have been part of the elite institutions that offered some safety and efficacy in voicing their opinions. Hardly a better understanding of "modernity."

This exploration of Vai literacy suggests that the reading process involves far more than cognition about written language and mental operations studied in psychological tests. Furthermore, literacy success—in this instance school-taught English—can contribute to thinking that misunderstands the world, and can thus create another kind of literacy problem. Finally, it is clear that finding the best instructional methods would have had little effect in a country in which only 50 percent of children went to school and Vai literacy was acquired by only a small portion of the male population and by almost none of the women. These outcomes had nothing to do with a failure to use the "best" instructional methods.

As these historical and cross-cultural examples suggest, the terms of the dominant debate are flawed in understanding the meaning of literacy, the cognition in literacy, the instruction of literacy, or literacy failure and success.

2

THE "NATURAL" ROAD TO READING

n the last decade of the eighteenth century, William Blake wrote "The Schoolboy," a poem about a boy who awakens on a summer morning and, like a "bird that is born for joy," wants to keep company with singing skylarks. Forced instead to go to school and sit under a "cruel eye," he soon forgets "his youthful spring" and becomes a caged bird, with drooping "tender wing," who cannot sing.[1] Written two centuries ago, the poem expresses a still familiar concern about the harm schooling can do to the wonder, excitement, and expression of children.

Reformers and traditionalists who have made appeals for children's natural disposition for learning have seldom allowed students to be as free as the birds, as Blake might have liked, but have assumed instead that if the instructional aviary were more attuned to children's natural mental makeup, intellectual pecking could be facilitated. This holds in the present dominant debate over literacy, in which all sides claim their mode of instruction is based on "natural learning."

Whatever the intentions of this claim about natural learning— whether by reformers seeking to open learning or by traditionalists wanting to cage it for students' best interests—all theories and instruction making such claims provide a flawed and limited interpretation of learning and teaching. I will also argue that to understand the mental processes involved in learning to read, the terms of the dominant debate need to be replaced by the categories I outlined in the previous chapter.

A Look Backward

In 1791, around the time Blake wrote "The Schoolboy," Friedrich Gedike, a German educator, proposed a new method of teaching reading that ran counter to the pervasive ABC approach. Instead of beginning with the alphabet, continuing through syllables, words, and sentences, and moving eventually on to books, he advised reversing the progression, or at least modifying it, by going from words to word parts. Echoing Rousseau's view in *Emile* that education should follow nature, Gedike argued that, unlike the ABC method, his was more harmonious with children's natural way of learning:

> As a rule, the synthetic method, which leads from parts to wholes, from causes to results, is more the way of dexterity and system than the way of Nature, made more for the purpose of putting in order what is already known and examined, than for finding out and examining. The analytical method which proceeds, on the contrary, from the whole to the parts, from the results to the causes, is incontestably the natural way of the human mind, and especially of the mind as it is first stirred into action.[2]

By immediately occupying children with whole ideas, he maintained, his method would prevent the boredom and indifference common in classrooms and would facilitate literacy learning.

These arguments did not impress German education leaders, who rejected Gedike's reform efforts on two grounds: Psychologically, the method placed excessive demands on students' memory because of the scores of words they were required to learn. Pragmatically, the method was not suited for the crowded classrooms of the day, which required discipline and a more systematic approach of instruction.[3] Gedike's reforms, in other words, were criticized partly because of existing conditions that would not have allowed for successful learning: had classroom conditions been different, the pragmatic criticism suggests, Gedike's method might have been more successful. For example, a teacher could have adequately monitored the words a child was learning to ensure that her or his memory was not being overloaded. In making this criticism, however, the educators must have assumed, reluctantly or willingly, that crowded classroom conditions had to be accepted as one of the givens within which any method would be used and assessed.

Given their assumptions and appraisal, the educators who gave a thumbs-down to Gedike's approach might have been right: in overcrowded classrooms, a tightly controlled method that progressed incrementally in small units would be better supervised and expected to yield better results. Since some children did learn to read using school textbooks, Gedike's criticism that the prevailing method was contrary to children's natural way of learning was at least partly deflected. The parts-to-the-whole method might not be the ideal way of learning and might even bore children, but it obviously was not glaringly antagonistic to children's thinking.

Rejection of Gedike in Germany did not dissuade United States educators dissatisfied with the lackluster alphabet approach from advocating a method based on the "more natural way of the human mind." Thomas H. Palmer, who served on a committee that examined teachers in his hometown of Pittsford, Vermont, wrote in 1837 that he was "much struck with the heavy, dull, vacant countenances of the pupils" that the alphabet method induced: "When the reading classes took their places, it was easy to perceive that the mind was no farther engaged in the exercise than attention to the pronunciation of the words required."[4] Palmer called for reading reform that used a whole-to-parts method that reflected the learning intrinsic to humans.

> This method, which may be termed the analytical system, is truly the method of nature. In her communications to man, she always proceeds from generals to particulars. We know a tree, and can name it, long before we become acquainted with its constituents, the leaves, limbs, trunk, and root.[5]

The need for whole meanings and instinctive learning was echoed by an author of a book on the sentence method (an extension of the word method): written language, like spoken language, should be learned "indirectly, while attention is directed to the thought expressed."[6] Other educators critiqued the alphabet method for forgetting that "children have minds."[7] By emphasizing particulars, the method taught them "not to think."[8]

Arguments about intrinsic learning and meaningful wholes forced only a small wedge into prevailing instruction. The word and sentence methods were promoted in various educational writings and used in many schools, but remained subordinate in the nineteenth century first to the alphabet method and then to the phonics method, which came into wide use in the middle of the century, especially with the introduction of the McGuffey *Readers*.

Why did these reform efforts fail? Part of the answer had to do with the availability of resources and conditions. As in Germany, these reforms were difficult to incorporate into existing classroom conditions. Also, schooling embodied assumptions about children and teachers that were antithetical to the reforms. Children's thinking, acting, and feeling had certain natural behavioral and mental proclivities that had to be controlled and guided for learning to occur. Rambunctiousness in children seemed, to teachers, parents, and policymakers, a natural quality of children that needed to be quelled for their best interests. Teachers "assumed that childhood was a precarious and undesirable state, and required vigilant tutoring and oversight. Children would learn to govern their passions, not only by being whipped or beaten into submission, but by attending to the tasks of formal learning."[9]

Another assumption about children held that although teachers would do the best they could for them, many children would nevertheless not become successfully literate. This assumption had a strong meaning for exercising classroom discipline. It was necessary not only for instructing those who would learn but for handling those who would not learn but were still expected to adhere to classroom disciplinary standards. Especially in classrooms with large numbers of students — by the end of the century urban classrooms held forty to forty-eight students — this double need for control was a constant challenge for teachers.[10]

Conditions not amenable to the reform efforts were exacerbated by the limited expertise of most teachers, who saw teaching, with its severe working conditions and meager financial rewards, as an interim job. For women, teaching often was an interlude between their own schooling and marriage. For men, it frequently was a way of earning money while going through college to prepare for other work. Structured, sequential instruction of skills met the needs of these teachers because it appeared to be efficient, required little training to use, and enhanced classroom control. The effectiveness of this kind of controlled instruction demonstrated its efficacy in the many children who learned through it. For the rest, it would have to be good enough.

The Quincy Method

In contrast to the reform efforts just outlined and the predominant reading instruction in nineteenth- and most twentieth-century schools were the reforms initiated by Francis W. Parker in the schools of Quincy, Massachusetts. Hired as school superintendent there in 1875, after the school board had found sizable reading and writing problems in children graduating from the eighth grade, Parker immediately embarked upon major changes. In the tradition of basing instruction on intrinsic ways of learning, Parker denounced conventional schooling for subjecting children, after their early years of "vigorous development" in "Nature's great methods," to "dull, wearisome hours of listless activity upon hard benches" that destroyed their "imagination, curiosity, and love for mental and physical activity."[11] As Merle Curti has written, Parker sought to cultivate

> the naturally divine motives which every child possessed. These motives, unless blighted by formal teaching methods, made every child an artist, a searcher for and lover of the truth, and an altruist. With the zeal of a true reformer, he set himself the task of devising methods and creating a spirit in the schoolroom that would nourish rather than kill "these native endowments," which stamped every child with the image of God.[12]

Parker created an education that sought to involve children actively in their own education and to use literacy critically, imaginatively, and practically. Like educators before him, he believed that the word method allowed children to learn in a "natural manner." As children had learned to speak in contexts that emphasized meaning, so too would they learn written language. Unlike previous proponents of the word method, however, Parker thought of the method not simply as a single reform in a separate academic subject, but as part of a new, integrated curriculum. Children would learn to read, write, spell, and think as they simultaneously learned about nature, society, history, geography, art, and literature.

Furthermore, although the curriculum defined general ways of teaching, Parker insisted that children should not be required to learn—could not learn—by a single method. Instruction had to be "marked throughout by intense individuality," which meant that teachers had to know their children as individuals.[13] Regimentation and uniformity were minimized; experience, spontaneity, curiosity, excitement, happiness, and individual opinion were encouraged. Children were given greater responsibility for their own conduct and for the work in class. Instead of punishment and competition, teachers emphasized intrinsic rewards and cooperation. For Parker, encouragement of individual thinking and discouragement of uniformity applied to both teachers and students. Teachers were encouraged to rethink and revise the curriculum, and were challenged to reassess their assumptions about how children learn and the purposes of education. The Quincy "method," Parker insisted, actually was a "spirit of study" and a system of "everlasting change."[14]

To what extent was the Quincy method built on children's "natural" inclinations for learning? Certainly children did not simply follow their natural inclinations. Rather, whatever might flourish in children was the result of work with teachers who were actively engaged in devising a sophisticated curriculum and encouraging children's learning. "Natural learning" did not mean that teachers simply facilitated— or, to use a contemporary term, "mediated"—children's thinking as they strove to master written language. For example, children were taught that true patriotism embraces the well-being of people in the entire world. Lessons explored the injustice and brutality in white treatment of Native Americans. Rebellion against oppression and injustice was regarded as commendable, not a crime. Overall, the study of history put more emphasis on equitable social relationships and less on military and political events. Children were encouraged to discuss their views, but teachers also discussed their own. Like all instruction that tries to eschew teacher authoritarianism and at the same time teach children about the world and themselves, Quincy teachers worked to maintain a difficult balance that would not pitch too far to one side or another. Teachers had to guide but not impose, foster but not require. Children could express their own ideas but not with the presumption that all views were equally good, not without being challenged. Parker's pedagogy did not merely make available conditions that allowed intrinsic inclinations to blossom. Rather, his conception of literacy learning had clearly defined ideas about the "uses" of literacy and the kind of thinking, acting, and feeling that successful literacy would achieve. The Quincy method offered teachers more opportunities to express and implement their ideas about education and encouraged an active infusion of adult ideals and guidance into the classroom.

Parker's reforms were relatively successful by two measures. First, the substantial truancy problems prior to his reforms were essentially eliminated. Second, a state survey showed that educational achievement in reading, writing, and spelling for Quincy students was superior to those in other schools in the county. Arithmetic achievement remained poor, but at the time of the survey Parker had not yet undertaken reform in that subject.[15] These measures of success did not mean that the new method was an unqualified success or fully satisfactory to Parker and others; still, its accomplishments were evident when compared with the failing system Parker had inherited.[16]

Laudable as Parker's successes were, and even though much can be learned from his achievements, equally important are the lessons learned from the Quincy method's not surviving long. Continuously faced with a school board and community that did not see his accomplishments as sufficient for providing him the financial support he needed, Parker began to feel disheartened and indicated he would not stay at his post. The board did little to change his mind, and in 1880, five years after his appointment, Parker left. Soon after, the Quincy schools discarded his reforms and reverted to conventional instruction.

I will have more to say about the reasons for the failure of this noteworthy reform, but since my assessment has to do with economic matters in Quincy, I will wait until Chapter 8, where I offer a fuller discussion of political-economic influences on literacy education.

Reading Instruction in the Early Twentieth Century

In the early twentieth century, ideas about basing literacy education on children's natural psychological makeup began to acquire a more scientific look. In a landmark 1908 book, *Psychology and Pedagogy of*

Reading, Edmund Burke Huey drew upon empirical studies of perception and thinking to offer a sophisticated argument for whole-to-parts reading instruction.[17] As the title of the book indicated, psychology and pedagogy were joined: insights into the psychology of reading were to be the basis for the pedagogy of reading.

Huey echoed the complaint that the logic of phonics instruction was not "natural to the child's mind" and that it interfered with the "child's formation of natural habits of reading." He cited research he believed demonstrated that meaning was fundamental for identifying print. For example, meaning could enhance how much a reader could apprehend in a single visual fixation. Experiments had found that the more meaning contained in letters or words (for instance, real words instead of nonsense words, or words combining to make a thought instead of unrelated words), the greater the number of words or letters a person could grasp in a single eye fixation. Applied to reading instruction, this finding meant that children could "recognize the whole word about as quickly as they recognize a single letter." Thus, children's learning was best served by beginning with whole meaning and sentences: "make thought lead" and allow analysis of constituent sounds and letters of words to "follow in its own time."[18] Phonics should be ancillary to meaning. Huey's approach to the psychology of reading established an orientation that continues to this day. Unlike Parker, who addressed the particular "meanings" that should be part of learning to read, Huey restricted his discussion of meaning to the natural psychological mechanisms that processed it. He had nothing to say about the meanings in meaning.

In the decades following Huey's work, methods emphasizing either meaning or skills, or amalgamating the two, held a similar conception of naturalness: a successful method worked because it was in accord with children's natural psychological processes for learning written language. By the 1940s the dissolution of any partisanship to meaning or skills was apparent in the most common reading programs: beginning reading started with a basic sight vocabulary, after which came instruction in phonics and other word-analysis skills, then work with increasingly longer stories.[19]

There were a number of exceptions to these instructional practices. One was the "activity," or "project," method, aimed at using children's interests as the foundation of the curriculum.[20] The method rose in popularity in the early 1920s, but mostly in private, experimental schools, and did not have more than a modicum of influence in the public schools. By the 1930s, with occasional exceptions, it remained only as a minor supplement to traditional instruction.[21]

As Parker's reforms had done, teachers using the activity or project method overstated children's natural learning as the starting point for their teaching. Children did not decide solely by themselves what activity or project they wanted to pursue, how they wanted to learn to read and write within these projects, or what they would learn through the projects. The approach was based on assumptions about children that were contingent upon a more active, orchestrated teacher involvement. Whatever their intrinsic tendencies for learning, children contributed to, but did not determine, or have sufficient influence in determining, their learning.

The failure of the method to take hold was not because it did not "work." There is evidence that it did work and that, if promoted, it could have worked even better. Its disappearance was due more to the fact that teachers who wanted to foster children's interests, creativity, and individual qualities had to do much more planning, be much more creative, and work much harder than traditional teaching had required. For instance, various facets of a given project had to be integrated, all children had to participate in the project, each child had to learn to read, write, and spell through the project, and special provisions had to be made for children who learned differently or at a slower rate. Above all, the project always, to one degree or another, required a genuinely participatory interaction between teacher and student. Unfortunately, most teachers who tried to use an activity approach did not get sufficient support from principals and school policymakers. Without this support—especially in terms of time, in-service education, materials, and class size—most project method teachers found that since they were working alone, what was required by the method was more than they individually could ever have sustained over the years.

The 1960s saw a reformulation of the natural learning view. John Holt wrote that, when learning to read, "in their own way and for their own reasons, children learn so much more rapidly and effectively than we could possibly teach them, that we can afford to throw away our curricula and our timetables, and set them free, at least most of the time, to learn on their own."[22] In a similar vein, Charles H. Rathbone wrote that children's learning is a result of their "own self-initiated interpretation" of the world. Children are their own agents—"self-reliant, independent, self-actualizing individual[s] who [are] capable, on [their] own, of forming concepts and of learning." The teacher is "mainly assistant to not director of the child's activity."[23]

This reformulation helped inspire the reform known as "open education," aimed at breaking down the rigid structure and preset curricula of classrooms. In theory, children would learn according to their "own nature," their "innate impulse" to achieve, to find out: "Provide children with sufficient materials which involve looking at words, talking, listening, writing, and reading, and they will somehow evolve their own best individualized reading 'program'; they will learn how to read."[24] The open educational approach encouraged children to self-select goals and activities, but like its reform predecessors, it raised the question of what was natural and what it meant for children to exercise natural choice. Children do not come to classrooms—open or otherwise—with a clean mental slate. They do not "choose" independently of an already formed mental organization of the world. They do not necessarily have the opportunity within classrooms to explore all facets of a topic. And if children's choices were contrary to what teachers thought they should choose, would teachers only serve as mediators and not attempt to alter the choice?

As had been the case for its forerunner, the activity or project method, the open education approach generated widespread interest, mainly in the late 1960s and early 1970s. In practice, however, it was introduced in only a relatively small number of classrooms. Larry Cuban estimates that in New York City at most 20 to 25 percent of classrooms were "open," even with a broad definition of the term.[25] The largest estimate of existing open classrooms nationwide reported that 60 percent of the schools in one community "had at least one open classroom." A survey of city superintendents throughout the country in 1974 found that an estimated 17 percent of classrooms in their respective cities used open classroom "approaches to education."[26]

Critics maintained that research showed that "students in open classrooms had significantly lower academic achievement than students in traditional classrooms," a "finding" that contributed to public hostility toward the reforms. Retrospective studies have repudiated this research, determining that "no clear conclusions" could have been reached "about the superiority of one form of instruction over the other." Nevertheless, both the erroneous reports and the failure of research to find a clear-cut, obvious literacy and academic subject advantage in open classrooms heightened opposition to the reforms.[27]

A familiar scenario unfolded once again. Open classrooms failed to gain sufficient support and resources, as well as a sufficient period of time to address and eliminate its problems. Open classrooms required teachers to do more work and experimentation than more traditional teachers had to do. Without support from their school systems, teachers dedicated to open classroom learning found the demanding work even more demanding; and teachers not fully committed to the innovations had little or no encouragement to become so. Feeling the pressure of test score comparisons, and having to squeeze changes within a few years, many open classroom teachers "quickly reverted to traditional methods, to authoritarian classroom control, and many soon left teaching."[28]

Natural Learning and the Current Great Debate

Nila Banton Smith observed in 1965 that the underlying assumption throughout the history of reading education, to one degree or another, has been that reading practices should be devised according to children's stages of development and "mental characteristics."[29] This assumption has continued into the current debate, as I have suggested, and is shared by reformers and traditionalists alike.

A chief contemporary example of the traditionalist version of natural learning is Jeanne Chall's comprehensive model of learning to read. Chall, a major figure in reading education, has argued relentlessly for conventional, skills-first education. Chall introduces her theory by asking, "How in essence do readers change as they advance from *The Cat in the Hat* to the financial pages of *The New York Times*?" Her answer is that readers move to this desired goal through a developmentally preprogrammed, hierarchical progression of stages, each with a distinctive cognitive structure.[30]

In Stage 1 (corresponding approximately to grades one and two), children are trying to gain control of the correspondence between symbols and sounds. Little attention is paid to the meaning of stories because without mastering symbol-sound basics, meaning cannot be achieved; conversely, thinking about meaning can only interfere with learning at this stage. With the mastery of basic sound-symbol relationships, Stage 2 (around grades two and three) emerges and meaning can be introduced. However, because of children's cognitive limitations, no more than a small amount of meaning is allowed through the instructional gates. So as not to overload a child's mental processes, says Chall, meaning must be controlled, confined primarily to content with which the child is already familiar. In Stages 1 and 2, "very little new information about the world is learned from reading."[31] Both these stages are conceived to justify nicely the use of a controlled, skills-first method.

Before proceeding to Chall's next stages, it is useful to see how her scheme might translate into actual classroom practice. An example Chall uses comes from a third-grade classroom she observed. The teacher was "businesslike and task-oriented, as were the children." The children read silently, answered questions, read orally, then sounded out difficult words. For spelling, the teacher wrote words on the blackboard, the students read them in unison, and individual students circled silent letters and defined the words. The teacher erased the words and the students spelled them from memory. A spelling test closed the activity. This, Chall concludes, "reflected a strong sense of the structure and organization" that is associated with reading improvement.[32]

At last, in Stage 3 (beginning around grade four and continuing to high school), children arrive at the first stage of "reading to learn the new—new knowledge, information, thoughts and experiences." Nonetheless, cognitive development continues to demand a tight grip on the instructional gates. Although children can now master ideas, the ideas need to be restricted to "conventional knowledge of the world essentially from one point of view."[33]

What is meant by "new" knowledge that youngsters learn from one viewpoint in Stage 3? Chall provides examples of "typical" materials:

She smoothed her hair behind her ear as she lowered her hand. I could see she was eying beauty and trying to figure out a way to write about being beautiful without sounding even more conceited than she already was.[34]

Early in the history of the world, men found that they could not communicate well by using only sign language. In some way that cannot be traced with any certainty, they devised spoken language.[35]

Presumably, the fragile cognition of youngsters at Stage 3 still prevents them from satisfactorily developing their own appraisal of stories depicting males changing the world while females primp. Meanwhile, the school years go by—now eight—and still nature militates against unbridling children's minds lest they stumble upon unconventional ideas.

Not until Stage 4 (the high school years) does reading finally include dealing with multiple viewpoints. Yet even here thinking is proscribed by natural mental development: students can think about a variety of perspectives, but not yet their own. Finally, at Stage 5 (usually in college or at age eighteen and above), readers do begin to develop their own views. They now are able to read what others say and "construct knowledge" for themselves, and create their own "truth." With this achievement, the last stage is completed.

Because Chall's progression of stages is an idealization of the long-standing dominant form of education, perhaps it is not surprising that she points to traditional educational practice itself as "proof" of the validity of the reading stages:

> Many practices in the schools seem to parallel the reading stages proposed here. One of the clearest parallels is that of school organization [in the past] two centuries. The primary grades—once called the language school—parallel Reading Stages 1 and 2. The intermediate and upper elementary grades (the middle grades and beginning of junior high) parallel Stage 3, reading to learn a variety of subjects and values. Academic work in traditional and contemporary high schools requires the broad reading that is characteristic of our proposed Stage 4. College-level work, when up to traditional academic standards, requires and gives practice in Stage 5 reading.[36]

In other words, the intrinsic learning stages have led educators to teach children in certain ways. School instruction, given the natural trial-and-error experiment that it has been, was devised through observations made by educators on how children's intrinsic learning abilities benefited from various kinds of teaching at various stages of development.

Without question, Chall's stages do resemble the traditional education that has "worked" for many years for many millions of children, but also not worked for millions of others, in terms of reading test score achievement. When considering its possible effect on children's development, many educators and parents might be likely to reject this pedagogy, regardless of claims about its connection to children's natural mental propensities. Who would want his or her child's early education to encourage little participation in initiating and creating learning activities; inattention to self; no exploration of multiple views; little experience making choices and solving problems; minimal experience developing, expressing, and contesting a viewpoint; contorted views of the world and opinions about it; an undervaluing of affect in learning experiences? These are hardly qualities to help children understand their own thoughts and emotions, feel secure about themselves, assess accurately the views of others, understand the world, and make sound judgments. Instead, educators and parents would be actively searching for alternatives, because what is natural to children's learning is simply and profoundly that they do learn and that they learn in various ways toward various learning and developmental goals. It is these goals that can be the standards for selecting a pedagogy fashioned in accordance with children's adaptable thinking.

Whole Language and Whole Meanings

Advocates of whole language—whose heritage is Francis Parker's Quincy method, the project method, and the open classroom approach—also make strong claims about how their approach is founded upon children's natural learning. Learning to read is served by putting children "at the center of the learning process" in a "literacy environment." Teachers can provide "multiple occasions to learn" as they "try to understand the way children are thinking, given the particular requirements children may have at specific moments of their evolution" to full literacy, proposes Emilia Ferreiro, a psychologist who has studied early literacy development.[37] Adults provide the environment and aid children in their literacy problem solving, but it is the children who ultimately devise their own solutions.

Some whole-language scholars stress placing social influences alongside biological ones in the concept of "natural." Nigel Hall, for example, emphasizes that the idea that literacy emerges naturally implies "some kind of maturational phenomenon, something that occurs almost inevitably as a result of biological programming." But children do not learn independently of social interactions. Children could not "learn to talk if deprived of access to purposeful oral language use. No child has ever learned to talk by being locked in a room with an endless supply of tape-recorded language."[38] Children require a social context in which people use literacy for a wide array of social purposes. "Thus the 'naturalness' is a function of social experiences where literacy is a means to a variety of other ends."[39] Even in Hall's more social interpretation of natural learning, however, children are independent learners who puzzle out meaning in social contexts.

In exemplary whole-language classrooms, teachers are active, but in an ancillary way. They become good observers of how children are attempting to solve written language problems and assist them in finding solutions. When a teacher observes that a child is having trouble with some aspect of reading, the problem is addressed then, with the teacher planning to address it again if the child continues to need assistance.[40] Through this "For Your Information" strategy, as it has been termed, a teacher conveys information about language "over and over again throughout the school day and the succeeding days, always within the context of meaningful literacy situations." By using this strategy, a teacher would be "confident that for those children who wanted and needed to receive this information it would be helpful, and for those children who had not yet begun to notice [certain aspects of language], there would be another day, another situation."[41]

Exemplary whole-language programs encourage children to choose the books they want to read and the way in which they want to write. The children may read to one another or read alone, or they may write alone and then share their writing with others. Over several days they may write twelve- to fifteen-page stories, which might be read by other children. The topic may be suggested by a teacher or may be one of their choice.[42]

This overview of whole language indicates much in its application of natural learning that is laudable. As Linda Christensen puts it, whole language seeks to empower "students to use their own voices, to plumb their lives for stories, poems, essays, to engage them in a dialogue with their peers about their writing, about literature."[43] Conversely, it eschews rigid, one-size-fits-all, docile learning. Still, for all its pluses, its emphasis on an intrinsic reading process contributes to a limited meaning of the term "whole." Even though ideas in language are always constituents of the whole and despite the emphasis whole-language advocates put on "meaning," they have surprisingly little to say about the specific ideas children naturally puzzle out and grasp.

This is not to say that whole-language teachers do not talk about the ideas in stories and children's interpretations of ideas or that teachers do not actively elicit children's expression of ideas. However, there is little said in whole-language writings about the ideas themselves that children confront, absorb, and express in their purported "natural" meaning-making efforts. For example, in a description of a youngster's behavior in his early literacy development, a teacher writes: He describes his pictures "in great detail orally. He tells a story: 'This is a Tiger Shark shooting. The Cobra shot at him and he missed. So the Tiger Shark shot at the Cobra plane and the Cobra hit himself and shot off one wing. And the Tiger Shark shot at the Cobra and blew it to smithereens.'"[44]

The youngster's writing is discussed solely in terms of his overall language development in his natural efforts to learn to write and read, his invented spellings, his development of sound-symbol correspondence, and the personal words he can sight-read. Yet the fact that the ideas generating the boy's writing are culturally created and certainly not "natural" has no place in the discussion. Discussion of the facilitative role a teacher should play as children naturally construct their own literacy is narrowly drawn. Nothing is said about any facilitative discussion or activities that would address the culturally created ideas of aggression and killing.

Facilitating children's meaning-making activities has been called "leading from behind," in which a teacher waits until a child attempts a task and then helps him or her accomplish it.[45] By assuming that children's natural learning inclinations should be the basis on which teachers facilitate learning, "leading from behind" does not address the ideas teachers might want children to consider or what they should do if children do not initiate a consideration of those ideas.

Whole language emphasizes that "learning is both personal and social" in classrooms or "learning communities," learning should be "functional," all learners should be "empowered," and the "experiences" of children should be "accepted."[46] These tenets sound good, but lacking specifics, the guidelines they offer are ambiguous. How is learning by using culturally given ideas "personal"? How is literacy "functional"? What is an "empowered" child? Which "experiences" are accepted?

These omissions do not characterize the thinking of all whole-language advocates. Carol Edelsky, for example, has been explicit about creating a whole-language pedagogy that "opposes social stratification and promotes an egalitarian social order." She emphasizes that whole language requires

> explicit statements about [its] political project and explicit discussion of the connection between its political stance and its theoretical positions on language and education. When people with a Whole Language perspective fail to explicate these connections, it is too easy for their theoretical positions to be used merely to create a "kinder, gentler" *status quo.*[47]

In a similar vein, Harvey Daniels asked how a whole-language approach can be built that is not depoliticized but has a "critical approach toward the society around us." Daniels noted the importance of choosing good literature that would be at "the core of kids' experience." Among this literature are good books that deal with homeless people, refugees, and other societal issues. "There's a lot of literature out there that is very political and extremely critical of this society," Daniels continued. "In fact, almost all good literature is critical. I don't know any good literature that takes the present state of affairs and spins a tale about how wonderful everything is."[48]

Unfortunately, views that explicitly address the specific ideas in written language in terms of goals for children's development are peripheral in whole-language discussions, as well as in the dominant debate over literacy.

"Natural Learning" Reform and Resources

The need to address the many influences external to the natural reading process is evident in Rexford G. Brown's survey of literacy education in the United States and Canada. Brown has been especially interested in reform efforts and has looked at classrooms using whole language to some degree. He found that although many teachers and principals had created alternative forms of learning guided by the students' own learning goals as creative and independent thinkers, on the whole most classrooms, he lamented, remained dry, mechanical, and authoritarian:

[The schools] do not provide the climate in which a literacy of thoughtfulness for all students is likely to thrive and spread; quite the contrary. Programs conducive to thoughtful, active learning are at the margins. Whole language-oriented schools are fighting upstream against heavy resistance.[49]

Why the failure to achieve more reform? "The most frequently given reason for not moving toward an instruction more conducive to thoughtfulness," concluded Brown, "was time."

We were told that there simply is not enough time in the day to challenge every student or provide personalized opportunities for learning. Teachers who were sympathetic to the idea of providing more challenges said that they did not have the time to prepare well for discussions, collaborative activities, or interdisciplinary lessons; they did not have the time to respond thoughtfully to 145 essays or projects.[50]

Susan M. Church, chairing a project on changing classroom teaching toward whole language, found that teachers in the project "commented over and over again about how privileged they felt to have time, with paid substitutes, to reflect on their work. One told me, 'I truly feel like a professional, like someone values what I know and can do.'"[51]

How time influences instruction and learning is also evident in discussions of language acquisition that compare learning to speak with learning to read.[52] Whole-language proponents have maintained that literacy education should be grounded in similarities between the two, but Dina Feitelson, quoting linguist Courtney Cazden, observes that the numerical ratio of adult to child in learning to speak and learning to read nullifies any analogy:

Language is typically acquired by a single child surrounded by several doting "teachers." This numerical relationship is reversed in the school setting. Here it is one teacher who has to instruct 25 and sometimes many more students. It is in part on account of the numerical disparity that Cazden feels that one cannot really generalize from learning to talk to learning to read. At home the child is exposed to "a rich set of pairings of meanings and sounds—for that is what language in the context of ongoing experience is." Rich sets of pairings of oral and written language are, on the other hand, "much less available" in school.[53]

Learning to speak, then, is an inapplicable model not because of its differences in children's cognition and language needs, but because more adults are involved when children learn to speak.

One may infer from this difference that if the number of adults available for learning written language were the same for learning oral language, the two could be more favorably compared and the following question could be posed: Since all children learn oral language, why do schools not use the oral language model or come closer to it? As the previous quote suggests, the likely answer runs something like this: It would be too costly to fund the adult-child ratio in the oral model. Leaving aside for the moment the question of whether or not funds could be made available, the theoretical point I wish to make here is that conceptions of natural literacy learning and teaching are contingent upon—rather than independent of—available resources.

"Natural Learning" and "Effective" Instruction

Because both traditional and reform instruction claim to be most attuned to children's natural mental makeup, literacy specialists usually propose comparing the respective claims by using the literacy achievement outcomes usually measured in tests. As one group of researchers put it, the "comparative effectiveness" of respective approaches is "the question" for "the majority of present-day practitioners."[54] Presumably, the instruction most in accord with children's thinking processes will be the fastest in promoting literacy test achievement.

A problem with this kind of comparison is that it does not adequately address the educational and developmental goals contained within each kind of instruction. Instruction aimed toward a particular set of goals may elicit a particular and corresponding composition of mental abilities. Since children can learn in various ways, another form of instruction with different goals may elicit a very different set of mental abilities. Thus, the success of one kind of instruction does not by itself demonstrate that it is better attuned to a child's natural mental propensity for learning to read and write.

Nor does the speed at which goals are achieved necessarily mean that the instruction that achieves the goals faster is superior (that is, more effective) or has a more direct connection to the mental processes for literacy learning. A form of instruction with more than narrow literacy learning tasks, one with a wider array of literacy and child development goals, may actually be "slower" or "less effective" in reaching some specific goals.

For example, the single goal of scoring well on achievement tests of skills, word recognition, and multiple-choice comprehension of given passages would be quite different from a second form of instruction with the multiple goals of: reading a specified range of books; demonstrating comprehension of the books through extensive discussions about them; expressing independent thinking in these discussions; producing different kinds of writing that demonstrate comprehension of the books, creative ideas, and spelling growth. These are just a few of the goals that could be established in literacy instruction.

This second approach would call upon a different set of mental abilities, not more natural abilities, but merely abilities different from those activated in the first approach. Although this second approach might be slower in reaching the goals of the first, its rate would not mean that it was less effective, because it would engage children in a broader set of goals.

3

ALPHABET SOUNDS

AND LEARNING TO READ

In recent years, researchers seeking to understand the thinking abilities involved in learning to read have claimed to have found a chief predictor of "individual differences in early reading acquisition."[1] This predictor, called "phonological awareness," has been considered a breakthrough in knowledge and instruction. As one review concluded: "After over a decade of research, we know more about relations between phonological awareness and reading than we do about relations between reading and just about anything else" and know that it plays "a causal role in the acquisition of reading skills."[2] More emphatically, Keith Stanovich, a prominent figure in the reading field, has observed that the investigations into phonological awareness have produced "a strong consensus" that it is "the cognitive process that best predict[s] reading progress in the earliest stages."[3]

Phonological Awareness

"Phonological awareness" (or "phonemic awareness") means knowing that phonemes (the smallest units of speech sounds) are separable and can be manipulated mentally and orally, as when blending or separating phonemes in order to identify words. Tasks demonstrating phonological awareness include:

- Blending phonemes: Asking someone to say or identify a word made by blending its phonemes (/b/, /a/, /t/ = bat).
- Segmenting phonemes: Asking what sounds are heard in a word (bat = /b/, /a/, /t/).
- Deleting phonemes: Asking what word would remain if a phoneme were deleted (remove /b/ from bat).

The importance of phonological awareness in literacy achievement seems logical because "learning to read and spell in an alphabet writing system depends upon the ability to conceive of spoken words as sequences of phonemic segments and to identify and locate those segments within words and syllables."[4]

Many researchers use terms like "predicts" and "depends upon" to denote the potent causal role of phonological awareness in learning to read.[5]

[R]esearch has shown that phonological awareness appears to play a causal role in reading acquisition—that it is a good predictor not just because it is an incidental correlate of something else, but because phonological awareness is a foundational ability underlying the learning of spelling-sound correspondences.[6]

But to the annoyance of those in the "strong consensus," the strength of evidence that has convinced them has not convinced everyone. "In some quarters of the reading education community" (read: whole-language advocates), complains Stanovich, his and similar work on phonological awareness has been "less than welcome."[7] Stanovich thinks this resistance is connected to the debate over teaching skills: if whole-language advocates agreed with the strong consensus, they would be acknowledging the importance word skills play in beginning reading and the necessity of direct instruction in skills.

There is no question that phonological awareness is a major explanation of reading success and failure. Indeed, one cannot find a discussion on reading in either the professional or popular literature that does not underscore the importance of the role of phonological awareness. In most cases, phonological awareness is seen as a "magic bullet," a straightforward determinant of reading success or failure: If you teach it, students will learn. But the robust role it is supposed to play seems to run counter to my view of the multiple, complex influences involved in learning to read.

Phonological awareness does play a causal role, but it is not an independent psychological process, and its causal role is different from that conceived by those in the "strong consensus." Seeing phonological awareness as a distinct psychological process distorts its role in beginning reading, proscribes instruction that can allow it to play such a role and minimizes the responsibility of social policy in fostering successful beginning reading. Understanding properly how phonological awareness affects beginning reading requires accounting for many more influences as well. I will begin to develop these arguments by looking first at the research supporting a causal relationship.

Evidence of a Causal Connection

Evidence of a causal connection between children's early phonological abilities and later reading achievement comes from a number of studies that used training programs to teach children to identify and manipulate sounds. One of these programs for preschool children with poor phonological abilities—such as not being able to distinguish phoneme sounds in simple words—emphasized skills such as categorizing sounds; for example, recognizing words that shared the same initial phoneme (cat, cab) and rhyme units (cat, hat, mat). The children were also taught to associate common sounds with plastic letters. The children's reading and spelling scores were approximately at age level (age eight), while those of a matching group, who received no such training, were below age level.[8]

Another phonological awareness training program found that preschool children in the program "significantly outperformed" untrained children in reading and spelling ability over the first three school years, suggesting that phonological awareness was the "single most powerful [determinant] of later reading and spelling progress."[9] Phonological awareness, said the researchers, was "a critical precursor of reading acquisition rather than a mere consequence of being literate."[10] Other studies have reported similar instructional effects and have agreed that phonological awareness is essential in beginning reading and can be attained with specific training. With phonological awareness beginning readers start to see writing not as arbitrary but as having a coherence and consistency. By analyzing speech into units and understanding that the flow of speech is actually combined parts, beginning readers are able to identify words they have not yet encountered.[11]

The skills-first theory of learning to read underpins much of the work on phonological awareness. Within this theory, phonological awareness abilities are thought to precede phonics competence. It is argued that beginning readers must first grasp the sound structures of spoken words (that is, acquire sufficient phonological awareness) before making connections between sound structures and the symbols and patterns of symbols of written words. Because phonological awareness is considered a requisite for associating sounds and symbols ("phonological recoding ability," in reading jargon), advocates of direct teaching of this skill hold that phonics instruction should not be introduced before the "default" strategy has been employed and phonological awareness has been attained. Doing otherwise, they believe, produces only minimal benefits. Although in practice this sequence is not rigid because the two abilities overlap, reading experts who emphasize skills in early reading insist that learning phonological awareness is the critical first step.[12] More specifically, phonological awareness is thought to fit into early reading by allowing beginning readers to get beyond their natural, initial strategy for reading words—their "default acquisition procedure" as one computer metaphor described it.[13] This does not mean that early readers read whole words. Rather, as psychologists Usha Goswami and Peter Bryant posit, they make associations between some part of the word they are reading and the whole word. Their initial strategy relies more on words as patterns or sequences of letters within words: "there is very little direct evidence that children who are learning to read do rely on letter-sound relationships to help them read words." Instead, they "take easily and naturally to reading words in other ways: they adopt a global strategy which means that they either recognize the word as a pattern or remember it as a sequence of letters."[14] In other words, beginning readers tend to grasp whole words as "logograms" (symbols representing an entire word), especially because they have difficulty relying on symbol-sound rules. This initial obstacle arises from the limitations of English, a language whose "simple letter-sound relationships do not work or only work very approximately with a large number of written words."[15]

The use of the logogram method will continue until the child is taught appropriate phonemic sound principles and begins to make connections between phonemes and the letters that symbolize them. Without this knowledge, beginning readers will be unable to break free of essentially memorizing part of a word and associating it with a spoken word.

What Phonological Abilities Are Necessary?

What I have just outlined appears fairly straightforward. However, when we begin to look at the details we find that a chief concern in work on phonological abilities is whether all or only particular ones are necessary for learning to read. Goswami and Bryant,[16] for instance, postulate that the critical phonological ability is learning to distinguish between onset (the opening unit of a word, as /c/ in cat) and rime (the ending unit of the word, /at/ in cat). They theorize that as youngsters attain phonological awareness, they first distinguish syllables in words, which provides them with an awareness of broad segments in words, but before they can attain the ability to distinguish phoneme sounds they must take an intermediate step. Detecting phonemes is difficult for beginning readers, except when the phoneme comes at the beginning of a word, but manipulating onset and rime requires breaking the word into fewer parts and is thus somewhat easier. For example, "cat" has one syllable and three phonemes (c-a-t), but the rime ending "at" is a phonological unit that lies between a phoneme and a syllable.[17] As children learn to read, Goswami and Bryant explain, they use their ability with onset and rime "to work out how to pronounce unfamiliar written words by drawing analogies between familiar and unfamiliar written words, and using these analogies to work out pronunciations for the new words" (such as did, kid, lid).[18]

This interpretation emphatically maintains that not all phonological awareness abilities are necessary for learning to read. Rather, propose Goswami and Bryant, after a youngster gets off to a start in beginning reading by learning a body of words and how to manipulate onset and rime, continued reading itself is "probably the most important cause of awareness of phonemes."[19] Even though their theory is orderly and logical—and highly regarded by many reading experts—Goswami and

Bryant do little to clarify whether phonological awareness abilities are causal. Critical of their interpretation, for example, are a number of researchers who claim that without first acquiring some phonemic knowledge—particularly the sounds of consonants at the beginning and end of three-letter words—the two-unit onset and rime can confuse beginning readers because they will not know where to make differentiations within words. Further criticism of the onset-rime theory comes from a study that found that among first graders who were proficient at manipulating onsets and rimes, 20 percent of them could not read words at the preprimer level. This study also made more complicated the question of what phonological skills needed to be learned by proposing that the relationship between phonological awareness and actual reading does not run in only one direction. Like Goswami and Bryant, they proposed that "basic word recognition" might itself foster the learning of "more complex forms of phonological awareness."[20] Other researchers have also suggested that phonological awareness and learning to read have a "reciprocal" not unidirectional relationship: some amount of phonological awareness may facilitate learning to read, but learning to read in turn plays a "causal role in the development of phonological abilities."[21]

The use of training studies for identifying the specific phonological awareness skills that facilitate learning to read has provided a number of contradictory answers. For example, the ability to blend phonemes ($/c/ + /a/ + /t/$ = cat) was identified as a reading "enabler" and a good predictor of later reading gains,[22] but a reexamination of the research failed to duplicate this initial finding. Instead, this study found that when kindergarteners taught to blend were compared with others taught to blend and segment phonemes ("What are the three sounds you hear in the word 'cat'?"), the latter group did better on a word-learning task, a measure more directly reflecting reading.[23]

Identifying specific phonological abilities that contribute to beginning reading is further complicated by the proposal that specific abilities might not have any fixed place in a sequence of reading achievement. Rather, their contribution is determined by the teaching approach. Teaching that emphasizes learning the connections between letter sounds and whole words would require greater knowledge of small phonemic units. In contrast, a method emphasizing the skill of dividing words into onset and rime components might make this skill a "stronger determinant in learning to read." Consequently, it may be "inappropriate to formulate theories of the relationship between phonological awareness and literacy in universal terms."[24]

We can conclude from these kinds of studies that if children were taught different kinds of phonological awareness skills without, at the same time, engaging in reading, writing, and other written language activities, certain kinds of phonological awareness skills might be considered "enablers" facilitating reading. The limitation of studies like these, however, is in their use of artificial tasks as opposed to the "real life" activities of young children. It is thus impossible to conclude that beginning readers would benefit most from phonological awareness skills of any kind, if they were taught separately and prior to experience with fuller reading and writing.

We have, therefore, two seemingly contradictory findings: phonological awareness is a causal ability, but is not—in the strict sense of the term—causal. The more phonological awareness training is incorporated with written language, the more substantial the results. One program achieved success by using the following array of activities: teaching phonemic analysis and blending by manipulating individual letters (e.g., changing sat to sam, sam to ham, ham to him), studying phonetically regular words, reading stories from phonetically controlled books, and spelling dictated words and sentences that were phonetically regular. Putting aside the question of whether or not these particular activities are the ones that should be used, we see that phonological awareness is "causal" in the sense that it contributes to reading achievement, but is itself attained through (or "caused" by) experiences with written language.

When we introduce the question of what kinds of written language experiences promote phonological awareness, we find that they do not necessarily have to be those just described. Although most studies on phonological awareness have been done by researchers supportive of direct instruction of skills and critical of whole language, the importance of phonological awareness is evident in a large portion of whole-language theory and practice. Clarifying this misrepresentation is, as we shall see, important.

Whole-Language View of Phonological Awareness

In her discussions of beginning reading, Marie Clay, a major figure in the whole-language movement, cites research on the importance of phonological awareness and readily acknowledges the correlations found between early phonological awareness and later reading development.[25] While critical of direct, systematic skills teaching, Clay's instructional recommendations agree with conclusions in phonological awareness research: children should learn the discrete sounds in spoken words, and as they learn to read, should make connections between sounds and letters. Although her instructional emphasis offers children wide experiences with written language, she does not adhere to this approach rigidly. Children who have trouble learning to read, Clay assumes, might benefit from some explicit teaching of phonological awareness.

Despite her recognition of the connection between phonological awareness and beginning reading and of the special assistance some students might require, Clay's interpretation of the meaning of this connection diverges from that of most advocates of phonological awareness training. She is concerned not only with teaching phonological awareness but also with how children want to learn and benefit from phonological awareness as they become literate. This divergence may seem minor but in fact is sharp because Clay wants to make young children active learners who "want to hear the sound segments in words and to search for these on their own initiative."[26] For her, phonological awareness is one part of a larger panoply of written language constituents, not a "stand alone" skill in which to train students.

The importance of phonological knowledge in whole-language education is also evident in what is often called "emergent literacy," an area of whole language concerned with early literacy development.[27] I will briefly summarize this work to show how it details the development of phonological awareness as part of young children's overall encounter with written language. Literacy experience can obviously begin with storybook reading in the first year of life, but I will begin around age four, when children often exhibit striking progress in their awareness of spelling and the function of letters.

Emergent literacy research has identified a pattern of young children's initial efforts to differentiate their scribbling from writing, and their progress in making their scribbles look more letterlike and contain letterlike strings. While this is taking place, the children begin to recognize a letter or two, often the initial letter of their own name. Continued experience provides them with the opportunity to begin to understand that the same letter in different words makes the same sound.

This, in turn, contributes to their learning additional letter names and how to apply them. With time and continued written language experience, children's writing displays a strategy in which syllables make up the "phonemic units" of a word, and a single letter is used to represent a syllable, as in the example that writing expert Donald Graves gives of a child writing SSTK for "This is a truck."[28]

Through further writing experiences children eventually recognize that syllables are insufficient units for writing and reading, and begin to make more complex phonetic connections. The spellings they invent generally reveal an increasingly acute understanding of the positions and sequence of consonants and vowels. Graves gives an example from a child's writing of the successive mastery of "grass": It begins with "g" and proceeds through further writings as "gs," "grs," "gres," and ultimately to "grass."[29] Through their writing activities, children learn that letters correspond to sounds smaller than a syllable, and they begin to analyze phonemes of words they write. Continuing to progress, children get to "know practically all the letters of the alphabet by name and eventually are capable of giving both the name and the sound value or the different sound values that the same letter can represent."[30]

Graves provides many examples, such as the following, of whole-language instruction that promotes phonological awareness abilities. While discussing a child's writing, a teacher says, "Here is 'fell' and 'down,' you got the first and last part. I'd like you to say each of these words slowly to see if you can spot any missing letters." The child says the words slowly but cannot find any, so the teacher goes on to the word "went," spelled "wet." The teacher says, "This is a hard one. The tricky 'n' is hard to hear but you are saying it. See if you can guess where an 'n' goes in 'went.' Say it slowly now." The child does so and replies, "Oh, right here. Between the 'e' and the 't.'" This exchange illustrates that, in whole language, through a teacher's guidance with sounds and letters previously "obliterated in struggles with more dominant features in the words," children can obtain and expand their phonological awareness and knowledge of sound-symbol relationships.[31]

We see that whole-language researchers and theorists are not indifferent to phonological awareness: what is different from the skills paradigm is their conceptualization of how phonological awareness develops and should be allowed to develop, and their concern with helping children construct phonemic knowledge within the context of written language.

Direct and Indirect Teaching of Phonological Awareness

A study comparing different approaches to teaching phonological awareness sheds further light on the issues of causation and instruction. Reading Recovery is an early intervention program that provides one-to-one daily instruction for approximately thirty minutes to youngsters who have been identified in the early grades—usually the first—as having difficulty in learning to read. Initially, some time is devoted to letter identification with plastic letters, but most of the session is used for reading books and writing, with children learning phonological awareness, phonics, and similar word skills within the reading and writing activities rather than through separate, direct instruction.

In one study, two forms of Reading Recovery were compared, a "standard" approach and another that included explicit phonological awareness teaching—that is, explicit instruction on letter-phoneme patterns. In the standard approach, after children could identify at least thirty-five of the fifty-two alphabet letters (upper- and lowercase), the time devoted to learning the letters was replaced by additional storybook reading in which word analysis activities, such as phonological awareness, were learned incidentally. In the modified program, the remaining time was devoted to direct teaching of phonological awareness. When the programs were compared, both groups performed similarly on phonological awareness tests and on other tests of reading and writing. Their progress continued to the end of the first year, when tests showed that both groups were reading at grade level.[32]

The researchers identified as important a learning rate difference between the two groups touching upon the question of the speed at which reading competence is achieved if phonological awareness is directly or indirectly taught. The modified Reading Recovery group learned skills and improved its reading and writing sufficiently for the program to end in eight and a half weeks. The standard group required eleven and a half weeks. This difference demonstrated to the researchers that the modified Reading Recovery group "learned to read much more quickly." Its systematic, direct instruction in sounds and symbols was "more effective than incidental instruction" that relied "on writing activities as the primary means of developing knowledge of the alphabet code."[33]

Whether direct instruction was "more effective" cannot be inferred solely on the basis of learning speed. Rather, this conclusion first requires answering the question: What literacy and child development benefits might accrue from a program that gives relatively greater emphasis to storybook reading? What might be the additional enhancement in reading pleasure, motivation to read, opportunity to think in greater depth about stories, confidence to discuss stories, and other important aspects of reading not assessed by the tests? Moreover, although this three-week difference does represent dissimilar speeds of learning to achieve particular goals and might be significant for school budgets, I believe it is trivial in view of the comparable literacy achievement at the end of the first year.

In a similar comparison, a Reading Recovery group spent an average of 60 percent of its time reading stories and other written material, compared with 30 percent for the group receiving direct instruction of skills. Approximately 15 percent of the Reading Recovery time was spent working indirectly on phonological, sound-symbol, and related word recognition and word analysis abilities, compared with 70 percent of the time for the direct instruction group. At the beginning of the next school year—several months after completing the programs— only the Reading Recovery students showed significant gains in tests of comprehension, writing, and word analysis and sound-symbol correspondence skills.[34]

This and related research do not demonstrate that Reading Recovery is a "magic bullet" program for poor readers.[35] They do, however, add support to the judgments that phonological awareness can be learned indirectly in comprehensive experiences with written language and through ("caused" by) adult-assisted written language experiences. Additional insight into these issues can be gained by examining the valuable preschool activity of storybook reading.[36]

Preschool Learning and Phonological Awareness

There is no question that preschool storybook reading contributes to eventual reading success: significant and positive correlations have repeatedly been found between it and later reading achievement in school. Additionally, storybook reading has been shown to expand oral vocabulary and strengthen an eagerness to read.

What might storybook reading teach children about written language and, in particular, about phonological awareness? Gordon Wells, who has studied language development for many years, has proposed that storybook reading gives children the opportunity to experience language's "characteristic rhythms and structures." Mimicking storybook intonation patterns is evident in young children's "pretend" reading.[37] Storybook reading can also make children aware that written language is symbolic of actions, people, things, etc., and that, unlike spoken language, it is language independent of context (that is, it is not like everyday spoken language that is related to situations and people associated to the language). Children learn that with decontextualized written language they must "treat the verbal formulation of the message as the chief locus of meaning, disregarding if necessary the immediate context and the personal associations; language alone is used to create experiences."[38]

Kindergarteners who had been read to frequently before they learned to read demonstrated a knowledge that written language, more than oral language, used participles (verbs used syntactically as nouns or adjectives; e.g., padding, ice skating), attributive adjectives (e.g., "The brown dog" instead of "The dog is brown"), and adverbial clauses (-ly adverbs to modify verbs: "He slowly followed them"). They also carry this knowledge "with them when they enter school and begin formal literacy instruction."[39]

Storybook reading also fosters greater attention to written language itself, thereby promoting phonological awareness. Storybook reading helps preschoolers "extend their letter and word recognition abilities, and learn about sound-symbol correspondences."[40] Reading researchers Steven Stahl and Bruce Murray offered one such scenario:

[Children might] first learn letter names, perhaps through hearing alphabet books read aloud or by singing the alphabet song, and then they learn to match individual letters with their names. As a part of teaching the letter names, sound values are taught. For example, a child might read an alphabet book in which letters are paired with pictures of animals containing their names. The parent or teacher who taught the letter names might also include beginning sound instruction with the letter name instruction. Alternatively because most consonants contain the phonemes most commonly associated with them in their names, learning a letter name helps children identify its sound value.[41]

Phonological awareness and sound-symbol knowledge is also promoted by children's experimentation with rhyming words in storybook reading, such as when "reading" phrases in stories with rhymes ("Good night room, Good night moon") and learning nursery rhymes ("Humpty Dumpty"). Children will ask an adult to find a word or phrase in a book they have heard, and they begin to see that words and letters reappear and that the squiggles are letters and have sounds. They experiment with identifying a word by first identifying a sound in it, and through this experimentation become increasingly aware that symbols represent meaning and that sounds and symbols are related.[42]

Studies of storybook reading and related literacy activities reinforce the view that acquiring phonological awareness plays an important role in learning to read, but within full early literacy experiences it is one among many interrelated and interdependent activities and accomplishments that comprise learning to read. Thus, attributing to phonological awareness a causal role in learning to read is an artificial abstraction of only one among many very important facets.

Storybook reading is but one example of the contribution of adult or mentor assistance (or "mediation") in promoting phonological awareness and other written language knowledge. Less obvious is indirect assistance that creates the conditions for seemingly "self-generated" experiences in learning written language. This assistance comes through buying paper, pencils, crayons, books, audiotapes for read-along books, magnetic letters on a refrigerator, games using animals and the first letters of their names, and other written-language-related materials.

Phonological Awareness as a Marker

Because both direct and indirect adult-supported experiences with written language can promote phonological awareness, we may go one step further and ask, "What are the sources (or 'causes') of these experiences?" A strong one is social class. It is no secret that children from lower-income homes perform less well in school than children from middle-income homes and that early readers are more likely to come from middle-income than lower-income families. There are many reasons for this, but in terms of learning phonological awareness and other aspects of written language, class generally carries with it different literacy learning experiences that influence school learning. Middle- and upper-income families, for example, tend to do more storybook reading, have more children's books and other literacy-education materials, introduce uncommon words, provide more cultural experiences related to novel concepts and vocabulary, and send their children to enriching preschool programs.[43]

Connections between these class influences and phonological awareness are easy to draw. In reading educator Eileen Ball's words:

> Preschoolers and kindergarteners who come from print-rich environments experience thousands of hours' worth of prereading activity before they enter kindergarten or first grade. Through these early literacy experiences, they acquire extensive knowledge about print and how print maps to speech, including knowledge about the segmental nature of speech. It stands to reason that children who, by comparison, enter school with a limited number of hours engaged in school-consistent interactions with print, have far fewer opportunities to discover how written language maps onto speech. One consequence of this limited interaction with print is that some children will enter school without the prerequisite phoneme awareness knowledge necessary to bootstrap literacy learning.[44]

Connections between social class, early literacy achievement, and phonological awareness do not mean that class is an invariable determinant. High literacy achievers can come from poor homes[45] and low literacy achievers from middle-income homes.[46] However, the strong association between class-related literacy experiences and literacy achievement points to another way of seeing phonological awareness: more than a cognitive causal factor in itself, phonological awareness is a "marker" of adult-supported social and literacy experiences that influence (cause) literacy achievement. Seeing phonological awareness as a causal cognitive process that promotes literacy leads to the misdirected and inadequate question: "What kind of training programs and specific experiences are required to teach phonological awareness?" When, however, we see phonological awareness as a marker, it is more likely to lead to the fuller, more promising question: "How can all children obtain the comprehensive written language experiences that will ensure continued achievement?"

4

EMOTIONS AND LEARNING TO READ

In the early part of this century, Soviet psychologist Lev Vygotsky observed that the study of psychology had been damaged by the separation of the intellectual from the motivational and emotional (or "affective") aspects of thinking. The terms "emotions" and "affect" refer to states such as happiness, shame, fear, disgust, annoyance, sadness, anger, equanimity, anxiety, depression, surprise, and love. Thinking, said Vygotsky, was transformed into an "autonomous stream" separated "from the full vitality of life, from the motives, interests, and inclinations of the thinking individual." By not identifying how emotions contribute to thinking, our ability to provide causal explanations of thinking was impaired. Vygotsky also emphasized the need to take into account the contexts in which this unity is created: "Every idea contains some remnant of the individual's affective relationship to that aspect of reality which it represents."[1]

Unfortunately, the field of reading in general and the literacy debate in particular have tended to disregard this unity. Rather than recognizing that cognition and learning are always intertwined with, and never independent of, emotions, thinking has tended to be conceived instead almost exclusively as "cognition"—that is, as a process of images, concepts, arid mental operations. Absent has been a distinction between models of cognition and the actual functioning of cognition: although models can isolate cognition as a means for understanding facets of thinking, in real life cognition is never an isolated mental process.

The Study of Cognition and Emotions
in Psychology and Education

The emphasis on cognition in the literacy debate parallels that in psychology and education. Until recently, psychological research on emotions was sporadic. Behaviorism, which dominated psychology for many years, shunned "internal states."[2] Cognitive psychology, behaviorism's replacement, emphasized "internal states" but did so insufficiently. As neurobiologist Joseph LeDoux has remarked:

> Cognitive science emerged recently, around the middle of this century, and is often described as the "new science of the mind." However, in fact, cognitive science is really a science of only a part of the mind, the part having to do with thinking, reasoning, and intellect. It leaves emotions out. And minds without emotions are not really minds at all. They are souls on ice—cold, lifeless creatures devoid of any desires, fear, sorrow, pains, and pleasures.[3]

Differing from this orientation is clinical psychology, for which emotions—depression, anxiety, mania, panic, psychosis, anger, aggression—are the stock-in-trade. In this respect, clinical and scientific psychology have had opposite emphases: aberrant emotions for one and behavior and/or cognition with little about emotions for the other.

The field of education has had a similar division. In "special" education, "emotionally disturbed" has been a long-standing category for describing and classifying millions of children said to have aberrant emotions causing unruly, disruptive classroom behavior and impairing learning. "Attention deficit hyperactivity disorder" (ADHD) has in recent years become a major special education category said to describe severe cognitive and emotional problems of inattention, hyperactivity, and impulsivity that interfere with learning.[4] In contrast, "regular" schooling, like cognitive psychology, apportions nonaberrant emotions little professional attention:

> Schools continue to operate on the theory that "cognitive" and "academic" are synonymous and both are apart from [emotions]. While goal statements may include concern for such concepts as self-esteem, social relations, and cultural awareness, the fact remains that curriculum plans are nearly always based on the learning of skills and content within various disciplines of knowledge.[5]

So too for literacy education. Diagrams depicting models of the reading process include "boxes" identifying affective factors, but beyond this kind of acknowledgment affective factors "receive little additional elaboration or explication."[6]

Reading education has consistently ignored learners' emotions despite the efforts of many educators who have indeed been concerned with how children feel when learning to read. "Dull," "boring," and "monotonous" have frequently been the educators' critical descriptions of reading instruction. Calls for "meaning-centered" literacy education have always presumed that children's learning should be positively connected with their feelings, and that children who are happy, enthusiastic, and motivated, who read interesting and enjoyable books, and who feel a connection between books and their own lives and interests are children who will more easily learn. Debates around multiculturalism assume that children will feel good about themselves if their heritage is represented in school work and that these positive feelings will, in turn, enhance literacy and other academic learning.

The criticism that educators have given too little attention to emotions also recognizes the ironic inveterate efforts of educators to control children's emotions. The history of schooling reveals that indifference to promoting certain emotional states was not a matter of oversight but part of a conscious conviction that teaching children to forgo happiness for later learning achievement was best for their learning and character. Following his survey of contemporary schools, educator John Goodlad remarked, "Our impression is that classes generally tend not to be strongly positive or strongly negative places. Enthusiasm and joy and anger are kept under control."[7]

The issue, then, is not whether or not emotions should be part of learning to read—they are always part of it! Rather, there needs to be a full, explicit debate over how and which emotions are, and should be, connected to thinking, learning, and teaching.

Emotions, Cognition, and Literacy

As a vehicle for understanding the complexity of the "continuous and interwoven fugue" between cognition and emotions,[8] especially in learning to read and write, and for insight into specific meanings of emotions, I will discuss the literacy progress of a student of mine, whom I shall call Earl. I have tried to look at Earl's cognition, emotions, and literacy not as static entities, but as they interacted and changed as he gradually became transformed from a poor reader to a good one. I hope I have met the challenge of Soviet psychologist A. N. Leontiev, who criticized Western psychology for being primarily "a registering science which merely analyzes the psychological processes" and urged it to become instead "a science of their mutability and transformation."[9]

Earl

Earl is an African-American man who grew up and lived in a middle-sized city in New Jersey, and was in his mid to late twenties when we worked together. His school records showed that starting at about second grade he had continuous academic and behavior problems. His behavior problems were substantial—he sometimes would throw chairs if he became angry—and assessments by school psychologists suggested that he might have had a "brain dysfunction." Despite his academic difficulties, Earl managed to stay in school and received a diploma from a vocational-technical high school. His reading level at the time of graduation was about second grade.

Following high school, Earl continued to be upset over the effect of his poor literacy ability on his work and everyday life. When he was in his early twenties, he enrolled with considerable trepidation in an adult education program that used volunteer tutors. For reasons that are not clear, he worked solely on arithmetic and had no reading instruction. His attendance was erratic, and he left after four months.

Earl's employment history consisted of a series of jobs each held for a short time until, at the age of twenty-five, he obtained a custodial job in a county social service program. He kept the job for about a year, and had it when we began working together.

The literacy program where we met provided a mixture of small group (around six students) and individual instruction. I was impressed by the motivation Earl displayed in both the first and second meetings, but he missed the third. Later, he called to explain his absence and we made plans for a fourth meeting. But he arrived late for that meeting, attributing his tardiness to problems with the bus schedule.

I responded by explaining that when he approached me with his intention to resume his education, I strongly believed he would be successful and made a firm commitment to him. Because of that commitment, I told him, he could expect that when we met I would be on time, would have work prepared for him, and would ensure that he would learn to read. In turn, I felt his commitment should be that he attend regularly, arrive on time, and be ready to do serious work. I said, in a tone that was reassuring rather than "managerially firm," that I anticipated nothing less than his unfaltering dedication to his educational progress.

From that time on, Earl's attendance was almost 100 percent, even though occasionally he came late. This change, I believe, was due partly to my expression of belief in his ability to learn and my dedication to helping him. These were expressions, in other words, not only of the thought I was prepared to put into his learning but of an affective pledge to him. It was a moment not only of connection between emotion and cognition in a learner but in a learner's interpretation of a teacher's assessment of that learning.

The importance of a student's perception of a teacher's emotions is evident in a study that asked children what they thought a teacher inferred in each of the following hypothetical scenarios: "A student failed a test and the teacher ([a] became angry; [b] felt pity; [c] was surprised, [felt guilty], etc.)." The students' reply to the question "Why did the teacher think that the student failed?" confirmed the researchers' expectations: "each affect was associated with a particular causal attribution." An expression of anger or surprise implied that the student had "not tried sufficiently hard." If the teacher felt guilt, the students inferred that this meant the teacher felt blame for the student's failure. Inferences interpreted as expressions of deficiencies in the student were made by children as young as five years old. By nine, inferences of lack of ability in the student were even stronger.[10]

Earl needed to hear an expression of my emotional commitment because his previous school failures were both cognitive and emotional. In the long, damaging process of becoming barely literate, a person not only does not learn to read and write, but "learns" that she or he has difficulty learning. In trying to learn, one also learns about oneself. Earl's later description of a conversation he had with his brother about his poor academic work in high school expresses some of the emotional consequences of his learning failure—his lack of self-confidence and his disbelief that he was capable of any educational accomplishments:

> My brother, who lived in Virginia, told me when he came up one summer and I was still in Voc-Tech—I was bullshitting my life away then, hitting the gym all the time—he said, "Brother, I'll tell you one thing." I said, "What?" He said, "You can learn anything you want to." That's what he told me. I said, "Yeah, man, right." You know, I didn't believe that shit. I was glad to see my big brother, but I didn't believe that shit, you know.

Earl's self-description was similar to that of Claude Brown in his *Manchild in the Promised Land,* in which he tells of his own experience and feelings as an unsuccessful student:

> I knew I didn't want to go to school, because I would have been too dumb and way behind everybody. I hadn't been to school in so long; and when I was really in school, I played hooky all the time and didn't learn anything. I couldn't be going to anybody's school as dumb as I was. [11]

As literacy failure continues into adulthood, these insecurities and feelings of mental deficiency increase. For example, a volunteer tutor in the Cuban Literacy Campaign of 1961, speaking with Jonathan Kozol, recalled her instruction of Nenno, a thirty-five-year-old campesino, and his continued struggle with illiteracy and feelings of inferiority: "He said to me, 'I am not intelligent. I will give you a prize if you can teach me to read.' During the months in which we worked together, it was as if he had to wrestle with his inner self, in order to turn himself into another human being."[12]

Earl's lack of confidence alternated with feelings that he might be capable of learning. These contradictory impulses are common in students who have not learned to read, so that left to draw solely upon their own motivation, they are likely to find that motivation insufficient for sustaining a commitment to learning. Necessary for literacy achievement is a transformation of emotions and self-perception.

Vygotsky has used the term "zone of proximal development" to differentiate between a person's "actual developmental level as determined by independent problem solving and his or her level of potential development as determined through problem solving" under guidance. This difference is the "zone." In a student's transformations, the zone of proximal development has usually referred to changes made in cognitive and academic achievement.[13] We see that it has a potentially additional meaning for emotional development attainable through guidance and support. Fear of failure may be changed to feelings of self-confidence; motivation may change from low to high; intellectual insecurity may become confidence in one's intelligence. These transformations can occur through a teacher's "scaffolding" and guiding these emotions so they are transformed to new emotional states a learner can achieve and sustain by himself or herself.

Earl Begins Reading

When choosing reading material for a beginning reader, an essential consideration should be its emotional influence: how should a student *feel*; what is the material's importance to the reader and what motivation will it engender? When we began work, as I said, Earl was reading at a second-grade level (to use the conventional measure). Finding material at that level that is of high interest for an adult is difficult. I wanted to choose material that, as Brazilian educator Paulo Freire has put it, would not be "idle chatter," but would help Earl develop a deeper understanding and critical view of, and deeper, clearer feelings about, the world that had shaped him.[14] The material I thought would help achieve these purposes was a set of biographies that included as subjects many black Americans. The men and women in these books were exemplary figures who overcame adversity and helped change the world, who had a high regard for education, and whose lives were partly changed through education. As Earl later reflected, the books offered him a history he wanted to know about:

> Once I started to come to school here I started to look at different stuff (about black history) but like when I was in high school, I

wouldn't be looking at no books or nothing like that. I was hanging out on street corners. I had heard about Malcolm, Huey Newton, Angela Davis, stuff like that. I was into that, but I couldn't read any stuff about what I was into then. My mind was always set that I couldn't read anything. If I could hear anything, I could repeat it. But if I had to read something, I would make an excuse, like I didn't talk so good. . . . I liked black history but I couldn't read, so that was my letdown.

Emotional effects are bound not only with cognition—not simply in facilitating or impairing thinking—but with motivation as well: motivation activates, impels, directs, and has a reciprocal relationship with cognition and learning.

The connections between learning and emotions have been well documented: poor learning can produce negative emotions; negative emotions can impair learning; positive emotions can contribute to learning achievement and vice versa. Research has demonstrated how induced negative emotions can hamper performance on cognitive tasks, whereas positive emotions have an opposite effect.[15] Similarly, research on very young children found that an induced sad mood increased the time it took the children to learn to respond to a task, and also increased their number of errors. Converse results were achieved by inducing a happy mood.[16]

Studies on language, memory, and story learning point to comparable important effects. Fifth graders recalled more adjectives when they were in a positive mood rather than in a sad mood.[17] A positive mood enhanced children's memory of televised story narratives and information about story characters.[18] Countless studies have demonstrated a connection between anxiety and academic performance: the more anxious a person is, the poorer his or her academic performance.[19]

The influence of emotions is the same for nonverbal learning: preschool children in a "positive mood" mastered a shape discrimination task more quickly and with fewer errors than did children in an induced negative mood. Youngsters identified as at risk for school failure were found to complete significantly more math problems accurately when in "positive-mood induced conditions."[20]

Illustrations of these connections were evident in Earl's learning. I first brought out six biographies, three about famous white Americans, and three about black Americans. From these Earl chose Martin

Luther King. The King biography was at about a fourth-grade level, a choice that might appear inappropriate, given Earl's tested reading level. I believed, however, that Earl would be able to read it. I have found that when students are interested in a book above their reading level—when their emotions are positive and high—they will read it more successfully, and learn more about written language skills, than they would reading an unimportant and uninspiring book at their tested reading level. Earl learned to read by always reading "beyond" his tested reading level: he read Malcolm X's autobiography and Claude Brown's *Manchild in the Promised Land* long before his level indicated that it was prudent to use these books in instruction. On the other hand, saying Earl "read" books beyond his "reading level" does not mean I simply gave them to him and asked him to read them aloud or to study them for future meetings.

To enable Earl to learn difficult vocabulary, concepts, syntax, etc., I used a number of instructional approaches, some of which I describe below (though not in detail). This pedagogy made the books more accessible, but at the same time, it was Earl's extraordinary effort—the emotional side of his work—that really helped him reach "upward," beyond the reading level determined by conventional testing. Again, it was both cognition and emotion that functioned in the "zone of proximal development."

Earl later said about this first book: "Reading King was a struggle, but I wanted to read it because I was comparing myself to King and thinking about the change from the street, and turning everything back around, how it's supposed to be. So I could relate to what he was doing."

Ideally, of course, the reading level of Earl's first book should have been more accessible to him but, as I mentioned, at a low-literacy level this ideal is not always possible to realize. Literacy instruction must, therefore, consider more than an incremental development from simple to complex words. Meaning, motivation, desire, and ardor cannot be separated from learning to read; it is not autonomous cognitive abilities that influence a student's mastery of written language. Look, for example, at Brecht's play *The Mother,* in which workers in prerevolutionary Russia are learning to read. The teacher begins with "three easy words": "branch," "nest," "fish." The students object to studying these words and ask instead for words they "need" for writing pamphlets and for organizing, such as "worker" and "class struggle." The teacher replies that they need to "begin with the simplest things and not at once with the hardest." "Branch," he says, "is simple." But a worker, recognizing the importance of meaning and passion for the learner, responds, "Class struggle is much more simple."[21]

"Automaticity" and Emotions

Earl became thoroughly engrossed in the King biography. He could read about a man he was interested in, but about whom he had never been able to obtain more than minimal information. He began talking about the history and struggles of black people, his admiration for King, and the aspects of King's life that he thought were important to follow. From the beginning he read and reread the chapters.

Models of early reading mastery have devoted considerable attention to the importance of "automaticity" — that is, unconscious, almost instantaneous processing of words and comprehension — which is considered essential for competent reading. One means of achieving automaticity in beginning literacy is by reading many different books; another is by "repeated readings" of the same book, allowing a reader to become increasingly familiar with the plot, ideas, characters, difficult words, etc. The repeated reading route to automaticity is both cognitive and emotional. Illustrated in Earl's desire to master information about King are his feelings of admiration for King and his connection to King's life. His aspiration to talk with people about King and black history initiated and propelled his self-determined repeated reading of the biography.

Earl now found he could talk with people about what he had read; literacy had new uses. Becoming the conveyer of written knowledge was a new role for Earl, one that began changing his self-perception and self-esteem.

Critique of a Concern for Emotions

Educators are far from united in the belief that emotions are critical to cognition and literacy. An attack on whole language and "touchy-feely, privacy-invading mush," and a call for an emphasis on phonics, "a method of reading instruction that had 70 years of experimental research behind it and which was successful in producing a literate population," concluded: "The bottom line is that today, education is not about literacy. It is not about proficiency at anything. . . . It's about mental health, stupid!"[22]

Chester Finn, who served in the U.S. Department of Education during the Reagan administration, offered a more elaborate criticism of efforts to boost self-esteem as a means of improving learning. In a chapter entitled "Bad Ideas Whose Time Has Come," Finn snickered at the National Education Association's call that "schools 'must structure esteem-building into the curriculum.'" He complained that he could rarely "pick up an education journal without encountering several articles" on self-esteem. Professional meetings were no better: "Rooms full of people" at "any of the zillion professional conferences each year" solemnly discuss "how best to foster self-esteem in children."

Finn maintains that his criticism is based on empirical evidence: the correlation between self-esteem and academic achievement is low or negative. Moreover, even where a positive correlation exists, he says, one cannot identify the causal link: does heightened self-esteem come from academic achievement or vice versa? Possibly, he speculates, the two "vary together" or are derived from other influences, "such as innate ability, social class, and prior accomplishment." Regardless, Finn believes that growth of emotions like self-confidence and self-esteem will come through academic accomplishments. If children are academically successful, if they learn what they are supposed to learn in school, they will feel good about themselves. Teachers should concentrate on teaching academic content and abilities; students' good feelings will follow.[23]

This denunciation misses the mark because Finn misconstrues the connection among self-esteem, other emotional states, and learning. Certainly children feeling good about themselves will not by itself cause successful learning. And, as I have said, the history of education shows that some children have managed to learn even when passive, indifferent, withdrawn, hostile, angry, insecure, or blindly obedient. Some have also learned with low self-esteem and an array of other insecurities. But the connection and solution are not, as Finn proposes, the one-two step of cognitive accomplishment followed by emotional gain. Nor, as he suggests, do the two "vary together" because of "innate ability." The research reveals the matter is quite different. Evidence, already cited, and neuropsychology that I will soon discuss suggest that cognition, emotions, and learning do not "co-vary"—rather, they interact. Surely there is a balance that children and adults must learn to strike between doing tasks that immediately generate good feelings and those that may not but that must nonetheless be done. Any undertaking, whether fixing a car or writing a book, involves arduous work that is not instantly fulfilling and festive. Yet recognizing this does not mean that learning should not be as emotionally positive as it can be or, more to the point, that educators should concentrate on learning and be indifferent to the emotional well-being of children. It is empirically incorrect and pedagogically callous to argue that children's feelings about themselves when engaged in learning to read and write should not be a primary concern of teachers.

Self-esteem and Fear of Failure

Helping Earl wrestle with his fear of failure required not only instruction focused on written language but, often, explicit exploration and interpretation of his feelings about himself. The following example of his effort to memorize sight vocabulary illustrates this. Shortly after beginning work with Earl, I introduced a sight vocabulary study method that, contrary to some whole-language precepts, does give a learner a useful experience of studying and learning words decontextually. Without special decontextualized attention to some words, I have found, students have great difficulty learning these words in context. That is, even when seeing the words in context, the words present sizable obstacles. If students work to master them both contextually and decontextually, however, success is swifter.

One way of identifying words he and I felt he needed to learn was to note the ones with which he had difficulty while he read out loud. From these words I selected seven, some that had strong meaning for him and some not high in meaning for him but which were frequently used and often obstructed fluid reading. I then wrote each of them on a three-by-five card, numbering them sequentially in a corner of each card. I made him a study tape by saying the number, pausing a few seconds in order to give him a chance to say the word, and then saying the word. This method gave him immediate feedback, reinforced his response, and enabled him to practice on his own as many times as he wished. Because Earl actively read the stories from which the words were chosen, he constantly had an opportunity, on his own, to see them in context. He went over the study procedure and I asked him to memorize a few words in class. Although he worked with the cards and followed the study method correctly, he had difficulty learning the words.

I suggested he might be having trouble because I was "watching him" while he tried to learn, and proposed that he take the seven cards with him and study them on his own, where he was likely to feel less pressure. I felt confident he would not have trouble learning the words, because in our work together he had, on several occasions, demonstrated good memory. I also did not think the tape recorder would be an impediment, because Earl had used it for other instructional assignments.

The following meeting I asked him for the cards and placed them before him one at a time. After he bumbled through the first four I asked him what his studying had been like and he replied he had studied the words but could not remember them afterward. I told him that perhaps he was having difficulty because the study method was new and he needed some time getting used to it. I reviewed the procedure and asked him to work with the cards for a few more days. When he returned, he still did not know the words.

Discussing his second attempt to learn the words, I asked him how and how much he had studied. Gradually, he admitted that he had not studied very much. In fact, a few minutes later he acknowledged he had not studied at all. He wanted to, he said, but different things kept coming up and he was unable to get to the words.

I had doubts about this explanation because Earl had been diligent with other work I had given him and, knowing his day-to-day schedule, I found it hard to believe he really did not have time. Knowing his school and personal history, I told him I had another explanation. Rather than not having time, I said, I thought he had not studied because he felt afraid. He asked me what I thought he was afraid of, and I answered, "Afraid to fail." I suggested that he was afraid because of insecurities he had about his intelligence and ability to learn. One time he had said about his reading experiences:

I was a wallflower, when you're a wallflower you feel like a wall flower, you're shut out, you be scared. I think it's being scared of learning how to read. That plays on a lot of people's minds.

'Cause when you're in school and you got to read in front of a
whole class and don't want to make no mistakes. Like if I missed a
word I'd feel embarrassed. You know how kids are, laughing, so
you're scared to read.

In one way or another all through his school years, he had been told
he was stupid and, I suggested, had come to feel so himself. We discussed his school experiences and various examples of how he had
been made to feel incompetent, how these feelings had remained, and
now made him insecure about his memory. I told him I had found his
memory to be good and mentioned several instances in our work
together, such as his recollection of story details, that showed this. Earl
appeared to be persuaded by my explanation, but I knew that listening
and talking are seldom enough to overcome these kinds of feelings and
guarantee successful learning. In this respect, of course, Finn is correct: boosting feelings is not sufficient for boosting cognition. However,
the solution for a learning problem is not to attend to cognition alone
but to address the "fugue" of emotions and cognition. To become convinced that one is smart and able to learn, one needs to prove the "theory" to oneself and others. Feeling the moment was propitious for this
demonstration and because our discussion had already begun to instill
confidence, I said, "I'm going to help you see how smart you are."
 I took the seven cards, held them so we both could see them, set my
stopwatch without calling attention to it, and began going through the
words with him. The first time through he memorized the words in
about four minutes, in the second practice period in two minutes, the
third time in twenty-two seconds. I showed him how easily and how
much he had reduced the time needed to memorize the words, and he
was astonished. "I guess I am smart," he said.

I told Earl to study the words each day and explained the need of
"overlearning" to ensure mastery. In our next meeting he quickly went
through the same cards correctly. We had a few more practice trials
during the next few weeks. By the third week he was up to twenty-three
words, which he memorized in seven and a half minutes in the first
trial and in three minutes and fifty seconds in the second. From then
on he never had difficulty learning new words and consistently learned
them on his own.

Essential in understanding Earl's "memory problem" (I had by now
firmly dismissed the suggested "brain dysfunction" diagnosis of his

childhood) was the necessity of seeing it not as a singular cognitive process but as tied to his emotions and the fuller experiences of his life. It was imperative to understand his mental functioning in connection with his school experiences, his self-concept, the various means of approaching the present task, our feelings toward each other, the ways in which I could mediate learning, Earl's feelings that inhibited learning, and so forth. Embodied in the seemingly simple task of learning a few words was a lifetime of detrimental experiences and emotions.

Leontiev distinguished between two kinds of meanings: "significance" and "personal sense." Significance is meaning in its independent objective existence as it has been developed in society. But this significance is only one part of the "double life" meanings have. In their "second life" meanings are individually subjective, both cognitively and emotionally.

Earl's work in this instance demonstrates the importance of making this distinction. An educational task has the pedagogical significance of mastery of an operation or of acquiring certain information for literacy development. For Earl, however, his personal sense of the task was not consonant with its significance because his personal sense of this and other tasks was infused by failure and anxiety. Unless this distinction was understood, his response would have been misunderstood: the instructional agenda would have been thought the same as the learner's agenda even though they were not. Whereas the instructional agenda was to memorize words, his agenda was to avoid having one more failure and revealing again his "stupidity."

Second, the episode illustrates that Earl's memory difficulties lay not only in his past experiences but also in his own actions. In other words, while the past may result in the internalization of failing experiences and harmful emotional states, a person may act to perpetuate his or her own victimization.

Third, a change in learning must occur through the unity of thought, emotion, and action. Change in Earl required more than transposing my thoughts to his. Just as faulty learning develops through actions, effective learning must also develop through actions. Therefore simply having Earl "think" and "feel" that he was smart was insufficient; he also had to act in the world as a changing person and master part of it. Throughout this process his changed actions and changes in thought and emotion were a progressive unity.[24]

The Neural Connections Between Emotions and Cognition

We have been looking at the learning a person does as a whole individual or, as it often is called, at the "behavioral" level. Now, for a fuller understanding of the relationships between emotion and cognition, and their influence in learning, we will look at the neural level—that is, at the neural networks that integrate emotions and cognition.

Based on neurological findings, strong arguments have been made against the conventional separations of cognition and emotions. Neurologist Antonio Damasio rejects this distinction by arguing that there are no "higher" and "lower" brain centers: the neocortex—the "high and new" brain—does not handle reason while the subcortex—the "low and old" portion of the brain—handles emotions. Rather:

> There appears to be a collection of systems in the human brain consistently dedicated to the goal-oriented thinking process we call reasoning, and to the response selection we call decision making, with a special emphasis on the personal and social domain. This same collection of systems is also involved in emotion and feeling, and is partly dedicated to processing body signals.[25]

Damasio maintains that neural substrates for cognitive responses associated with neural substrates for emotions are acquired connections that emerge from the unique experience of an individual, which may be similar to, or at variance with, that of other individuals. With the repetition of subsequent experiences, the emotional responses— often nonconscious, automatic, and involuntary—are activated in various parts of the brain.[26] However, the activation is actually a full body activation of the endocrine systems, the heart, blood pressure, and other regulators of the body that affect cognition and emotion. In other words, as opposed to more traditional models of thinking, it is not the brain but the totality of the person that is the unified whole of thinking.

Damasio's arguments lend further support for teachers to see thinking and emotions as integrative and interactive processes and to address multiple goals of cognition and emotion in every facet of learning. All learning activity must be pursued, modified, or eliminated according to the many influences that shape thinking. Damasio's interpretation helps in understanding some of the neural underpinnings of Earl's transformations and progress.

Another leading investigator of the interconnections between emotion and cognition is Joseph E. LeDoux, who has identified brain pathways that carry sensory signals to sites of emotion and cognition. More specifically, the thalamus, an area that relays sensory information, conveys sensory stimuli to the amygdala, a site of basic emotional memory, and to the cortex, where cognition occurs. From the cortex the stimuli go on to the hippocampus, a site involved in memory and linked to the amygdala. Hence, stimuli do not have to come to the amygdala from the neocortex in order for an emotional reaction to occur. Stimuli, LeDoux established, can go to the amygdala through various routes, either from the initial sensory stimulus or via signals from the cortex and the hippocampus. LeDoux observes:

Placing a basic emotional memory process in the amygdalic pathway yields obvious benefits. The amygdala is a critical site of learning because of its central location between input and output stations. Each route that leads to the amygdala—sensory thalamus, sensory cortex and hippocampus—delivers unique information to the organ.[27]

In other words, there is more than one route to emotional learning, and an emotional response can precede a cognitive perception and response:

The thalamus activates the amygdala at about the same time as it activates the cortex. The arrangement may enable emotional responses to begin in the amygdala before we completely recognize what it is we are reacting to or what we are feeling.[28]

Because the neural "emotional system can act independently of the neocortex, some emotional reactions and emotional memories can be formed without any conscious, cognitive participation at all."[29]

We form emotional memories from emotional events, and the emotional memory itself can be elicited through an event similar to the initial event. The "emotional memory underlying" a phenomenon may be dormant but not erased. "Apparently extinguished," the emotional response can be reinstated. Emotional memory is not "declarative" memory—that is, memory of "explicit, consciously accessible information." Rather, emotional memory most likely operates independently of our conscious awareness. Nonetheless, and most important: "Emotional and declarative memories are stored and retrieved in parallel, and their activities are joined seamlessly in our conscious experience."[30] Thus, emotions "exert a powerful influence on declarative memory and other thought processes." The amygdala "plays an essential part in modulating the storage and strength of memories."[31] Again, we can see the implications of these findings for Earl's "memory" problems. An implication for literacy education—and education overall—is that we begin to see how, at the neural level, an emotional response can enhance or impair cognition and literacy learning. For example, input from the thalamus to the amygdala, based on prior positive or negative experiences, may impede or foster declarative memory, the kind of memory required for retrieving and consciously using information for decoding and comprehending.

Emotions also affect working memory, the active memory used for a current task.[32] For example, negative emotions (conveyed from the amygdala and parts of the limbic system) can impair the activity of the prefrontal cortex, an area of the brain involved in working memory: "That is why when we are emotionally upset we say we 'just can't think straight'—and why continual emotional distress can create deficits in a child's intellectual abilities, crippling the capacity to learn."[33] Of course, positive emotion can facilitate working memory.

These neural relationships are important for understanding Earl's fears and the contribution made by emotions in the formation of his responses to situations. LeDoux's work suggests that neural pathways are set so that a situation may evoke an emotional response that may be helpful, or a rapid negative emotional response can precede cortical cognition and impair learning, memory, and thinking.

Instruction, Black English, and Emotion

Instruction teaches someone both about a specific area of learning and about himself or herself. It can "teach" the feeling of being a learner or a nonlearner, powerful or powerless, worthy or unworthy. Nowhere is this more evident than in the use of Black English (or "Ebonics") in instruction.[34] The incorporation of Black English into a reading curriculum, a teacher's attitude toward Black English and how that attitude is expressed, and school judgments and classifications of students using Black English all contribute to how black students see themselves as learners and whether or not they learn. Some of this was evident in Earl's work with phonics.

My recognition of the importance of phonics knowledge in beginning reading does not mean (as must be clear by now) that I advocate a "phonics-first approach" or that phonics knowledge is more essential than other language knowledge. With these caveats, I have no question that unless phonics is part of literacy learning, the beginning reader will reach a point where "cracking the code" becomes difficult. The principle should always be that learning phonics should only take place in a context of meaningful reading and writing.

In our work, I found that Earl could not distinguish and pronounce all the phonics sounds of standard English. For example, he could not distinguish short "e" and short "i" as in "pen" and "pin." He pronounced both as a short "i"—that is, "pen" and "pin" were both pronounced "pin"—a common pronunciation in Black English. There is no problem in communication, of course, because the words are homophones in Black English and understandable in context, as are standard English homophones such as "groan" and "grown."

These pronunciation differences are not a problem in reading instruction unless the teacher chooses to make them a problem. For example, I could have identified Earl's auditory perception and verbal expression of short vowel sounds as a problem of auditory discrimination, visual-auditory association, verbal encoding, etc., and treated him as someone with a language deficiency or dysfunction. Had I done this and insisted upon linguistic code switching as he was learning to read, I am certain I would have created innumerable reading and emotional problems, and am equally certain I would not have eliminated his "phonics problem."

Instead, I chose to have Earl pronounce print as he spoke it, allowed his language to be the basis for phonics instruction, and taught conventional phonics only insofar as it was consonant with his language. His pronunciation was corrected and changed only when his attempt at decoding a word did not coincide with his natural language. For example, he pronounced the "r" blend "br" as "buhr," an error frequently made by beginning readers, regardless of language divergencies. Therefore, it was appropriate to teach Earl the pronunciation of "br" as in "brink," as he naturally said it, rather than as "buhrink."

An interesting development occurred after about a year and a half of instruction. By this time Earl's reading had advanced approximately three years, which meant he had an expanded sight vocabulary and greater familiarity with sound-symbol associations. Reintroducing the short vowel sounds of standard English, I found that Earl could now distinguish and pronounce each of them after ordinary instruction. Apparently, the pool of sight vocabulary had given him the material to identify new sounds inductively, and phonics instruction had increased his facility with sound-symbol association.

The dire effect of a teaching method on a student's language, social background, self-concept, cognition, and learning was aptly depicted by Dickens in *Hard Times*. In the book, schoolmaster Thomas Gradgrind, instructing his "little pitchers," looked around his classroom and said:

"Girl number twenty . . . I don't know that girl. Who is that girl?"

"Sissy Jupe, sir," explained number twenty, blushing, standing up, and curtsying.

"Sissy is not a name," said Mr. Gradgrind. "Don't call yourself Sissy. Call yourself Cecilia."

"It's father as calls me Sissy, sir," returned the young girl in a trembling voice, and with another curtsy.

"Then he has no business to do it," said Mr. Gradgrind. "Tell him he mustn't. Cecilia Jupe. What is your father?"

After learning that her father worked with horses, Gradgrind plunged onward toward his pedagogical goal: "Give me your definition of a horse."

Thrown into the greatest alarm, Sissy could not respond.

"Girl number twenty unable to define a horse," said Mr. Gradgrind, for the general behoof of all the little pitchers. "Girl number twenty possessed of no facts, in reference to one of the commonest of animals! Some boy's definition of a horse. Bitzer, yours," . . .

"Quadruped, Graminivorous. Forty teeth, namely, twenty-four grinder, four eye-teeth, and twelve incisive. Sheds coat in the spring; in marshy countries, sheds hoofs too. Hoofs hard, but requiring to be shod with iron. Age known by marks in mouth." . . .

"Now girl number twenty," said Mr. Gradgrind, "you know what a horse is."

She curtsied again, and would have blushed deeper if she could have blushed deeper than she blushed all the time.[35]

Had I seen Earl's phonetic limitation as an indication of a language disability, such as "phonological dyslexia," not only would I have taught the same lesson taught by Gradgrind, I would have been wrong. Not only was his language adequate for learning to read, but in the process he had also developed skills that made him somewhat "bilingual" by advancing his competence with standard English. Furthermore, in our work together his facility with language was demonstrated in numerous ways, such as his paraphrasing portions of a story or his imagery in describing effects. Yet, misunderstanding his phonics abilities, increasing phonics work for which he was not yet prepared, and failing to appreciate and emphasize work in other language areas in which he was exceptionally capable, not only would have promoted failure in phonics but would also have fostered emotional turmoil that undoubtedly would have had extensive repercussions for his cognition.

Changed Literacy and Emotional Meanings

Beginning with the first biography we read together, Earl connected his reading to his own life. He could see that his education was advancing and he was acquiring a confidence and wholeness he had not known.[36] As Earl read the biographies, each added to and changed his thinking, emotions, and overall life in some way:

Phillis Wheatley was a person from Africa and people thought Africans were supposed to be in cages. They had a picture of a monkey in a cage that was supposed to be a black person. But she came a long way. I never knew she was the first black woman poet. But knowing about her and the way I can talk . . . maybe one day I can write poems.

Malcolm was a person experienced like Claude Brown. He experienced gun fights, he experienced armed robbery, he experienced using ladies, making them sell their bodies. . . . But Malcolm was smart and he turned himself around and was in front of the Nation [of Islam]. . . . That made me think about turning things around.

I can relate to some of the street life Claude Brown did and seeing him change from the street life. . . . Reading [*Manchild in the Promised Land*] made me feel good because I never thought I could read something like that in my whole life.

King had a nature for all kinds of people . . . his nature was for helping. He made me see how much black people have put out, black people always had respect and they kept on going.

These books and other biographies about figures such as Sojourner Truth, Frederick Douglass, and Harriet Tubman gave Earl a historical perspective he had not had, and a fuller understanding of racial and class oppression, and how blacks have struggled against it. The political became personal; the personal, political. From these books he began associating his learning with other sources of information: he read an article about Jesse Jackson, whom he admired; during Black History Month he listened to Malcolm's speeches on the radio; on Martin Luther King's birthday he found a story and picture of him and his children in *Jet* magazine. These paths raise a question about the array of emotions that should be part of learning. What should students feel strongly about? Where do negative emotions enter into learning? What should students love and what should they hate? With what should they empathize and what should they despise?

Sometimes it was not stories but a single word that had special emotional meaning for Earl and led him to an exploration and clarification of himself. For example, when he first read the word "worrying" he said, "So that's what the word looks like. That word's played a big part in my life. If I hadn't worried so much I'd have been somewhere." He went on to talk about how his excessive worry over problems had hindered him from finding solutions for them. From this ensued a discussion about problems that deserved worry, those that did not, the societal causes of many "personal" problems, the self-blame connected to worrying and problems, and current problems about which he was worrying.

The interaction and development of literacy and emotions was an ongoing process:

Right now I feel totally different. Even my outlook on things is different. People talking to me, I feel more important to myself. I feel more important because once you get some education you feel better about yourself. Everything seems different.

I remember when I first came here I wanted to get my education, but I wanted to get it and go. But you don't get education and get it and go. You get it second by second—it takes time, it takes discipline, you got to relax. You got to get it little by little . . . Education is almost like everyday living, like you got to get up and breathe.

James Beane has emphasized, "Education must be affective and cannot be otherwise. Affect enters the curriculum in any experience that influences (or attempts to influence) how young people see themselves, the world around them, and their place in that world."[37] I have suggested throughout this chapter that the contribution of emotions to learning and teaching must be part of the debate over literacy. If it is not, the debate will continue to be what Earl's learning would have been if "cognition" had been its center.

5

MEANING, COMPREHENSION,

AND READING SUCCESS

Does the stress on meaning in whole language provide sufficient opportunity for teaching skills? Does the skills emphasis in traditional education infuse a notion that merely "reading" words has little to do with thoroughly comprehending them? Does a skills emphasis bore children by discouraging their interest in the meaning of what they read? Can meaning and skills be balanced in reading instruction? The controversy over how much meaning should be emphasized in beginning reading takes the form of these important questions, which represent sharp divisions at the center of the literacy debate, but also some common ground. No side proposes that meaning is unimportant, and all sides seem to agree that the key instructional questions are about how to teach meaning, how much of it to teach, and when to teach it.

This focus has contributed to giving minimal attention to another question about meaning, one that dwells at the far periphery of the debate: precisely what do children need to think about and what ideas should they acquire or reject as they learn to read and write? The neglect of this question implies another area of common ground based on a tacit agreement that the dispute over meaning need not include issues of the specific nature of meanings in reading and writing.

I argue that this "missing" question about specific ideas and ways of thinking must be at the center of the debate because to neglect it is only to ignore the specific meanings that are always part of literacy education. The question is also pertinent to the questions of which literacy approach is "best" and what is meant by "successful" literacy education. Without identifying and assessing ideas and ways of thinking implicit or explicit in a given literacy approach, literacy outcomes judged successful for some may be totally unsatisfactory for others.

Meanings Past

Lack of explicit attention to the ideas that are always integral to any learning process is a fairly new phenomenon in the history of literacy education. As historian Harvey J. Graff shows, those who crafted reading education over the centuries have been unambiguous in the meanings they wanted books and teaching to convey. Literacy was used "for reasons of state and administration, theology and faith, and trade and commerce."

> From the classical period henceforth, leaders of polities and churches, reformers as well as conservers, have perceived [that] unbridled, untempered literacy [was] potentially dangerous: a threat to social order, political integration, economic productivity, and patterns of authority. But increasingly they also concluded that literacy, if taught in carefully controlled formal institutions created expressly for the purposes of education and supervised closely, could be a powerful and useful force.[1]

In the early American colonies, reading textbooks reflected particular purposes. *The New England Primer*, intended to change children from unregenerate "young vipers" into God-fearing Christians who were afraid they "should go to hell," contained religious and moral materials, including catechisms, the Lord's Prayer, and the Ten Commandments.[2] Toward the end of the eighteenth century, the content available in reading textbooks was more moral than strictly religious, but continued to be directed toward character formation. In the words of one author of a reading text: "the great end of education, that of forming the younger and tender minds to virtue and usefulness, is promoted by no branch of science more effectually than by learning to read."[3] The moral instruction in *The American Spelling Book* by Noah Webster, which sold more than twenty-four million copies from its publication in 1790 through the mid-nineteenth century, is illustrated in the following story: An old man finds a "rude" boy stealing his apples and asks him to come down from the tree. When the young "saucebox" persistently refuses, the man is forced to pelt him with stones, which does the job. Moral: "If good words and gentle means will not reclaim the wicked, they must be dealt with in a more severe manner."

With the rise of industrialism and its accompanying economic and political turmoil in the early nineteenth century, the schools were used to instill proper socialization, morals, and habits in poor and working-class children. By teaching them respect for the law, the church, and the Republic, they would be "more docile, more tractable," and would grow to be adults "less given to social discord, disruption and disobedience."[4]

For mid-nineteenth-century school reformers, moral education was an essential goal: "The cultivation and the transmission of cognitive skills and intellectual abilities as ends in themselves had far less importance for early school promoters than the problems" of moral development.[5] The effect these moral conduct stories were expected to have can be seen in the following concluding passage of a tale about a crow and a dove, from the Sanders *School Readers*, a widely used reading series:

> The crow is an unclean bird, and it puts us in mind of bad children who like to steal and do mischief; but the dove is a quiet, harmless, clean bird, and it puts us in mind of good children who always like to do right. Bad children often try to lead good children astray, and persuade them to steal, as the crow did the dove; but no good children will go with them to do anything wrong, for fear they might become as bad as they.[6]

In the mid-nineteenth century, partly because of criticism that reading instruction failed to engage students sufficiently, stories about children's ordinary experiences began to replace reading textbook stories containing strong, explicit morals. The inclusion of both kinds of stories was evident in the "Analytical Series," published in the 1860s. For example, children read a clear moral tale about a boy who did not get up early enough to kill a fox that had killed one of the family's lambs. Too late he regrets not following his father's admonition that "early to bed and early to rise, makes a man healthy, wealthy, and wise."[7] Another story told about John and Jane, forerunners of Dick and Jane:

> Here are John and Jane at play. How happy they look! Do you know what this play is? It is a see-saw. When one goes up, then one comes down. And so it is, when one comes down, then one goes up. And as they go up and down they sing, "See-saw, here we go, up and down, just so."[8]

Even though this kind of "real life" story, without expressed moral messages, was intended to hold greater interest for children, most were insipid and socially narrow. Still, by the end of the century the majority of stories in many beginning reading textbooks were of this kind. The 1897 edition of *Stepping Stones to Literature* had stories about George and Mary: "George has a little sister. She lives on the farm, too. Her name is Mary. Mary likes to feed the chickens."[9]

To be fair, all the textbook stories were not this bland. Some had charming stories about the beauties of nature, for example. Overall, however, most tended to be colorless and to project implicit visions of morals and behavior. By 1916, the vision of gender roles that was commonly found in reading textbooks is illustrated in following passage:

> What can a little girl do?
> A little girl can read in her book.
> She can sweep with her little broom.
> She can wash her doll's dresses.
> What can you do, John?
> "I can drive the cows to the meadow."
> "I can make a kite and a box."
> "I can ride to school on my bicycle."[10]

Supposedly depicting only the "normal" run of children's experiences in the simplest of sentences, these stories of white characters who led easy lives and followed established social roles were filled instead with assumptions about gender, race, class, happiness, and life's goals. The stories did, of course, reflect the experiences of many children, but while seemingly no more than objective mirrors of life, they also implicitly legitimized and reinforced notions about how people should and should not live. This was done not only through a superficial "reflection" of life but by excluding other characters and ways of living, and other assumptions about happiness, what was prized, and what was insignificant.

Meanings Now

In recent years, stories in reading textbooks are no longer based on the delightful lives of George and Mary or Dick and Jane. Now, "ethnic and socioeconomic diversity has appeared, and Mother is out of her aprons and Father has taken off his dress shirt and tie." Nonetheless, as a review of these textbooks concludes, despite efforts by publishers to make the stories more interesting and relevant, they remain, on the whole, lackluster.[11] Many teachers using these textbooks have attempted to counter this blandness by adding trade children's books in instruction, and whole-language teachers rely entirely on children's books. But even children's books are not without problematic moral meanings.

Despite the publication of many outstanding books for children, the majority continue to depict, as school reading primers always have, a moral imperative that reinforces the organization of the societal order. In his analysis of contemporary best-selling children's literature, Tom Engelhardt describes the absence of social context, except for "the Great Here—predominantly a land of suburban, middle-class malls or, at best, rural areas. Reading these books, one could easily imagine the city had yet to be invented." There are exceptions, in stories portraying more ethnic diversity and exploring problems such as racial prejudice and the endangered environment. Yet, overwhelmingly, the stories are very much about small events, and the implicit moral message is in the characters, whose lives are narrow, individual, and minimally if ever controversial.[12]

Each year, an issue of *The Reading Teacher*, a leading journal of the International Reading Association, contains teachers' choices of worthwhile children's literature. Many of the choices reveal a concern for important topics: concentration camps, the bombing of Hiroshima, the civil rights struggles of the 1960s, homosexuality, and political activism. In contrast, numerous other choices indicate that many teachers are untroubled about meanings in books that promote acceptance of, adherence to, and even praise of society's more dubious values. There are stories with traditional gender roles (princesses who get to marry princes or kings), and those with now outmoded views of American history (George and Martha Washington at home, with no mention of their slaves; the "westward movement" and pioneers; customs of Native Americans but little about the decimation of these peoples). There are books in which wealth is fancifully wished for (how a million dollars would change one's life), and those that encourage sympathy for the wealthy (the complicated life of a millionaire).

The same journal shows relatively more concern with the validity and value of meanings in its monthly thematic bibliographies, often prepared by teachers. For instance, selected for the theme "Living in Harmony" are books aimed at "exploring different perspectives on how we can work towards achieving harmony in our world."[13] The books are about living in harmony with nature, people, and animals; living in harmony by celebrating diversity; and searching for harmony and justice in the world. The latter subtheme contains biographies of Mohandas Gandhi and Chico Mendes, the Brazilian activist defending the rain forest. Other theme articles cite books about "cross-cultural understanding," about "changing lives" (changes that occurred through social changes, growing up, changing the world, and making new beginnings), and about "systems" (family, ecological, political).

Nonetheless, these bibliographies also recommend stories consonant with the dominant ideology. For the theme "Movement in U.S. History," a story about a young girl in Plymouth is recommended. The book describes shops in a Pilgrim village and the difficulties of life in this early settlement. One suggested activity is a "time line of the book according to when settlers banded together for survival." The students are encouraged to study Native Americans by exploring "critical ethics," such as looking at the meaning of "discovering" a land already inhabited. Beyond this ethical issue, no mention is made of any of the "survival" problems of the Indians: how the Massachusetts Bay Colony took their land, and how white "explorers" deceived, attacked, and massacred whole villages of Indians, often using Christian rhetoric as justification. The recommendation omits any hint of interpretations of the "settlers" contrary to those in the book.

Besides teachers' choices, each year *The Reading Teacher* presents "Children's Choices" (a project of the International Reading Association and the Children's Book Council), which lists the books for children and adolescents that ten thousand youngsters from different regions of the United States have chosen as their favorites. Selected on the basis of teachers' written accounts of children's responses to them, the one hundred titles in "Children's Choices" (winnowed down from a list of eight hundred) are a major source for book selection by teachers and librarians.

Reading educator Patrick Shannon, in a review of thirty randomly selected books from "Children's Choices" lists of several years, found that twenty-nine had individualist messages and only one offered a perspective "balanced" between responsibility to oneself and the community. Shannon found that whether a book

> was about an individual or a group, about animals or people, about the city or the country, about males or females—the authors of these books promoted concern for self-development, personal emotions, self-reliance, privacy, and competition rather than concern for social development, service to the community, cooperation toward shared goals, community, and mutual prosperity or even a balance among these social attributes.[14]

These are not simply books to be read for an "enjoyable" experience. Rather, they depict certain values and social relationships that come to be the "natural" way of being in the world, the "natural" order of the world, since no foil or other possibilities are explored. "Children's Choices" offers no information about what role, if any, teachers played in formulating children's tastes in choosing these books. Possibly for teachers, as well as for authors and publishers, the meanings in these books seemed beyond question if not unquestioningly "natural."

Herbert Kohl's analysis of Jean de Brunhoff's *Babar* provides insight into the significant underlying meanings in a children's "classic," a book seemingly intended only for entertaining and captivating children. This book has touched countless children, as it did Kohl, who writes that he "loved the book, identified with Babar, and found an abiding affectionate place for him in my heart." When he revisited the book as an adult, however, Kohl saw that woven into the fabric of this story (about an elephant who is befriended by a "Rich Lady" after his mother is killed by a hunter) are strong portrayals of sexism, racism, and colonialism.

In *Babar*, children learn there are different social classes, and that the Rich Lady belongs to the better one. Trying to recall his childhood response to the story, Kohl suggests that he "got the impression that people who served the rich weren't as good as the rich." He goes on to observe that, made powerless by the Rich Lady's money, Babar "does what he is told, is as passive as a paper doll and as uncomplaining." Eventually Babar returns to his home in the jungle with all the "accoutrements of civilization and access to the Rich Lady's purse" and assumes "power over other, less fortunate elephants."

After Babar returns home, Kohl explains, he finds "a crisis in the elephant patriarchy; the old king has died." By this time Babar has civilized his cousins, who acquire European upper-class dress and lord it over the naked, uncivilized elephants. Upon seeing Babar, the elephants exclaim, "What beautiful clothes! What a beautiful car!" and soon choose Babar as their new king. He has "learned so much living among men," the elephants say admiringly. Kohl observes that what he "learned" is how to buy things. The moral is clear: "power lies with money."

Kohl proposes that the content of *Babar* is sufficiently troublesome to prompt adults to consider whether children should read the book:

> The use of symbols and possessions to legitimize authority is dangerous and antidemocratic. It suggests to children that blind acceptance of authority is good behavior. The question of whether one encourages a child to accept or question authority is a major one in child rearing. [The book] makes a thoroughly undemocratic way of governance seem natural and unquestioned.[15]

Babar exemplifies the observation of Mem Fox, an Australian teacher and children's book writer: "There's no such thing as a politically innocent picture book." An example she offers is the "apparently innocent text" of her book *Wilfrid Gordon McDonald Partridge*, the story of a small boy who tries to understand the meaning of memory so that he can help an elderly friend regain hers. *Wilfrid*, says Fox, "reinforces the Dan Quayle/George Bush notion that real families have two parents, not one parent, three parents, or four parents, all of which are becoming increasingly common family configurations. The political message is a conservative one." Still, she wryly adds, the book does "hint that the world, as it is, need not be so, at least in one respect": a white "masculine, sports-loving cricketer" male is allowed to cry.[16]

Reading these stories "successfully" might mean that children will achieve many of the goals of literacy education—comprehending the plot, learning word skills, enjoying reading, and so forth. But "successful" comprehension of the meanings in such books could lead not only to a misunderstanding of the world but also to a form of literacy "problems" quite different from the conventional definition of the term.

"Meaning" Defined

In the literacy debate, meaning tends to be defined through a set of general categories, such as comprehending main ideas, comprehending facts, understanding story structure, and using mental imagery.[17] The comprehension of meaning is discussed in terms of how prior knowledge, background experience, and topic interest can affect it.[18] Researchers have sought to understand the strategies for obtaining meaning used by "proficient and less proficient comprehenders"[19] and the teaching methods for making students better "reading comprehenders."[20] In *Beginning to Read*, Marilyn Jager Adams discusses "text comprehension" as "a hierarchically layered process."[21]

There is nothing inherently wrong with these perspectives and approaches, other than their giving little attention to what should be comprehended or what good comprehenders comprehend. While this omission might not be unexpected on the skills-emphasis side of the debate, it is found as well on the whole-language side, where meaning in literacy education supposedly is the driving emphasis.

Neglect of exploring the meaning of "meaning" is apparent in the area of whole language focusing on "emergent literacy" (the reading and writing activity preceding formal school instruction). Work on emergent literacy sees reading and writing as abilities that "emerge" in children through their participation in meaningful literacy-related social activities within real-life settings. These meaning-driven activities have been extensively studied, but the specific meanings children obtain or should obtain in these activities has received little attention in the emergent literacy literature. In an illustration of literacy experiences that can stimulate "precocious literacy development," a Coca-Cola label is used because of children's familiarity with advertisements of the commodity. The label is cut out for the children, who read it and compose sentences, such as "Coke is a very refreshing drink," or "Coke is a very refreshing drink for babies," or "Buy caffeine-free Coke because it's good for your children." Another commercial label prompts the sentence, "Nestlé's chocolate is the best in the world." A media resource outside of the classroom is the news, from which the following was composed in an emergent literacy class in the 1980s: "Margaret Thatcher is the most important woman in England."[22]

What meanings emerge through this emergent literacy? For the commodities, the children have essentially absorbed and mirrored the commercials and the tastes as marketed. For the news comment, the word "important" is defined only in terms of political position and power. No alternative meanings are included, such as how Coke contributes to ill health, what it means to be "refreshing," what food is good for children, what effect the Nestlé company has had on the Third World, or what "important" effects Thatcher's policies have had on working people in England. Presenting these consumerist and politically charged meanings as neutral, harmless, or inconsequential fosters flawed comprehension based on dominant meanings only.

Many whole-language advocates describe meaning and its comprehension in similar neutral categories. An example is Marie Clay's discussion of mastering written language. For Clay, as children begin to be more independent in comprehending meanings in their social settings, they achieve a "stage of independence" where less outside help is needed "to confirm whether [they are] right or wrong or [have] a good quality response."[23] Nothing is said about the specific meanings that are comprehended, and how they might organize children's thinking, or how the "independent" comprehension children achieve may only be within the range of meanings available to them.[24]

"Thinking Skills"

Similar deficiencies are found in programs that teach thinking skills. Used in many classrooms as part of reading comprehension instruction, the skills taught include: similarities and differences, sequencing, classifying, drawing analogies, deductive reasoning, and logical connections. These classifications of skills reveal a frequent coupling of thinking skills with prevailing social and political assumptions. For example, a story on the bombing of Hiroshima is meant to teach "decision making," even though most of the story space is devoted to President Harry Truman's explanation of his decision to drop the bomb, a decision supported by the story's own interpretation of events. Students do have the choice of going to the library to research other options, but unless they are skilled in research methods, the school or local library has books with alternative interpretations, and the students are motivated to seek out explanations contrary to the ones given, the students are likely to be led only through Truman's explanation. The "sample student response"—reinforcing Truman's view that within the givens his choice to drop the bomb was the best one—offers the following thinking, comprehension, and inference template:

> Loss of life is the most important consideration. Cost is important also, as is poor morale, since that could affect our ability to wage war effectively. That the Soviets might enter is also important, because of the impact partition of Japan might have on the balance of power in the Pacific. That war contractors will do well, however, is not too important in this context since they are a special interest group and whether the war continues, and how it continues, affects the country as a whole.[25]

While this is not the place for a critique of this interpretation, I do need to point out that there are other assessments of both Truman's options and the claim of the necessity for dropping the bombs, which killed hundreds of thousands of civilian men, women, and children. Had these assessments been available to students, the opportunity for very different meanings and comprehension outcomes would have been possible.[26]

Reader Response Theory

All dominant theories of meaning making have been influenced by a theory that emphasizes how readers *extract* meaning from reading material—rather than simply obtaining meaning that is *in* the material. This theory, known variously as "reader response theory" or "schema theory," conceives of reading as an activity mostly of a reader's making. Reader response theory does not deny there is meaning *in* written material, but it deemphasizes the import of this meaning in favor of the meaning a reader makes from the meaning he or she brings to the text:

> Meaning is mostly supplied by us through our familiarity with [meaning] formations we learn elsewhere. The printed page

does not determine the meaning we make from it. There is little or nothing there to comprehend "in" a text. There are many meanings to be made from it by reading it in different ways, i.e., by contextualizing it differently.[27]

The "click of comprehension" occurs when there is a connection between what is on the page and "the concepts stored" in one's head. Comprehending written ideas is

limited and colored to a large degree by the concepts already stored in memory. Thus, contrary to conventional wisdom, which states that comprehension is the process of getting meaning from a page, comprehension is viewed as the process of bringing meaning to a text. It is this process of bringing meaning to a text which accounts for the fact that the same text can be interpreted so differently by so many people.[28]

The structures of ideas already stored in memory, serving to interpret new information, are sometimes called "schema." The ideas in texts can become "affixed" to a structure of ideas in the head, but for this to occur, the existing ideas must be "stable, clear, discriminable from other ideas, and directly relevant to the to-be-understood" ideas in the text.[29] Comprehension and learning are, in other words, an affixing of new ideas to already stable ideas.

One facet of this theory that is not generally addressed is the origin of, and ideas in, stored knowledge. An example of this omission is an analysis of the term "ship christening," used to illustrate the structure a schema may take. For a reader to understand the term fully, reading educators Richard Anderson and David Pearson explain, the schema requires several component meanings, such as the ones in the following phrases: to bless a ship, in dry dock, involves a new ship, done just before launching, bottle broken on the bow, and done by a celebrity.[30] Activation of this schema during reading would mean that its parts (or slots) would be "instantiated"—that is, filled with particular information. Noting the "constraints on the information with which a slot can be instantiated," Anderson and Pearson give the following example:

Presumably, for instance, the "celebrity" slot could be instantiated with a congressman, the husband or wife of a governor, the secretary of defense, or the Prince of Wales, but not a garbage collector or barmaid.[31]

To these categories of exclusion, one might add a shipyard worker.

While this schema example is, of course, considered to be the conventional definition of the term "ship christening," we must ask if this definition is benign and neutral—or could "successful" comprehension of the term also mean faulty or limited comprehension? Anderson and Pearson recommend:

> To get a feeling for how a model of schema activation of this type might work with text, consider the following two sentences:
> Princess Anne broke the bottle on the ship.
> The waitress broke the bottle on the ship.[32]

A reader's intuition, they say, would likely interpret the first sentence as a ship christening, the second as an incident in the ship's dining room. By not providing additional explanations of why the schema slots happen to be filled this way, the deeper meanings of the schema are not probed. Why is it, one might reasonably ask, that a waitress (or garbage collector or barmaid) would not christen a ship but a celebrity would? The answer is not that Princess Anne had more to do with building the ship than did the waitress or garbage collector. It is more likely, in fact, that garbage collectors and waitresses might have helped a great deal more than Princess Anne. The difference, of course, has to do with hierarchical power and privilege.

This example shows that although schema theory does deal to some extent with specific ideas and ways of thinking and meanings, it does so in a very circumscribed way. In the christening example, how is the social hierarchy that is reflected in the slots created in the minds of the reader? Certainly not by the reader's independent choice. Rather, the slots contain socially formed understandings. In narrowing the focus on the fit between mental slots and reading text, the question of how the meanings come to exist both in slots and in text is ignored. Schema theory does not consider that the "old knowledge" used to acquire new knowledge might be contributing to either comprehension or miscomprehension. A click of comprehension may occur, but simply because there is a click—say, between the schema created by George Bush's explanation of why the United States began the Gulf War and an article on the war—does not mean that the schema allows for accurately comprehending the text. The failings of reader response theory point to the need for teachers to address both the ideas in literacy materials and the ideas and ways of thinking that students bring to their reading.

An example of an educational theory and program that uses schema theory to support infusing specific meanings into literacy education is the "cultural literacy" of E. D. Hirsch, Jr., author of the book of the same name. Hirsch sees the mind as a cultural literacy dictionary, and the educated mind as one that has extensive schema, with many cross-references among them. He argues that children need to learn a multitude of facts in order to build their schema, and is forthright in advocating that schools provide these facts by acculturating children with traditional "core knowledge": "To thrive, a child needs to learn the traditions of the particular human society and culture it is born into."[33] Hirsch's notion of traditional information is evident in his depiction of United States history. His "facts" portray a nation propelled by a harmony of interests, despite internal and external pushes and pulls, that in the end work out for the good of all. Deemphasized in this harmonious view is labor history, women's history, immigrant history, class discord, challenges to capitalism, political dissent, and the continuous struggle over the purposes of the nation.[34]

A more detailed sample of the skewed ideas in the core knowledge is provided in Bob Peterson's examination of the information Hirsch wants students to know about Daniel Defoe's *Robinson Crusoe:* "Hirsch seems content that students know who wrote *Robinson Crusoe* and when, and understand its plot line and major characters. This kind of 'just the facts, ma'am' approach may produce people good at playing Trivial Pursuits but doesn't produce critical thinkers." Peterson, a fifth-grade teacher and educational activist, points out that although Defoe's novel is "infused with a belief in the inherent superiority of white people" and "constantly refers to non-white people as 'savages,'" Hirsch has students read the book "as part of a unit that explicitly equates 'discovery' with 'adventure,' not with colonialism." Peterson acknowledges that *Robinson Crusoe* "has an undeniable place in the literary canon" but asks why it could not be read so that children could, for example, "be taught to question Defoe's use of the term 'savages' as a way of exploring the social dynamics of the time?"[35]

Hirsch's cultural literacy is an example of how important it is that questions about specific ideas and ways of thinking be at the center of the literacy debate. Do literacy educators agree with Hirsch's "facts"? Should other ideas and ways of thinking be included? Do these facts contribute to miscomprehension of the world? What does successful attainment of this delimited and skewed body of information mean for measures of "successful" reading achievement?

Noam Chomsky and the Meanings in Language

Noam Chomsky's writings on linguistics are frequently cited in the literacy debate.[36] Most of these writings do not deal directly with schooling and learning to read, but literacy educators have used them to draw parallels between children's acquisition of oral and of written language. Referring to an interview with Chomsky in *The Reading Teacher*, the editor of that journal noted, "We feel the interview offers readers a glimpse into the thinking of Chomsky, a person whose work has revolutionized the way language is studied."[37]

Ironically, although his work has contributed to certain aspects of literacy theory, virtually none of it has been applied to issues about meaning. To understand why, we need to look again at the *Reading Teacher* editor's comment, which says that Chomsky's work on language has profoundly changed the way language is studied. However, an examination of the entirety of his work on language reveals that the editor's observation should actually have been: A portion of Chomsky's work has been used in language and literacy studies to revolutionize a portion of how language and literacy are studied. The portion that has definitely been used is Chomsky's seminal writings on syntax and generative grammar, on the relationship of language and the mind, on the system of rules of language that appear to be biologically fixed and invariant, and on the defects of behaviorist explanations of how language is learned. Most of this cited work usually comes from publications from the 1950s and 1960s, such as *Syntactic Structure*[38] and *Aspects of the Theory of Syntax*.[39] Ignored in most of literacy work—and most pertinent to a discussion of meaning and comprehension—are Chomsky's views on the semantics of language. Remarkably, the writings on literacy that reflect "the way language is studied" by Chomsky provide little hint that Chomsky gave any thought to the ideas and ways of thinking embedded in language.

This omission is remarkable because much of Chomsky's work in recent decades has been devoted to the semantics and comprehension of written language, work that should be relevant to literacy educators, certainly as much as his earlier work has been. The reason for this omission, I believe, is that drawing on Chomsky the "semanticist" means discussing work that is passionately political in its critique of the print medium that buttresses the dominant—and dominating—ideas and actions of the societal order. Chomsky has written many books and countless articles on the distortions, omissions, choices, and emphases in written language (and other media) that serve to shape the public's miscomprehension of power, ideology, force, and innumerable political events. "Manufacturing consent" is the phrase Chomsky and co-author Edward Herman borrow from Walter Lippmann to describe, in their book of the same name, this shaping of public thinking.[40] Citing Chomsky the semanticist—exploring the ideas and ways of thinking he analyzes—requires asking critical, controversial, and difficult questions about the content of reading texts and about children's thinking. Agreeing with this Chomsky means concluding that print and other media promote not only understanding but misunderstanding as well. The task of "ideological institutions," says Chomsky, of which the schools are one, is to "channel thought and attitudes within acceptable bounds, deflecting any potential challenge to established privilege and authority before it can take form and gather strength."[41] To cite the "uncited" Chomsky in the literacy debate would mean being explicit about ideas in children's literacy education.[42]

Addressing Specific Meanings and Success

The literacy debate must be expanded to include specific questions on what children need to think about and what children need to acquire or reject as they learn to read and write. A first step in this process is to assess the ideas available and unavailable in literacy education. Second, we must study the array of ideas that can, in theory, be included in the classroom. Third, we must assess how these ideas organize thinking. Fourth, we must consider how teachers and students who choose to include alternative ideas in literacy education might find themselves in conflict with powers that serve as guardians of acceptable ideas. And fifth, we must assess the miscomprehension that is part of "successful" literacy education and reevaluate definitions of "success."

6

LEARNING CAPACITY, CHILDREN'S

FUTURES, AND READING ACHIEVEMENT

A s reading educators continue to argue over instruction, perni-
cious assumptions about children's capacities based on theories
of predestination have harmed both the instruction and the
literacy of millions of children. Although educators throughout this
century have not sufficiently addressed the sources and impact of
these assumptions, many, regrettably, have helped perpetuate them.
Until the literacy debate addresses the full scope of these assumptions,
no instruction will be sufficient for evading their damaging effects on
children.

Learning Capacity and Predestination

The first theory of children's learning capacity that claimed to be scientifically grounded was that of psychologist G. Stanley Hall, who in
1883 founded one of the first psychology laboratories in the country
and in 1891 organized the American Psychological Association. Drawing upon his empirical studies of the development of children's knowledge, Hall criticized educators for failing to understand the nature of

children's thinking and its implications for curricula. Only through knowledge of children's minds, he admonished, could a proper curriculum be formulated.[1] Like other educational reform recommendations at the turn of the century, Hall's emphasis on studying children had a positive, progressive ring. It eschewed preformulated schooling and called for instruction that would be child-focused and attentive to children's individual differences and needs.

Beneath the surface of Hall's theory, however, were postulates less congenial to the education of all children. Schooling based on knowledge of children's thinking meant teaching children in proportion to their mental capacity and bearing in mind their "probable destination," determined primarily by the place they already occupied in the societal hierarchy. As Hall looked out on the large number of children in the schools, he discerned not just a small portion of youngsters with low mental ability but a "great army of incapables, shading down to those who should be in schools for the dullards or subnormal children."[2] To be sure, Hall was not a one-dimensional determinist. His recommendations to build education on children's natures meant avoiding teaching information before children were ready to process it mentally, giving more attention to children's interests, and allowing more time for play and recreation. His strong belief in the hereditary determinism of mental capacity ultimately meant, however, sorting and unequal education. In educational practice, "individualization" of instruction meant devising curricula according to students' differing mental abilities—thus guaranteeing very different academic achievement outcomes among students.

The theory or, more accurately, the conclusion that children could be differentiated by their mental capacities was put into nationally recognized, functional form in 1916 as the Stanford-Binet intelligence test. Using the earlier work of French psychologist Alfred Binet, Stanford University psychologist Lewis Terman, who had studied with Hall at Clark University around the turn of the century, claimed that the test measured fixed mental ability—meaning that "the feeble-minded remain feeble-minded, the dull remain dull, the average remain average, and the superior remain superior."[3] He also claimed that the instrument had a "high correlation" with school achievement and could, therefore, "predict with some degree of approximation" a child's future academic development.[4]

Terman's belief in fixed mental ability led him to repudiate interpretations that attributed low intelligence to environmental influences. After summarizing a study in which teachers, when asked to list the causes of academic underachievement, named, in descending order of importance, "poor home conditions, physical defects, transferring from another school, retarded mental development, difficulty with the English language, lack of application, irregular attendance, laziness, late entrance, and delinquency,"[5] Terman explained why "mental retardation" should be first and how it led to the circumstances that appeared to be causes:

> Feeble-minded children do often come from poor homes, since often the parents of feeble-minded children are themselves feeble-minded. For the same reason, feeble-minded pupils shift frequently from one locality to another and attend school irregularly. Because such children are feeble-minded, they enter late, show little application in their school work, and tend to become delinquent.[6]

His explanations, claiming to be based on scientific findings, were infused with racism and classism. He called attention, for example, to the mental deficiency "very common among Spanish-Indian and Mexican families of the Southwest and also among negroes. Their dullness seems to be racial. Children of this group should be segregated by special classes. They cannot master abstractions, but they can often be made efficient workers."[7]

The racial and ethnic prejudice Terman and other leaders in the testing movement often expressed in their writings did not deter educators from believing in the analytic and predictive power of intelligence tests. By the mid-1920s, just a few years after publication of the Stanford-Binet, it and other IQ tests were used in most U.S. cities to classify children into ability groups.[8] In Detroit, for example, children entering first grade were given an intelligence test because school personnel believed it measured "fundamental differences in native ability" and was an invaluable "instrument of classification."[9] Academic failure of children in Oakland, California, was attributed chiefly to their "mental inferiority." In a copper-mining city in Arizona, intelligence testing "found" that children—mostly of Mexican background—first thought to be doing poorly academically were actually performing on a par with their intellectual level.[10]

Racial and class prejudices were not the only impulses for tracking students. Predestination and partitioning often seemed to arise from the humanitarian motives of educators and reformers who, in fact, rejected hereditarian interpretations. One of these social critics was Leonard P. Ayres, who, in his 1909 book *Laggards in Our Schools*, pointed to environmental circumstances to explain much of school underachievement. For many schoolchildren, however, the distinction, as the saying goes, was one without a difference. Concerned about appalling social and school conditions, Ayres expressed a view common among reformers of his time: the challenge of academic failure required the reformulation of schools—and tracking—to meet differences in students' "abilities" created in large part by social conditions.[11]

An excellent summary of much of the reform thinking in this early-twentieth-century "Progressive Era" is Scott Nearing's 1915 book, *The New Education*, which articulated the benevolent voice of sorting children by their socially predestined individual differences. "The ultimate truth," insisted Nearing, is "that every child is an individual, differing in needs, capacity, outlook, energy, and enthusiasm from every other child." This translated, as a Cincinnati school superintendent put it, into one curriculum for a wealthy suburban district "up on the hill" and quite another for the children "in the heart of the factory district," where manual training and domestic science courses began in second grade rather than, as they ordinarily did, in the sixth. These curricula differences were justified because the majority of poor children were not likely to be in school after the sixth grade. Liberal Progressive Era social critics such as Nearing caustically criticized oppressive social class relationships but still made recommendations for tracking children based on their likely future places. Using education in a mining village as an example, Nearing offered the following answer to those who criticized basing education on societal destination:

> To be sure this [training] course would not make the boys railroad presidents or United States senators; but even that is not a drawback because, incredible as it may sound to many old-fashioned ears, the vast majority of the boys will be miners and mechanics. The question is, therefore, shall they be good miners or bad ones? United States senatorships bother them not a whit.[12]

Reading Tests

Reading education's part in "scientifically" sorting children by their "capacity" and "predestined futures" arose within the growth industry of academic achievement tests.[13] Only three years after its 1922 publication, the Stanford Achievement Test for students in all grades reached annual sales of 1.5 million copies.[14] From the beginning, the reading subtest not only provided a measure of the academic area educators regarded as most important and most predictive of future school success; it also served to validate IQ testing. Grouped by mental ability, students were taught to read according to their "mental capacity." In turn, achievement tests "demonstrated" that children in each group had attained reading levels commensurate with their respective abilities, thereby justifying the initial testing and sorting—and the reading failure of millions of children.

From Assumptions and Classroom Outcomes

How do theories of predestination influence instruction and, therefore, different outcomes in literacy achievement?

The assumed wisdom in the instruction of children with dissimilar reading abilities is that these children require dissimilar types of instruction. Teachers further assume that poor readers require immediate responses to their errors, more time for the learning of basic skills, and less time to express their thoughts about what they have read. The opposite assumptions hold for good readers. For example, when two first-grade reading groups—one of high and the other of low ability—were given informal tests of letter recognition: "high- and low-group readers performed equally well on the tests. But the latter were nonetheless given extensive drill in letter recognition, while the high-group counterparts were beginning to read sentence texts."[15] The low group was given extensive phonics and word identification drills, and teacher corrections of oral reading errors focused on sound-symbol correspondences and word recognition. In contrast, teachers are "far less likely to interrupt good readers than poor readers" if they make an error in comprehension, regardless of the type of error.[16]

Another difference in instruction is the way poor and good readers practice reading. Among second graders, for example, good readers were more likely to have opportunities to read longer portions of a story and to read silently. They also spent more time discussing the meaning of what they had read and were more challenged to demonstrate an understanding of what they had read. Poor readers, on the other hand, had "fewer occasions" for extended reading and were less encouraged to demonstrate an understanding of what they had read.[17]

This difference in instruction has affected the amount of time spent reading. Poor readers, who would seem to need the most time reading, actually spend less time than good readers. One study found that the time children in low-ranked groups spent reading was approximately one-third of the time spent by a high-ranked group.[18] Other research reported that "good readers, on the average, [read] more than twice as many words per session as [did] poor readers."[19]

Assumptions about children's fixed characteristics are related to the levels of achievement they will be expected to reach. One study found that poor readers were four times more inattentive than good readers in the spring, but not in the fall. Further analysis confirmed that the inattentiveness was associated with being taught as "poor readers" and not with the students' individual characteristics (such as maturity level, past inattention, sex, reading aptitude, or socioeconomic status).[20] The teachers saw none of this and instead attributed the inattention to the children's personal defects, describing them as "unmotivated, immature, distractible, and hyperactive."[21]

As poor readers progress through the grades, they are described in increasingly unfavorable terms. Comments on report cards for the first four years of school revealed that while the students were described rather specifically in kindergarten as having particular needs in reading, classroom participation, and school socialization, by third grade the same students were more likely to be described by negative, single phrases pointing to their behavior, such as "disruptive" and "withdrawn." In contrast, by third grade, "top-rank students were clearly afforded more particularistic and elaborate evaluations."[22] In theory, poor readers can become good readers, but in practice this seldom happens. As poor readers pass through the grades, although they improve relative to where they had been scholastically, they remain in the same ranking relative to other readers.

Assumptions about capacity have been predominant in literacy education. A study of reading instruction in several school systems found that teachers, administrators, and other school personnel described the "overall goal of the reading program as insuring that each child is reading 'to the best of his or her ability at that level of development.'" Children's capacity and potential were assumed to be "fixed, measurable, almost tangible human characteristics that everyone can recognize and act on." Even though whole groups did not learn to read very well, policymakers, administrators, and teachers felt assured of having "done their jobs well" as long as they believed the "best" teaching had been provided for the children. As one teacher put it, you take the child "along as far as he possibly can go."[23] Not surprisingly, students often internalize assumptions made about their abilities: children in poor-reader groups tend to look disdainfully at themselves and at members of their group, to feel like "social outcasts."[24] Comprehensive reviews of the traditional grouping of children by reading achievement have failed to demonstrate a clear academic benefit in this approach, particularly for poor readers. Jeannie Oakes, who has written extensively on tracking, summarized the research this way:

> Considerable evidence challenges the widely held norm that tracking and ability grouping effectively accommodate students' differences—at least in terms of boosting schooling outcomes. For more than 70 years, researchers have investigated this "bottom line" question, producing a literature that is voluminous and of varying quality. Yet the best evidence suggests that, in most cases, tracking fails to foster the outcome schools value.[25]

As children move from grade to grade, "the gap between high- and low-group students widens."[26]

Eliminating Grouping and Tracking

The last few years have seen a number of political and advocacy groups—from the national Governors' Association to the Carnegie Council to the Children's Defense Fund—recommending eliminating grouping and tracking. In principle this recommendation is commendable, but by itself it is likely to be little more than a failed methodological fix, a cost-nothing reform.

In their use of a variety of groupings for many activities aimed at meeting children's diverse needs, whole-language classes are a step in the right direction. No replacement of traditional grouping, however, can eliminate the influence of the deeply ingrained assumptions about capacity and predestination that are embedded in this society and flowing into schools and classrooms. Although laudable, better ways of mixing children and encouraging teachers to change their own attitudes and practices will not eliminate classroom stratification because school grouping is not a primary cause, but an expression, of flourishing assumptions. As educational researchers Jeannie Oakes and Martin Lipton note, "tracking structures are firmly grounded in widespread and historically rooted beliefs about human capacity and about individual and group differences."[27] The beliefs include a national politics that blames the poor for their own problems. Political analyst Michael Parenti has observed:

> Throughout the ages, the affluent have argued that the poor are the authors of their own poverty, that indigence is caused by the profligate and demoralized ways of the indigent. In seventeenth-century England, impoverished people were thought to be not the victims of circumstances but of their own "idle, irregular and wicked courses." Little has changed since then. In 1995, right-wing Republican leader Newt Gingrich reduced poverty to a matter of personal inclination: "I am prepared to say to the poor, 'You have to learn new habits. The habits of being poor don't work.'"[28]

Similarly, economist Martin Carnoy addresses the question: "Are blacks to blame?" Most Americans today, he says,

> are convinced that blacks have been given every chance to succeed, and have even been pushed ahead of whites by affirmative action and government subsidies. Despite this help, they seem to fail at the economic game. Is it not logical that there is something wrong with them, not the system?[29]

Unless assumptions like these and the societal stratification that promotes them are changed, achievement outcomes are likely to remain fairly fixed. Reading instruction might not use formal groups, formal testing might be eliminated, children might not have labels of one kind or another, and there might not be basal readers. Instruction might mix skills and meaning, or might employ whole language and cooperative learning that mix children in many ways. Nonetheless, these modifications will not by themselves eliminate the treatment of children according to what is assumed to be their mental capacity, and predestined educational approaches will continue to fit them to their futures. As former Associate Director of the Carnegie Council on Children Richard deLone pointedly put it, in his book on children and inequality:

> Nor is it sufficient to argue that socially derived assumptions of teachers are the cause of differential treatment. Rather, the institutional apparatus of schools is explicitly designed to provide differential treatment. Teachers who have differential expectations for students, and who treat students accordingly, are merely reflecting practice built into the basic institutional fabric of the system they work in. It would be improbable for them to do otherwise. It is unlikely that these patterns will alter within schools unless they first change in the broader society.[30]

Reading instruction will continue to be predicated on the assumption that students should be helped to move from where they are educationally to only as far as their "capacity" can take them. This is far from a societal and educational commitment to moving children to a high level of achievement.

Finally, it needs to be said that much of the criticism of grouping has been that it does not work—that is, it has not fostered a high level of literacy for all children. While this is true, let us consider the meaning of "work" more fully. Grouping has worked insofar as it has strengthened the societal hierarchy. Certainly for policymakers whose decisions reproduce class and racial relationships, grouping has worked. And for maintaining a social structure in which people born into a social class are strongly destined to remain in that class, it has most certainly worked.[31]

Small Futures

As I have said, assumptions damaging to children find their way into educational policies that impair instruction and prevent the best-intentioned and most skilled teachers from contributing sufficiently to children's literacy achievement. A vivid example is Head Start, begun in 1965 as a War on Poverty program and based on the premise that providing poor children with basic medical, educational, nutritional, and emotional assistance would help improve their chances of future academic success.[32] Reflective of other national policies, Head Start policy over the last three decades has displayed a modicum of concern for the children the program has served, but a larger indifference toward ensuring that those same children obtain all they require for future academic success. Moreover, the history of the policy displays an intrinsic callousness toward millions of other children eligible for, but not at all served by, the program. Head Start policy assumes—and helps assure—that Head Start children are likely to have what Richard deLone called "small futures."

In the face of this policy, Head Start and similar preschool programs with comparable objectives have not been without their successes: participants were more likely to have higher literacy scores, less likely to end up in special education, more likely than their peers to be in the right grade for the right age, and more likely to go to college or be employed.

In the Perry Preschool Program in Ypsilanti, Michigan, for instance, a program patterned after Head Start though not part of it, program participants outscored control group youngsters on achievement tests at age fourteen and had higher literacy scores at age nineteen. Seventy-one percent of children completed twelve or more years of school, compared with 54 percent of the control group. Program children were less likely than the control group ever to be in a special education program—for girls the figures were 8 percent versus 37 percent, for boys 20 percent versus 40 percent.[33] In long-term intervention projects that extended a Head Start program, participants continued to score significantly higher on literacy tests than did children not in these programs.[34]

Studies like these counter the frequent claim of critics that the effects of Head Start and similar preschool programs "fade out" in the early school grades. Rather, as a reassessment of studies purporting to support this criticism eventually concluded, "there is considerable evidence that preschool programs of many types—including Head Start—have persistent effects on academic ability and success. There is no convincing evidence that these effects decline over time."[35] On the other hand, these results do not mean that Head Start and similar preschool programs are sufficient for ensuring full future academic success for their participants. Head Start youngsters do not, on average, do as well as middle-class students, partly because they attend lower-quality schools. One study found that the schools of former Head Start participants were "unsafe places where average achievement levels are low, the educational climate is unstimulating, educational resources are limited, and relations between staff and students are not harmonious."[36]

The history and debate over Head Start shows that what happens in the classroom affects literacy outcomes. At the same time it also shows that effectiveness of classroom teaching and literacy success is strongly determined by power and policy outside the classroom. Vivid in this history is the fact that regardless of evidence that preschool programs for poor children can be beneficial, Head Start has always been underfunded. At the beginning of the program, observed Edward Zigler, one of Head Start's founders, "the amount budgeted per child was too little to allow for a quality educational program."[37] By 1980 underfunding worsened, and Zigler was

especially concerned about the cutbacks in staff, hours, and services. Class size had increased from 15 to 20 children and the overall expenditure per child expressed in constant 1967 dollars had declined from $835 in that year to $813 in 1980. The average Head Start salary was $6,280, with a large percentage at minimum wage, and low wages were contributing to increased staff turnover. The federal regional staff charged with monitoring local programs had declined by at least 25 percent since 1970, at the very time that the program needed more staff to prepare for its first significant expansion in many years.[38]

In the early 1980s, the Reagan administration persistently tried to fold Head Start into block grants, which would essentially have destroyed the program by requiring it to compete with other programs for the reduced amounts of money allocated for those grants. Only a great public outcry forced the administration to back down. Nonetheless, the Reagan administration went on to dismiss all recommendations for restoring staff-child ratios and class size, upgrading professional quality of staff, increasing salaries, and making other quality improvements.

In fiscal year 1991, Head Start funding was raised by $399 million, to $1.95 billion, and the next fiscal year by about the same amount, to

$2 billion. These increases were helpful, but they provided resources to serve only about 31 percent of the children eligible for the program (541,000), according to congressional estimates. Underfunding of the program has always meant that it has served a minority of eligible youngsters: from 1965 to 1992, 11 million poor children had been in the program, but 50 million who qualified were left out.[39]

Insufficient funding of Head Start has led to larger classes than those in much more successful preschool programs.[40] Said one Head Start official, "A long-term disregard for the effect of inflation" resulted in an actual 13 percent decline in per-child expenditures from 1981 to 1989. Furthermore, because the appropriation disregarded cost-of-living increases for the staff's generally meager pay, grantees were forced to fund these salary increases with money they would rather have used for much needed improvement in other program areas. Staff pay still remained low and continued to contribute to a high teacher turnover and, in turn, to the dilution of program quality. Inadequate funding has ultimately meant that the full array of educational and support services required to overcome the effects of poverty could not be provided.[41] Moreover, since the need for more intensive services has actually risen because of deeper poverty, Head Start programs face a greater than ever need to respond to the effects of neighborhood crime, inadequate housing, poor nutrition, substance abuse, and child abuse. Unprecedented demands have been put on Head Start staff for one-to-one counseling, assistance to families, and dealing with troubled children in the classroom. As one Head Start worker observed, "We look back to the poverty of the early 1970s as the good old days. Poverty is getting uglier."[42] Under President Clinton, Head Start received $3.5 billion in fiscal 1995 and $3.6 billion in fiscal 1996 for about 750,000 children (about 36 percent of those eligible that year), still far, far short of the funds required for full, quality programming for the ever growing number of children eligible for the program.[43]

This history suggests that, judged solely by conventional measures of literacy success, millions of children will not become adequately literate because resources are not available. This failure is due to political policy, not to a lack of knowledge about what will provide fruitful preschool learning.

The argument that even Head Start's shortcomings can be overcome by increased funding has been countered by those who influence or reign over social policy, with claims about "reality" and poverty: Head

Start must compete with other programs for insufficient money. This explanation is not far from that given by those who are not supportive of the program, such as conservative critic John Hood.[44] "In the context of limited resources" rather than that of "the ideal world," Hood contends, there are insufficient funds for preschool programs. He recommends a voucher system for school choice and welfare reform "aimed at altering family behaviors." When Head Start critics were questioned about the demonstrated success of the Perry Preschool Program, they claimed that the findings were invalid because the Perry program spent nearly twice as much per child as the average Head Start program ($7,300 per child versus $4,100).[45]

My support for Head Start does not mean that I believe quality preschool programs are a complete answer for overcoming the effects of poverty on academic achievement. As much as quality preschool programs are essential, they can be regarded at best as necessary but not sufficient measures. Edward Zigler speaks of the class limitations of Head Start and cautions supporters not "to oversell the effectiveness" of the program. It is important in concluding to restate that although Head Start looks relatively successful when its participants are compared with similar children not in Head Start or comparable programs, its successes dim when Head Start children are compared with their middle-class peers: "compared to their wealthier peers, the Head Start children [remain] disturbingly behind."[46] The terms of the present literacy debate offer little hope for changing this.

7

READING DISABILITIES

AND LEARNING TO READ

In recent years, theories of predestination have acquired a seemingly more sophisticated form than those of their predecessors. The theory of reading disability is one such example. This theory proposes there are mild to severe neurological deficits in many otherwise normally intelligent children who do not learn to read and write. It explains reading failure by narrowing the focus onto the smallest part of the reading process—a brain "glitch." Instruction and all other circumstances in a youngster's life may compound the problem, but none is its primary cause. According to some estimates, more than 20 percent of schoolchildren (at least 10 million) are reading disabled.[1] Those with this disability can be helped, the theory goes, but "the disability persists into adulthood."[2]

The proponents of this theory are those who emphasize skills. They believe that phonological awareness is the chief skill impaired by neurological damage and that an extensive program of skills instruction is essential for the reading disabled. Because the research tied to the theory is heavily neuropsychological, employs sophisticated technology, and has the look of formidable hard science, it is beyond the expertise of most reading educators. Consequently, even though the theory gains most of its active support from those who advocate heavy skills instruction, many teachers more sympathetic to whole-language instruction regard the theory as credible and tend to accept its assumptions about predestined reading underachievement. This chapter will examine the reading disabilities research in order to assess the validity of the theory, the assumptions it generates, and what role it should play in the debate over literacy.

"Reading Disabilities"

"Learning disabilities" (LD) is the broader umbrella term into which fall the synonymous terms "reading disabilities" and "dyslexia." A person may have a math, handwriting, or other academically related disability, but most youngsters defined as "learning disabled" have problems with reading and writing. A "learning disability" originates within a child, not from social circumstances (such as poor teaching or family difficulties), emotional problems, sensory problems, or problems in personality or attitude (such as having an antipathy to school).

In *The Learning Mystique*, published in 1987, I reviewed learning disabilities research that had studied neurological dysfunctions in every conceivable way: dysfunctions in perception, language, attention, eye movements, and brain structure and function. Family, twins, and chromosomes had been studied to find genetic causes. All of these possible explanations had been explored separately and in combination. Despite its voluminous size, this research had failed to validate the neurological deficit explanation (or assemblage of explanations) that supposedly described the hordes of children diagnosed as learning disabled. In 1987, having spent more than a decade working with, and running programs for, children and adults labeled "learning disabled," I was all too familiar with the severest learning difficulties. So I did not draw this conclusion lightly. No doubt some children do have a "learning disability" that interferes with learning and academic achievement. Research suggests, however, that millions of children had been misdiagnosed as learning disabled.

A reading of the "evidence" tendered over many decades can discern recurrent patterns. One of these patterns is a confusion of correlation with causation. Differences in brain functioning between normal and learning disabled children have been identified. Although I do not question these differences and indeed I expect them from groups with varying skills, I maintain that they do not imply neurological abnormality. For example, if two groups of normal people were doing a task, but only one were competent in it, analysis of brain activity during the task would show differences, not dysfunctions.

Another pattern in the research might be compared to a climb over a mountain range, with peaks marking announcements of new evidence of neurological deficits. However, a slide toward the valley commences when replication studies suggest that the original conclusions were less true than claimed. The slide continues as additional research further diminishes the strength of the initial findings. Finally, after more replication studies, the explanation is rejected. A classic example is the clinical EEG. Around the mid-1960s, when "LD" was formally established as an educational category, researchers asserted that 95 percent of the children diagnosed as learning disabled had EEG abnormalities. A couple of years later the percentage dipped to 62 percent. When researchers recognized that earlier studies were not double-blind ones, and that EEG findings previously thought to be abnormal were in fact normal, the percentage dropped again, to 37 percent in 1970 and 32 percent in 1973. Today, the inability of the clinical EEG to distinguish the learning disabled is overwhelmingly accepted. But that has not been the end of it. Proponents of the EEG went from the valley to further peaks containing more intricate versions of the EEG (evoked potentials, neurometrics, BEAM mapping). Regrettably, those who have traversed this trail have failed to consider the possibility that the expected destination of explaining LD has not been reached because they started and have remained on the wrong conceptual route.

Despite these failures, research attempting to find a brain deficit has continued. In the pages ahead I will assess the work done since *The Learning Mystique*, concentrating on highly regarded studies published in major psychology, science, and learning disabilities journals. General observations are insufficient because the strength of the arguments rests on the data, analyses, and conclusions of the empirical research. Therefore, only a detailed examination of this research can determine if claims have been better documented in recent years.

Defining "Reading Disabilities"

A fundamental problem of all research on "reading disabilities" has been the lack of valid criteria for identifying the reading disabled. To date, when youngsters diagnosed as reading disabled are compared with others defined simply as "poor readers" because their problems are not considered to be neurologically caused, test results fail to distinguish between the two groups. Without criteria to identify the reading disabled, there is no certainty that the "reading disabled" subjects in a given study actually share the same kind of problem.

A frequently used standard for identifying children as reading disabled has been "discrepancy scores"—that is, the discrepancy between scores in tests of intelligence and those of reading achievement. Discrepancy score diagnosis assumes that if a person is not reading up to the expected level as indicated by an IQ score (children who have a "middle average" IQ score of 100 would be expected to read at average grade level), and if that person's social and educational circumstances were judged adequate or above average, the likely cause of that person's reading problem would be a neuropsychological deficit rather than low general intelligence or poor environment.

Although this is a preeminent means for classifying and labeling millions of children, the discrepancy formula does not hold up under empirical scrutiny. When the test performance of children categorized as reading disabled on the basis of a discrepancy formula is compared with that of poor readers and normal readers on a variety of reading, spelling, phonological processing, language, and memory tasks, children classified as either reading disabled or poor readers do not differ, and both groups score below normal readers.[3]

Another problem identifying the reading disabled is the assessment of the "exclusionary" factors—such as social, educational, or emotional difficulties—that might cause reading problems. Current studies, like past ones, consistently state that exclusionary factors have been sufficiently explored before being discounted, but a close reading of how subjects are selected frequently reveals the insufficient examination of exclusionary influences. For example, a two-year study identified fifty-two reading disabled children at the outset of the research. The researchers eliminated environmental factors as causes of the literacy problems because the children came from "predominantly middle- to upper-middle-class areas of Los Angeles and Orange counties"[4]—but their conclusions bear closer examination. Eleven moved during the study and, of the remaining forty-one, only twenty-one agreed to participate for the entire length of the study. Thus, only twenty-one remained for testing at the end. One might think that, in a group in which over 20 percent of families had moved within a two-year period and nearly 50 percent of the remaining families had refused to continue participating in a study that might have shed light on their children's problems, the researchers might have raised some questions about exclusionary factors. Could moving from school to school, with having to adapt to new classrooms, peers, teachers, and possible inconsistencies in teaching approaches have affected the subject's reading and writing? Did the large percentage of family opposition to participation suggest anything about family dynamics that could have influenced literacy achievement? At the very least, these events should have dampened the researchers' satisfaction.

A Dutch study also dismissed exclusionary influences, emphasizing that in the Dutch schools reading disabled children received "phonetically based reading skills" instruction, as did all beginning readers. This meant, the researchers concluded, that group differences were not likely to have arisen from differences in reading method.[5] They did not postulate that a "one method fits all" approach might have been the cause of reading problems for some Dutch children in the first place.

Sally Shaywitz, a prominent learning disabilities researcher, and her colleagues rejected the long-held assumption that boys are more likely than girls to be reading disabled. They found that schools identify boys as reading disabled more often, but the actual prevalence was nearly identical for both sexes. The inconsistency lay in the failure of the schools to recognize the problem when it occurred in girls. Schools that participated in the project displayed astonishing misunderstandings of children! For example, teachers rated boys as having more problems in language and academics than their female peers, even though the ability and achievement of both groups were comparable. Behavior problems, more than reading problems, determined whether children were classified as reading disabled.

Presumably, the failure to identify and address the reading problems of a substantial number of children might indicate something about poor teaching and school practices, which in turn might raise questions about whether schooling contributed to the reading problems in the first place. But not for these researchers. Instead, their appraisal was confined to surveying the actual prevalence of this disorder which, to them, was "biologically based." On what basis did the researchers conclude that these youngsters had this kind of disorder? They offered no evidence of faulty neurology; children were classified as reading disabled solely by the discredited discrepancy formula (reading test scores were lower than IQ scores).[6]

Deficit-Driven Research

Several years ago, learning disabilities expert Mary Poplin used the term "deficit-driven" to describe the tendency in learning disabilities research to interpret all test results as indicating a deficit regardless of what the result might be.[7] An illustration of the continued applicability of Poplin's phrase is a study on the purported "timing" problem that reading disabled children have in processing language.

A timing problem refers to the relatively slower pace at which the reading disabled read words within text, a problem in word recognition that supposedly impairs the reader's ability to string words into meaningful sentences. To study this hypothesized timing problem, three groups were compared: one of reading disabled children; another of "garden variety" poor readers (a term used for poor readers whose problems are not due to neurological deficits); and a third of average readers. The "garden variety" poor readers read slightly better than the reading disabled, and the average readers read much better than both groups.

On a naming test, each child was asked to name a picture as accurately and quickly as possible. If a child named any picture incorrectly, the examiner afterward showed the missed item, read a list of four words, one of which correctly named the picture, and asked the child to make a multiple-choice decision. The naming test scores for the reading disabled were below that of the good readers but were not statistically different from that of the "garden variety" poor readers.[8]

Similar naming test scores for reading disabled and poor readers would seem to represent similar cognition and a similar failure, but not for these researchers, who concluded instead that although there were no score differences, there were "significant differences for the reasons underlying the depressed scores."[9] This interpretation was based on differences in multiple-choice test results, in which the reading disabled were more likely to choose the correct answers. According to the researchers, this suggested a deficit because many of the reading disabled appeared to know the word prior to the multiple-choice test but could not retrieve it. Ordinary poor readers, on the other hand, "frequently miss a word because they do not know it, rather than because they cannot retrieve it."[10]

Not content with restricting their interpretations to the testing they had actually done, the researchers offered a speculation (a "speculative framework" they called it) that handily extended their chief hypothesis: they proposed that the reading disabled may have a "word retrieval" deficit possibly in the "anterior frontal areas" of the brain![11]

There are exceptions to deficit-driven research, and the distinction between differences and deficits is not lost on all researchers. When it is not, studies can shed light on the necessity of distinguishing between differences and deficits in order to grasp the complexity of the connection between brain activity and reading behavior. One such study was an EEG investigation that found considerable differences between the EEGs of reading disabled and normal readers when they read silently and out loud. However, rather than ascribe these differences to a biological deficit, the researchers suggested that the differences may lie in the way each group performed the respective tasks. The EEG differences "may not be a specific index of the underlying deficit in the reading disabled. It would be simply a sign that they are not using the same strategy as the normal readers, but not a sign of what keeps them from using it." In other words, according to this study, there is nothing in the differences that necessarily points to brain deficits over experiential deficits.[12]

Phonological Deficits

In the last decade much of the reading disabilities research has been directed toward finding brain abnormalities related to phonological deficits. The belief that phonological deficits are the cause of reading disabilities is clearly stated in a National Institutes of Health (NIH) guide for applicants seeking grants to support reading disabilities research. Summarizing the state-of-the-art findings, the guide concluded:

Reading disabilities reflects a persistent deficit in linguistic (phonological) skills and basic reading skills. Disabled readers do not readily acquire the alphabetic code when learning to read, apparently due to deficiencies in the processing of phonological information. Converging evidence show[s] that deficits in phonological awareness reflect the core deficit in reading disabilities.[13]

Similarly, in an article on reading disabilities published in *Scientific American*, Sally Shaywitz asserted:

> Over the past two decades, a coherent model of dyslexia has emerged that is based on phonological processing. This phonological model is consistent both with the clinical symptoms of dyslexia and with what neuroscientists know about brain organization and function.[14]

Claims of finding "evidence for aberrant auditory anatomy" that creates phonological deficits that lead to reading disabilities have been made by prominent learning disabilities researcher Albert Galaburda and his associates. Galaburda's research has appeared in leading medical and psychology journals, is repeatedly cited in reviews of research on the neuropsychology of reading disabilities, and has received considerable national media attention. Galaburda, who for over a decade has been reporting abnormalities in the brains of deceased individuals said to be reading disabled, has sought to provide evidence for the phonological deficit theory by studying a region of the brain called the medial geniculate, which processes arriving sounds as part of the auditory processing system.

Measuring the size and number of the neurons in the medial geniculate of five reading disabled and seven normal readers, Galaburda reported finding:

- The neurons in the left side of the medial geniculate of the brains of the reading disabled were significantly smaller than those in their right.[15] No such asymmetry was found for the normal readers.
- Compared to normal readers, the medial geniculate on the left side of the brains of the reading disabled had more small neurons and fewer large neurons.

The relatively smaller neurons that were in greater number on the left side of reading disabled brains were said to support the "behavioral findings of a left hemisphere-based phonological deficit in reading disabled individuals."

If we look closely at the data on these reading disabled and control brains, a different interpretation is possible. It might be true that in the brains of the reading disabled the neurons on the left side were significantly smaller. However, this description is true only when size is averaged. Looked at individually:

- The size of the neurons of three of the seven brains of normal readers showed the same left-right relationship as that of the reading disabled: that is, the average neuron size was smaller on the left side than on the right (left/right: 224/250, 241/250, 221/234).
- The left/right neuron size patterns of a normal reader's brain (241/250) and a reading disabled brain (240/253) were virtually the same.

Given these similarities, we may ask: How did these three normal readers learn to read if they had the same neuron pattern as the reading disabled? How is it that Galaburda found that "the brains of reading disabled show[ed] an abnormal asymmetry" but the brains of these normal readers did not?

Another important comparison is the neuron size in the left side of the medial geniculate:

- Two of the brains of the reading disabled had average neuronal sizes in the left side that were *larger* than or about the same size as that of five of the normal readers: 240 and 237 for the reading disabled vs. 224, 226, 236, 221, and 241 for the normal readers.

Thus, if the neuron size patterns for a reading disability appear to be related to smaller neuron size in the left side, how is it that these five normal readers did not have "abnormal development"?

A critique of this research could also include questions about the validity of the criteria for determining that the five deceased reading disabled persons had actually been "reading disabled." Galaburda and his colleagues say that these persons had been diagnosed with reading disabilities using "test batteries for intelligence and reading achievement," but they provide no test scores or other specific descriptions from the diagnoses. Their study also states, without any suggestion that the diagnostic validity of the IQ/reading test scores discrepancy formula has not been substantiated, that "in every case, there was a large discrepancy between intelligence (average or above in all cases) and reading achievement."[16] Failure to document the "reading disabilities" of other deceased persons used in Galaburda's earlier studies has also been a problem.[17]

Cerebral Blood Flow Studies

Many reading disabilities researchers have looked to new technologies for examining the brain in order to obtain more substantial evidence of the neurological causes of reading disabilities. A sophisticated technology that has been used in research on language and language problems is the positron emission tomography scan (or PET). A PET procedure begins with the injection of a radioactive isotope (oxygen 15) into a person's vein. The isotope accumulates in the brain in proportion to the amount of blood flow involved in a mental task, such as reading words. A PET camera detects the blood flow and that information is transformed into color representations of the relative activation of brain regions. Variations in blood flow are equated with degrees of brain activity, and in this way researchers can gauge the relative involvement of each part of the brain during a task. A similar method uses a radioactive tracer (xenon 133), which is inhaled and then also employed to ascertain the blood flow in various brain regions.[18]

PET and similar techniques have provided considerable insights into brain structure and function. With respect to reading disabilities research, however, as with previous studies using lesser technologies, the use of PET to establish neurological deficits that lead to reading disabilities poses a major problem: in any study, a technology cannot be better than the research methods employing it.

One PET study found that, when doing a rhyme detection task, a reading disabled group showed significantly less activation than did normal readers in the left areas of the brain (temporoparietal regions) involved in analyzing and synthesizing speech sounds.[19] Do these findings demonstrate that the reading disabled have phonemic deficits *because* of impaired brain regions? Or, rather, do they demonstrate, as in the EEG study previously discussed, that the reading disabled have differences in blood flow *because* of their phonemic analysis abilities? From the results, there is no way of deciding.

The difficulty in interpreting data is equally evident in a study using the xenon-inhalation method that looked at two areas of the brain. One, Wernicke's area, is involved in processing phonemic sounds and is thought to be where memory of these sounds is stored. It also contributes to the comprehension of written and oral language. The other, the angular gyrus, is involved in combining information from different sensory modalities, visual and auditory in the case of written language.

In a group of adults who had been normal readers in childhood, success on a written language task was related to the degree of activation in a brain area that processes phonemic sounds and comprehension (Wernicke's area). Conversely, adults who had been poor childhood readers, even if they became better readers in adulthood, exhibited a reduced response in this area. Almost the reverse was true for the groups in activating the areas involved in combining visual and auditory information (angular gyrus): the good childhood readers were more likely to inhibit activation of that area, while poor childhood readers were more likely to activate it.

The researchers remarked that a correlation between reading problems and poorer activation of Wernicke's area was not surprising because that area plays a part in the comprehension of written language. What did seem to be a significant difference between the reading groups was the varying activation of the area that combined visual and auditory information (again, it was low for the good childhood readers and high for the poor ones). This correlation purportedly provided "the first large-sample evidence [of] a chronic neural deficit, persisting from childhood" in the reading disabled.[20]

Possibly this is true, but there is another interpretation, one, as I have been emphasizing, that views brain activity in its interaction with learning, behavior, and social relationships. The brains of good readers, because they rely primarily on the meaning (semantic) cues of language, and minimally on symbol-sound relationships (that is, they do not have to "sound out" words, as poor readers have a propensity to try to do), show activation of the areas involved in semantic comprehension and less activation of those areas that process symbol-sound (visual-auditory) relationships. The brains of poor readers, because they tend to rely more on symbol-sound relationships, are more likely to show more activation of the angular gyrus. And even the brains of formerly poor readers, possibly because of an ingrained reliance on "sounding out" strategies stemming from their years as poor readers, and having a very different history of learning to read from that of normal readers, are more likely to show a similar activation.[21]

The deficit-driven impetus found in PET research on reading disabilities is evident in another study. Normal and disabled readers were given a task in which they had to associate an item with a category (for example, a reader had to decide if an apple was an animal, a body part, or a food). When performing the task, both groups had greater left than right hemisphere activation in the brain regions. This similar asymmetry, concluded the researchers, failed to "support the idea that severe reading disabilities in adults are characterized by underactivation" of the regions. So far, so good for the reading disabled.

The study also revealed that normal readers had relatively more symmetrical activation. This finding differs from a long-held assumption in reading disabilities theory that the source of reading disability lies in *symmetrical* hemispheric activation, which prevents one hemisphere from playing a dominant role in language processing. One might expect the authors to criticize the theory; otherwise the finding in their study would suggest that the more asymmetrical brains of the reading disabled subjects were more normal than the more symmetrical brains of normal readers. Neither conclusion had to be considered, however, because the finding in a visual perception test came closer to substantiating the researchers' original theory. In this test—a "line orientation" task, not a reading test—the reading disabled showed relatively greater right hemispheric activation than did normal readers. From this data, the researchers concluded that the reading disabled brains might be defective because the test results indicated a failure to integrate information and efficiently distribute language processing tasks between the hemispheres.[22]

Another PET study found overwhelming similarities between the brain blood flow activity of normal and disabled readers. The investigators' summary, however, expressed greatest interest in the few differences and, as in most reading disabilities studies, the differences represented deficits. Where a finding contradicted previous interpretations of purported neurological deficits in the reading disabled, the data were simply mentioned and passed over in favor of other findings that indicated deficits. For these investigators, no matter what size the blood flow activity (high or low) and no matter where the asymmetry (right or left), if there was a difference it was always presumed to represent a neurological failure in the reading disabled.[23]

MRI and Reading Disabilities

A technology employed in studying the connection between brain structure and reading disabilities is magnetic resonance imaging (MRI), a technique that provides a graphic depiction of brain (or body) tissues.

Several MRI studies have looked at the region of the brain called the planum temporale. This region in the left hemisphere includes Wernicke's area, which, as previously described, functions in analyzing and synthesizing speech sounds and in the comprehension of written and oral language. Because of the part it plays in phonological awareness, this brain region has been of great interest to many reading disabilities researchers.

Evidence of a structural brain defect in the reading disabled seemed to be found in an MRI study that reported a larger left than right planum temporale in 70 percent of normal readers (twelve of seventeen), whereas only 30 percent of disabled readers showed this asymmetry (six of nineteen).[24] For the rest in both groups, the size of the areas was equal or approximately equal. The percentage of asymmetry in the normal readers was roughly that found in the general population (65 percent larger left than right, 11 percent larger right than left, 24 percent approximately equal size).[25]

The percentages of asymmetry and symmetry in this study appear to suggest an abnormality in the reading disabled associated with phonological awareness, but other data in the study offer the basis for a different interpretation. First, the symmetry differences in both groups were due to size differences of the right planum temporale; *the size of the left was essentially the same for both the reading disabled and normal readers.* Consequently, if a phonological processing deficit is at all associated with the left planum temporale, it is not because the region is smaller.

Second, symmetry was found in 30 percent of normal readers, indicating that in itself symmetry of the planum temporale does not necessarily lead to poor reading.

Third, the researchers themselves offered a caveat for the MRI method used to measure the symmetry of the region, recommending "caution" when measuring it "by an indirect method like ours."[26] One reason for the measurement problem is a lack of clear-cut boundaries of the planum temporale: the exact location of the boundaries of the region and the precise location of areas within the region are in dispute.[27] The consequences of arbitrary definitions were evident in a study of the brains of human cadavers that found a strong leftward asymmetry using a classical anatomical definition of the planum temporale. However, by including the often omitted far rear portion of the structure, an alternative definition was possible and, when used in this study, the asymmetry found through the classical definition disappeared. In fact, the rear portion seems to demonstrate a reverse symmetry. Because of inconsistencies in definition and measurement techniques, several studies have contradicted each other, casting doubt on the associations between reading disabilities and the structure and asymmetry of the planum temporale.[28]

Finally, much of the research reporting a relationship between the planum temporale and reading disabilities may be wholly flawed because of a failure to take into account the ages of the subjects. When taken into account, however, "no statistically significant neuroanatomical differences" were found between the reading groups because "age was positively correlated with structure size," and the normal readers were slightly older. Even as little as a three-month age difference between groups produced substantial brain size differences through childhood.

Also of importance was the finding that the size of a particular brain region correlated with overall brain size. Thus "when brain size differences were controlled, no significant differences were found" between reading disabled and normal readers on a variety of brain measures, including the surface area of the planum temporale. The researchers emphasized that "for a regional brain difference to be meaningful, it must be independent of overall differences in brain size, else the finding is nonspecific (and incongruent with current theories of reading disabilities)." A failure to account for age and overall brain size may explain the contradictory findings in previous neuroimaging research on reading disabilities, the study concluded.[29]

There is, of course, nothing wrong—and everything right—in looking at connections between brain structure and function and serious literacy problems. With respect to the planum temporale, however, we see the now predictable rise and decline of another "finding." If there is no association between hemispheric asymmetry and auditory processing, this research direction is fruitless in achieving its underlying aim of finding structural brain deficits linked to phonological processing.

Genetics

Discovering a gene responsible for the neurological defect underpinning reading disabilities has been a persistent research goal. Numerous studies have reported finding that reading disabilities run in families, but whether the cause of these familial patterns is experiential, genetic, or both is simply not explained by discovering literacy problems across generations. A single dominant genetic model has not explained the pattern of reading disabilities in families, but this failure has not prevented continued publication of claims that "dominant inheritance is the most likely genetic mode" transmitting reading disabilities.[30]

In *The Learning Mystique* I criticized and rejected a more sophisticated mode of research that claimed to find a gene for reading disabilities on chromosome 15.[31] My criticism was based solely on my analysis of the data, but later replication research failed to find evidence for the gene and additional work by the original researchers led them to abandon their earlier claims altogether.[32]

The importance of observing a pattern of that theory's rise and eventual fall is not only in confirming a common pattern, but in seeing once again the attention given by the media to the original research — thereby reinforcing the view that the "problem" is inherited. The media's failure to report the demise of the researchers' original claim, of course, is even more interesting, and contributed to the impression that there is a chain of evidence supporting the biological basis of reading disabilities.

Unflaggingly in pursuit of finding the reading disabilities gene, the researchers who claimed to have found it on chromosome 15 have reported, again with accompanying media attention, that it is, in fact, on chromosome 6.[33] In considering this study, we must keep in mind that it is a single study not yet independently replicated. As geneticist Neil J. Risch said about the methodology of this research: "These are fishing expeditions. There have probably been a dozen findings for such behavioral genetic linkages. Not a single one has been [independently] replicated."[34]

"No Evidence" Evidence

For a final word about claims that purport to be backed by evidence, let us turn to Sally Shaywitz's contention that reading disabilities are a neuropsychological disorder. In *Scientific American*, after an elaborate description of reading disabilities as a phonological deficit created by "cognitive processes carried out by a specific network of brain cells," the only evidence Shaywitz offers is her MRI studies that claim to have found that men and women have a different locus for phonological processing in their brains. Even if this were true—and it is too early for it to be considered certain—this finding only describes gender differences and provides no information about processing in the "reading disabled." Shaywitz sees her finding, however, as the "possible neurobiological 'signature' for reading" and as one that may bring with it a "more sensitive measure of the disorder" and "the future promise of more precise diagnosis of reading disabilities." She sees "the discovery of a biological signature for reading" as "an unprecedented opportunity to assess the effects of interventions on the neuroanatomical systems serving the reading process itself."[35] To date, Shaywitz and her colleagues simply have not offered research validating these claims and expectations.

"Reading Disabilities" and the Literacy Debate

Biological explanations of "reading disabilities," although unsubstantiated, have been employed in the literacy debate to buttress claims about phonological deficits and the need to emphasize skills in beginning readers. Most literacy educators have little expertise in evaluating the claims of the "explanations," which therefore serve as ultimate reinforcers of assumptions among teachers about inevitable "small futures" for the "reading disabled." The persistence of the biological "explanations" further damages the literacy debate by diverting attention from factors and practices that can prevent severe reading problems in children.[36]

I have worked with adults whose problems have been explained as buried in the workings of their brains and whose educational achievement was presented to them as limited by their "defect." I have further seen these adults struggle with despair and feelings of hopelessness sometimes leading to suicidal behavior, and it will therefore be no surprise that I find this inflexible, overdrawn "explanation" especially abhorrent.

8

MONEY, POLITICS,

AND LEARNING TO READ

Before the Civil War, only a very small minority of slaves were allowed to learn to read. In the North, African-Americans fared relatively better: some northern private schools supported by religious organizations and philanthropists were open to African-American children, and public schools in a few northern communities were integrated. Overall, however, even these northern schools served few black children.[1] Nor did the end of the Civil War see a great leap forward: five years after the war, the combined number of black children who attended school reached approximately 10 percent, and by the end of the century, about 70 percent still received no schooling.[2] This was the scenario while educators were disputing various instructional alternatives.

If the question were posed: "Why did most black children not learn to read and write during the nineteenth century?" the answer would not be found either in an examination of the methods for teaching reading or by drawing upon the "reading process." Rather, the answer would lie primarily in an examination of the political-economic system and the racist culture. Only by accounting for these forces can there be any meaningful discussion of the internal aspects of teaching and learning. In the nineteenth century it would have been absurd to expect answers for solving the literacy plight of black children to lie in discussions of "how best to teach." Within this stark historical example, reading educators today would not think of disagreeing with the need to understand political-economic influences on literacy. In contrast, the terms of the present literacy debate, its focus on instruction and the "reading process," eliminate consideration of any compelling need to account for political-economic influences. In this chapter, I will argue that accounting for these influences is necessary because now, as in the nineteenth century, literacy achievement is determined as much or more by the needs of those who control society's political economy than by the instructional approaches teachers choose.

White Working-Class Children

Although education of most white working-class children in the nineteenth century was relatively better than that for black children, its deficiencies still illustrate the effects of decisions made by those who controlled the political economy. For instance, an 1837 law in Massachusetts required children under fifteen years of age to receive three months of schooling per year before being allowed to work in the factories, but these and similar compulsory school attendance laws, as well as child labor laws, were largely disregarded by business owners. By 1850, hardly a third of white school-age children attended school, a percentage lower than that of twenty-five years earlier. Despite the support businessmen gave to the common school, compulsory schooling laws for factory youths were generally unenforced and children typically worked eleven to fourteen hours a day: "manufacturers complained that a shorter work day would harm business."[3] In Chicago, compulsory education legislation was defeated "five times between 1871 and 1881" and though a law was finally passed in 1883, it was weak and did no more than require that children between eight and fourteen attend school for merely twelve weeks each year.[4]

For those who had political-economic power and benefited from child labor, there was no advantage in educating children. On the contrary, low literacy abilities of child workers had an additional "advantage" of tying children to the only kind of work that a meager education would later offer them as adults. There was also no reason for businessmen to pay adults adequate wages that would end their dependence on their children's income. Without an adequate wage, parents faced a troubling choice: they could allow their children to take advantage of the literacy education formally available to them, or they could send their children to work and keep the family income above dire levels. "The inevitable tendency," for many families, "was to slight education, to mortgage the future for the present; immediate concrete earnings looked larger and more inviting than future indefinite opportunities for the children of the family."[5]

The rise of the common school—that is, schools for the "common," not rich, children—from its beginning was marked by inadequate funding. Nineteenth-century policies aimed at getting the most pedagogy from barest funding meant overcrowded schools, both urban and rural. During the winter, when farm work slackened, a rural schoolhouse meant for thirty might have had sixty or seventy students instead. Toward the end of the century, urban classrooms had forty to forty-eight students per room. Thus, millions of children might of course have obtained more education than had the previous generation, but it would nonetheless still be less than the best that could have been offered.[6]

The Cost of Literacy Education: Francis Parker and the Quincy Schools

Even the exceptional instructional reforms of Colonel Francis Parker, superintendent of schools in Quincy, Massachusetts, in the late 1870s—arguably the leading educational reforms of the century—could not sway economic policy that moved in another direction. We will recall from Chapter 2 that by 1880, five years after his appointment, Parker had left the Quincy schools, which soon afterward reverted to conventional instruction. Why did this happen? How could the board terminate Parker's documented achievements and scrap his celebrated "Quincy method," which tens of thousands of visitors had come to observe?

Educational historian Michael Katz notes that "a fact of critical importance in nineteenth century educational reform was the assumption that economic frugality and improvement went hand and hand."[7] For the Quincy school board this translated into paying teachers poorly. For Parker, in turn, this meant training teachers only to have them lured to other communities for *relatively* better salaries. Parker's headaches were increased when the school board took the further step of reducing salaries of new teachers, thereby making it even harder for him to attract quality teachers.

Facilitating a low-cost Quincy budget was "the feminization of the teaching force."[8] By the time Parker took control of the Quincy schools, feminization, especially in the elementary schools, had become a fact of life.[9] Two years before Parker was hired, the Quincy school board had written that "the best results will be obtained at the least expense" if women worked in schools under the direction of a man.[10] For a school board set on pursuing "a gradual reduction in the instruction budget," using low-salaried female teachers was considered a budgetary achievement.[11]

The board's decisions were not wholly callous and sexist. Quincy, like the rest of the country, was feeling the effects of the depression since 1873.[12] Unemployment was high, workers opposed paying more taxes, and the tax base had decreased. Granite workers who had lost jobs or had their salaries reduced understandably saw any tax increase as taking bread out of their children's mouths. Thus, the reigning assumption that economic frugality and educational improvement were naturally complementary was accentuated by financial exigencies. With justification, the board did complain that Quincy "could not afford to pay salaries and have a per pupil expenditure rivaling" those in nearby wealthy towns.[13] On the other hand, not all of Quincy was poor: the wealthy of Quincy continued to have money but chose not to come forward to save the reforms. Reinforcing this choice was a school board that failed to express any anguish over the effect that ending the reforms would have on children or to propose greater taxes on the rich to support the reforms.

Parker's annual reports to the board complained about the need for stability and warned that excessive economic measures would undermine his reforms. He "accused the School [Board] of false economy," adding that "Quincy paid for the training of teachers and other towns reaped the rewards."[14] The board, in turn, not only ignored Parker's admonitions—it added insult by refusing his request for a salary increase. Frustrated, Parker resigned to become supervisor of schools in Boston. With him went thirteen teachers. A few years afterward, the Quincy reforms had essentially disappeared.

This overview suggests that the exemplary Quincy reforms were not killed because of deficiencies in instructional method. Parker had succeeded in improving the classroom. His reforms in reading instruction were far ahead of their time (many reading educators today are struggling to achieve changes comparable to the Quincy method). Although he had his critics, Parker attained the academic improvements expected of him when he was hired. Despite these achievements, the school board's primary focus was elsewhere. When the board had to choose between its budget and the educational reforms, their choice was clear-cut. Parker was not blind to the assumptions about finances that underlay the board's failure to support him, but he was helpless to influence them. Changes in instructional method, without changes in the political-economic power and policy upon which the reforms were contingent, proved fruitless.

Money and Literacy Achievement Today

How do the lessons from Quincy apply today?

Judging from the views of the American Legislative Exchange Council, an organization of conservative state legislators, they do not apply at all. If anything, the council might say, current school spending and educational outcomes vindicate the frugality of the Quincy school board. Now, plenty of money is spent on schooling, but increased per-pupil expenditures, the council maintains, have not produced a corresponding jump in student achievement.[15] Frequently cited in support of this kind of claim is the work of Eric A. Hanushek, a specialist on education finance. Summing up his sizable statistical analyses, Hanushek states:

> Even a cursory examination of the historical patterns of student performance and school finance highlights a central mystery of the educational debate. The nation is spending more and more to achieve results that are no better, perhaps worse. The standard nostrum of educational reformers—that additional resources should be devoted to each student's education—belies the fact that per-pupil spending has increased steadily throughout the century.[16]

Hanushek emphasizes that he would be in favor of adding financial resources if there were evidence that they would improve academic performance, but he concludes that today's schools do "not use resources well" in promoting student achievement and, most fundamentally, that current knowledge does not offer a guide for effectively spending money. He concludes that differences in school spending are unrelated to student performance. Hanushek recognizes that this judgment "defies common sense [and] conventional wisdom," but he maintains that his research has led him to oppose spending more money on school resources, teacher salaries, smaller class sizes, and so forth.[17]

Business Week echoed this conclusion in a 1992 article that provided graphs demonstrating how "the U.S. keeps spending more on students but their performance has declined."[18] And at the Heritage Foundation, a conservative think tank, a conference on the question "Can Business Save Education?" similarly decried the waste of increased money put into elementary and secondary education in recent decades.[19]

Strikingly absent is the logical conclusion that if money does not in fact matter, then students in wealthy districts would lose nothing academically if their districts were to distribute a substantial portion of their school budgets to poorer school districts. Not surprisingly, those who live in wealthy districts do not offer this recommendation. Researchers may muster evidence favoring the counterintuitive judgment that money does not matter, but the wealthy continue to act as though their intuition were sounder than apparently empirically supported opposite conclusions. And they do so for a good reason: research on school spending does support their intuition!

One strong piece of evidence comes from Larry Hedges and colleagues, who reexamined Hanushek's data using more sophisticated statistical methods requiring more stringent data.[20] Hanushek used a method called "vote counting" to tabulate and assess the data. In his "vote counting" method, Hanushek took studies of educational spending and looked at how the particular spending in the study correlated positively, negatively, or not at all to student performance, and attributed a "vote" to each of these three. By counting votes he then determined the extent to which the expenditures correlated with school performance. Using this method, Hanushek concluded that few studies showed a positive effect of school expenditures on student performance. For Hedges, however, a "vote counting" analysis had numerous problems that impaired its use as evidence, especially the failure of a "vote" to indicate the strength of the correlation between expenditures and performance. To correct these problems, his reanalysis of Hanu-shek's data did account for variables such as the weight a single study might have on the overall conclusions.

Doing so, Hedges and Rob Greenwald found, contrary to Hanushek, that "school resources are systematically related to student achievement and that these relations are large enough to be educationally impor-tant."[21] These positive relations occurred not only for per-pupil expen-diture but for teacher experience and teacher/pupil ratio, the last two both implying financial costs. The reanalysis led Hedges and colleagues to conclude that "increasing expenditures and teacher experience will increase student outcome."[22] For instance, a per-pupil expenditure increase of $500 (approximately 10 percent of the national average) was associated with a statistically substantial academic achievement outcome.

Hedges and Greenwald also observed that "home environmental variables" that "involve a parent (or parents) expending time participat-ing in or facilitating activities with children that enhance learning" appear to have declined in the past quarter century, due to pressures such as the need for parents to work more to obtain sufficient income. Schools, in turn, have greater pressure to compensate for this decline in informal home educative activities. Hedges and Greenwald argue that

achievement would be expected to decline over the 1970–92 period because of the decline in favorable home environment. The fact that achievement has not declined substantially (and has increased substantially for some subgroups) is evidence *for*, not against, the positive effects of increasing school expenditures. We argue that, as family structures have changed, increases in school expenditures have substituted for [these] informal educational resources.[23]

In a study of Texas school districts, with a huge sample of over 2.4 million students in almost 900 districts, Ronald Ferguson also found evidence for "how and why money matters."[24] Financial resources helped schools hire competent primary school teachers who strongly influenced children's reading achievement: the more skilled the teacher, the higher the reading achievement in the early years. Also linked to academic achievement (and money) was teacher experience: teachers with five or more years of experience contributed more to higher student academic achievement than did less experienced teachers. Money mattered because districts that were able to pay higher salaries for both beginning and experienced teachers were able to handpick better teachers; in turn, better teachers positively affected student achievement. When the student/teacher ratio was reduced to 18:1 or below, student achievement increased, especially in the primary grades.

Particularly important in Ferguson's research was the finding that these expenditures on teachers and classrooms could compensate for the reduced contribution that less educated parents may make in preparing their children for formal schooling or in assisting them with their schoolwork. These expenditures were comparable to the effect parental education had on academic achievement. Rather than bolstering "counterintuition," the research strongly supported "the conventional wisdom that higher-quality schooling produces better reading skills."[25]

The claim that the nation has unproductively "thrown money at the problem" of academic achievement mostly refers to the increase of real school spending by 61 percent from 1967 to 1991. However, a close examination of this spending, by Economic Policy Institute analysts Richard Rothstein and Karen Hawley Miles, offers a different conclusion.[26] Of this new money, only about 28 percent went to regular classrooms. About 30 percent of the money to regular classrooms was used to create smaller classes, but the reduction in teacher/student ratio (about 1:24) did not reach the level identified as essential for academic improvement.

Salaries for regular education teachers rose 23 percent, with most of the increase going to teachers who had greater experience and more advanced credentials than teachers had in 1967. The salary increases, in other words, strongly reflected higher average placements on salary schedules. Overall, salary scales barely kept pace with inflation and did not, over these years, generally offer increasingly higher pay for the same level of experience and credentials. Had teaching experience remained at 1967 levels, average salaries would have represented a decline in the subsequent twenty-five years.[27]

Approximately 38 percent of the new money went to special education, mostly for children categorized as learning and emotionally disabled. For any calculation of school spending and academic achievement, these funds cannot be pooled into a per-pupil calculation for regular education: "it is dishonest to suggest that special education funds should produce academic gains for regular students and, when they do not, claim proof that money spent on public schools is wasted."[28]

On the whole, the money spent has yielded comparable returns over the years: the modest growth in regular education expenditures has produced a modest increase in academic achievement (determined by test scores) for students as a whole and possibly somewhat more for minority students.

Class Size

Reducing teacher/student ratios ("class size") in the early grades is an excellent way to promote literacy.[29] Evidence comes from a huge body of research called Project STAR (Student/Teacher Achievement Ratio) and related class-size research in Tennessee.

The centerpiece of Project STAR was an extensive series of studies on class size comparing students in three kinds of classes: small (13–17 students) and regular (21–25 students), half of which had a full-time teacher's aide. At the end of first grade, youngsters who had been in small classes had reading achievement scores two months ahead of the students in regular classes without an aide, and one month ahead of students in regular-sized classes with an aide.[30] Thus, even when a regular class was augmented with a teacher's aide, small classes proved superior in promoting literacy achievement. Through third grade, students in small classes continued to score significantly higher in reading and math than did students in the other two class-size types, whether compared by community (rural, urban, inner-city, suburban) or by race.

White students scored on average higher than minority students in reading and math, although on some measures the minority children in small groups had scores within or near the range of scores for white children. The advantage of small classes was greatest for minority students, who always outscored the minority students in regular and regular/aide classes. Overall, minority children in small classes had a pass rate of 64 percent on a reading test, compared with 45.4 percent for the average of regular and regular/aide classes. In suburban schools, 74.7 percent of minority children in small classes passed the reading test, compared with 53.1 percent in other class sizes. Clearly, "few well-defined interventions have shown as consistent an impact as this one on the performance of minority students in inner-city settings, not to mention both their minority and nonminority peers in other settings."[31] Similar results have been found elsewhere.

When Project STAR pupils returned to regular-sized classes in fourth grade, the Lasting Benefits Study tracked their progress and found that in every grade through the eighth, students from Project STAR small classes "showed clear, consistent, and statistically significant advantages over Project STAR students from the other two" class sizes.[32] Superior academic achievement held not only in reading and math, the two areas tested throughout STAR, but in spelling, study skills, science, and social studies, all areas tested from grade four onward.

A third phase of the project was Project Challenge, an application of Project STAR in Tennessee's poorest counties. To evaluate Challenge, the average rank of the Challenge school systems was compared to the state's school systems. Among Tennessee's 138 systems, "a ranking of 90 would be below average" (not so good), "a ranking of 69 would be average" (that is, in the exact middle), "and a ranking of 50 would be above average" (good).[33] During the four years of the project, second-grade pupils in these counties continued to move upward in the rankings. In reading they went from a ranking of 98.9 in 1989–90 to 78.5 in 1992–93. In math, the respective rankings were 85.2 to 56.6. Among the many interesting results of these studies is the finding that small classes can benefit beginning readers even in the face of poverty's undermining effects.[34] There are many ways of improving school systems and many are the necessities calling for money to promote education; Project STAR shows the crucial importance of money and one way to improve literacy achievement. What is not evident is why the benefit occurs.

Why Do Smaller Classes Make a Difference?

Exactly what happens in smaller classrooms is, unfortunately, not clear from the research. What seems apparent, however, is that reduced class size allows for instruction not especially unique but nonetheless not easily done in larger classes. For instance, a study of Project STAR's "effective teachers"—teachers whose students ranked in the top 15 percent of largest achievement gains in reading and mathematics—revealed many qualities that could reasonably be expected of all effective teachers regardless of their teaching conditions. These teachers closely monitored student learning progress; when children did not learn, they used alternative strategies in reteaching; they had high expectations for student learning; they were enthusiastic; they had a sense of humor that promoted learning; they had a love for children; they used a broad range of resources and activities; and they had excellent personal interactions with their students.[35] Again, these are not phenomenal qualities for teachers, yet of fifty "effective" teachers, only three had large classes.

Cost of Smaller Classes

Smaller classes by themselves will not be sufficient for improving instruction and learning. There is no question, however, that money spent on small classes would be money well spent. This statement raises the familiar question: even if smaller classes are worthwhile, how can schools and the nation afford them? As one school board member put it in plain dollars-and-cents terms: "Reducing class size generally entails increasing personnel costs, and that can be prohibitively expensive for most school systems."[36] This view has been echoed by other critics who are quick to sidestep the evidence on academic progress and assert instead the pragmatic, realpolitik need to find more "cost-effective" approaches: reducing class size may be academically worthwhile but it is "not economically feasible."[37] Since school budgets cannot "realistically" foot the bill required for reduction of class size, is "reducing class size the best use of funds earmarked for education?"[38] The indisputable answer is implied in the rhetorical question.

Jonathan Kozol described another version of this "realism" in regard to class-size reform in the Chicago schools:

> In 1988 a number of Chicago's more responsive leaders told the press that cutting class size ought to be a top priority and indicated it would cost about $100 million to begin to do this. The rebuttal started almost instantly. Efforts to improve a school by lowering its class size, said then-Assistant U.S. Secretary of Education Chester Finn, would be a "costly waste of money. There are a lot of better and less costly things you can do and get results." Reducing class size would not be "a very prudent investment strategy," said Finn, who sent his daughter to Exeter, where class size is 13.[39]

Tommy M. Tomlinson, a member of the Reagan-Bush administrations, likewise stressed economic feasibility in his review of class-size research: "Reducing class size to any degree is a very expensive proposition; reducing class size to the point where student achievement would likely benefit to a reliably significant degree is prohibitively expensive."[40] Tomlinson urges a cautious public education budget. Rather than reduce class size, said Tomlinson, educational policy should begin by "assuming a limited amount of resources" as the given, then determine how to "arrange the various elements of the teaching-learning situation so that teachers can teach at some minimal level of acceptability and students can learn in the most conducive educational environment."[41]

Insufficient Educational and Social Spending

Despite cries that spending money on reducing class size would be "prohibitively expensive" and that educational spending is already excessive, the United States spends proportionately less on elementary and secondary education than do most other major industrialized countries. Among sixteen such countries, the United States ranks fourteenth in spending on K–12 education as a percent of the Gross Domestic Product (the output of all goods and services). Moreover, when adjusted for inflation, federal spending on elementary and secondary schools decreased 15 percent during the 1980s, according to the National Center for Educational Statistics.[42] For the United States to bring educational spending up to the average level of other major industrial countries, it would have to increase spending by more than $20 billion a year—a sum roughly equal to the entire federal education budget.[43]

The financial resources devoted to education should be considered in light of a 1995 General Accounting Office report estimating that $112 billion is needed to build and repair the nation's schools, thousands of which require extensive reconditioning or replacement. Yet in 1994 state legislatures appropriated only $3.5 billion and local governments $7.1 billion—less than 10 percent of what has been estimated to be necessary for meeting minimal standards. Continued efforts to secure a mere fraction of federal funds needed for school infrastructure have been refused.[44]

Of course, financial support for schooling is not uniformly bad across the nation. An examination of the differences between the per-pupil expenditures within states demonstrates huge gulfs between the wealthiest and poorest school districts. For example the difference between high and low per-pupil spending in California is $11,740 vs. $2,692; in New York $19,238 vs. $3,127; in Colorado $13,617 vs. $3,740; in Texas $14,514 vs. $2,150; in Illinois $14,316 vs. $2,253; and in Montana $10,495 vs. $1,975.[45]

New Jersey is typical of the educational economics that favors the affluent.[46] After two decades of legal battling to eliminate the spending differences between the mostly prosperous suburbs and poor urban and rural school districts, the State Supreme Court ordered the creation of a plan to end spending differences. Rather than comply with the intention of the order, Governor Christine Todd Whitman, after overseeing a major income tax cut that favored the wealthy, said the state would determine the cost of a constitutionally mandated "thorough and efficient education" rather than

> chasing the ever-higher spending levels of the richest suburbs. It has become increasingly clear that making a direct link between high spending and high achievement leads to a false conclusion. A great deal more goes into a successful education than an expensive education program.[47]

Putting this elusive "chasing" another way: Whitman's plan offered minimum funds for a minimally adequate education for many of the nonrich.[48] Especially ignored in this formulation was the need to take into account the reduction of other resources. Poor children and their families are increasingly neglected in state and federal budgets, so equal education requires that school spending for the nonrich must be at least at the level of wealthier districts. Certainly the argument that spending alone may not produce the same academic success across districts has a ring of truth. Whitman attempted to prove her point about a lack of a "direct link" between money and achievement by pointing to a district with high test scores that spent slightly below the state average per pupil. This district, however, just happened to be one of the state's wealthiest! Instead of underscoring her argument, the district actually could be used as evidence for the need for allocating funds for community programs that would help ensure the cognitive and developmental needs of all children.

The predicaments of black children and white working-class children in the nineteenth century are duplicated by the poverty spreading across the entire lives of many of today's children, with a decrease in "social health" for millions of children and adults coinciding with the trend of indifference to the educational well-being of these children. Marc Miringoff and his associates at the Fordham Institute for Innovation in Social Policy have tracked the statistics for sixteen social problems over several decades. Their "Index of Social Health" provides "a comprehensive view of the social health of the nation." Comparing the present to earlier years, the institute found there was no longer a connection between indices of social well-being and the Gross Domestic Product, a measure of economic growth. From 1959 until the mid-1970s, social health and the GDP had similar patterns, but since then the trajectories have diverged sharply: while the GDP has risen by 79 percent, the index has declined 45 percent. Among the sixteen social problem categories measured at their index lows were: children living in poverty, child abuse, the number of people without health insurance, and average weekly earnings. Thus, while the nation's economic growth has increased, its social health has worsened. Moreover, the gap between rich and poor has, in recent years, been at its widest recorded levels.[49]

The number of children growing up in poverty continues to increase. In 1994, 21.8 percent of persons under age eighteen lived in poverty.[50] That equals 15.3 million children, 2.7 million more than in the late 1980s. With the exception of 1988 and 1989, when the percentage dipped slightly, the percentage of children in poverty has been over 20 percent since 1981, with no sign that it will decrease and every sign that it will stay approximately the same or increase. For African-American children the poverty rate is 43.8 percent, for Latino children 41.5 percent, and for white children 16.9 percent.[51] A focus on the higher percentages of child poverty among minority groups can miss the fact that the majority of poor children (9.3 million) are white.

In many urban areas, poverty is especially severe. In 1989 the child poverty rate in Buffalo was 38.9 percent, in Atlanta 42.9 percent, in Fresno, California, 36 percent, in Laredo, Texas, 46.4 percent, and in Detroit 46.6 percent. In cities with populations of at least 100,000, 26.2 percent of children are poor. Twenty-eight percent of urban children are poor around the time they enter school.

And children living in urban areas are not the only geographic group in need, nor do they comprise the greatest number of poor children. In 1990, 22.9 percent of rural children—more likely to be white—were poor, a percentage higher than the overall rate of U.S. children in poverty.[52] Moreover, when poor children living in rural areas are combined with those who live in the suburbs, their "total number (8.4 million) is larger than that of poor children in metropolitan central cities (6.9 million)."[53]

One of poverty's many manifestations is impoverished school conditions. The more inadequate the resources in a school district, the higher the percentage of poor students. For example, in districts with 16 percent of students lacking reading resources, none of the students were poor; where 59 percent lacked resources, more than 30 percent or more were poor.[54]

Poverty is also linked to limited preschool learning opportunities. Children are more likely to attend preschool if their families are affluent rather than poor: in the most affluent counties, preschools are available to one in five three- to five-year-olds; in the poorest counties, the rate is one in seventy-seven. Inequality exists regionally and geographically: there are twice as many preschool programs for poor and working-class children in the Northeast than in the South; and more preschool programs for urban than for rural children. A major reason for these disparities is money: working-class and poor communities have few subsidized programs and little money to pay for nonsubsidized programs.[55]

The effects of class conditions on reading and academic achievement are vivid: students' average academic achievement scores increase in proportion to their positions in socioeconomic groups. For example, only 8.4 percent of students from socioeconomically "disadvantaged" families attained reading levels in the upper fourth of scores in contrast to 45.7 percent of students from socioeconomically "advantaged" families. Conversely, 44 percent of "disadvantaged" students compared to 11.1 percent of advantaged students were in the lower fourth of scores. Children from "average" socioeconomic backgrounds had percentages approximately in between those of the other two groups (for example, 23 percent scored in the upper fourth in reading).[56]

What can money buy that will promote cognitive, academic, and literacy growth? The Children's Defense Fund has many answers. Money buys good food and adequate nutrition that can prevent learning problems: iron deficiency can impair problem solving, attention, and concentration; moderate undernutrition can make children sluggish and distracted.[57] Money buys safe and decent housing: high housing costs can reduce a family's money for food. Frequent moves from house to house disrupt schooling. Poor housing conditions are linked to health problems that in turn interfere with consistent, attentive learning. Money "buys opportunities to learn," stimulating toys, books, and high-quality child care. Money reduces family stress, depression, and conflict. "Distressed parents tend to nurture their children less effectively" and contribute to family breakup. Parental stress in turn is linked to impaired language development, slower preschool development, and increased school problems. Money also buys transportation and communication. Decreased mobility may hamper a family's ability to reach "child care, medical care, and other services" for children, contributing to the health and developmental problems that impair learning.[58]

The emphasis in these figures has been on poor children and families, but working people above the poverty level are suffering as well. Less money is spent today on social services that benefit the nonpoor. This "class assault from above"[59] is increasingly hurting children at middle societal levels as well as those in poverty. This trend demonstrates that there is much, much more to ensuring literacy achievement than instructional method.

Doing Poor Children No Favor

Studies on literacy learning of children from different classes and linguistic cultures have concluded that there are differences in the types, meaning, and function of respective literacy activities but not that any of them is better or worse than any other. These studies say that the literacy activities of middle-class children differ from those of lower-class children only when literacy is equated, for example, with storybook reading or with numbers of books read and available. Lower-class families engage in their own considerable literacy activities.[60]

Reading educators Denny Taylor and Catherine Dorsey-Gaines describe the abominable life conditions that pose huge hurdles for poor families trying to engage their children in literacy activities, and note that there is a "decline of social, political, and economic support for poor families that constitutes the greatest long-term threat to the children's well-being." The predominant assumption throughout their analysis, however, is that children's literacy does develop in these conditions of poverty and that their literacy is one of difference rather than deficit. The poor children in their study were "active participants and interpreters in a social world in which texts are written and read." The homes of the children "were literate homes."[61]

This interpretation attempts to counter the view that poor children lack the capacity to learn or that poor parents care less than rich ones about their children's learning and education. Regardless of how grim the realities of life may be for children in poor families, these children nonetheless grow up "with literacy as an integral part of their personal, familial, and social histories."[62] Similarly, Marie Clay says that "lack of opportunities to learn about print does not imply deficits in the child or in his preschool culture."[63]

Well-meaning as this view is, it ignores all of the conditions of life that promote not merely "differences" but deficiencies in literacy. These deficiencies and the underachievement they cause are only consequences of poor children's social environment and do not lead to less mental capacity. These deficiencies do mean, however, that many children from poor families do not have the opportunity to learn as much about written language as they could in different social conditions. To claim otherwise, to speak only of relative differences, to suggest that poor children's health, nutrition, housing, and material well-being can suffer, that their families can suffer class, racial, and other assaults, and to conclude that their literacy achievement will be excluded from the effects of these assaults does these children no favor.

Acknowledging this socially created underachievement in children who have no inherent deficiencies simply recognizes the adverse preschool and school conditions that hinder literacy growth. What is the impetus of the long struggle for adequate preschool programs, for example, if not the recognition that all children, because of divergent conditions and experiences, may not be starting at the same level of written language ability when they enter school?

Similar well-meaning but misguided interpretations come from efforts to identify "the factors that relate to achievement in literacy among children in low-income families" in order to "seek better ways to help low-income children who achieve less than they should." These factors were looked for in families that overcame huge social class disadvantages and beat the odds: "low-income families that had produced successful school learners." By isolating "the factors that may actually be producing an effect" on literacy, all other low-income children may be helped to learn to read and write, the researchers proposed. Thus, the overall conditions of poverty were accepted—as though the material conditions of children who learn in higher social class homes could somehow be made inconsequential—and, ironically, ways for improving literacy within the givens of poverty were sought.[64]

Among the homes of poor black children Reginald Clark found high academic achievers whose parents strongly encouraged academic pursuits, allocated resources for learning, monitored learning activities, frequently talked to their children, set clear rules and norms for achievement, and interacted warmly with their children. Nonetheless, the ability of particular families to overcome great obstacles does not, for Clark, imply that programs aimed at boosting "family strength" or "parent education" are adequate solutions to literacy problems "when the family's basic socioeconomic needs are not met."[65]

Those who favor instructional solutions to literacy problems assume that with exceptional instruction, poor children can overcome all impoverished conditions. This is theoretically possible—there are a few exemplary programs for poor children that have achieved considerable success—but the overriding prospect is that the resources that were not initially available for promoting poor children's well-being in their early years will continue to be unavailable. It is naive to think that sufficient resources will ever be poured into the schools to compensate for those lacking outside of school. Again, the distinction must be made between asking "What is the best way to teach reading?" and "What needs to be done to ensure that children learn to read?"

Where Is the Money?

There is money for high-quality literacy education and the overall well-being of all Americans, but it simply has not been made available to all! Locating the money requires understanding the distribution of wealth, the policies that support the distribution of wealth, and the uses of money allocated for public purposes. Comparisons between the distribution of wealth in the United States and other industrial nations show that the United States has not only greater economic inequality but that inequality has been increasing since the 1970s. Among industrial nations, the United States has the highest level of income concentration and leads other nations in its number of millionaires and billionaires while at the same time the child poverty rate is four times the average of Western European countries.[66]

Many working people and their children have felt the effects of this upward redistribution of wealth and income. The median wage for working men has fallen 11 percent from the mid-1970s, and for the young it is even worse: wages are down 25 percent for men twenty-five to thirty-four years of age, and 32 percent of these men do not earn enough to keep a family of four above the poverty line. Within two-parent families, working women have made up for family income loss, and through the 1980s have even kept median household incomes slowly rising through their increased working hours. This direction has not been sustained in recent years: since 1989 median real wages for women working full-time have been falling, contributing to a decrease in overall family income. Middle-income working people—those earning between $20,000 and $50,000—have also felt the reverberation of lower real income. Middle-income people saw a 44 percent increase in their salaries in the 1980s, an impressive figure until compared with the 1980s inflation rate of 71 percent, resulting in an actual decline in median household income to below that of the 1970s.[67] In contrast, the 71 percent inflation rate could not have been more than a small annoyance for those earning between $200,000 and $1 million, whose income increased 697 percent; and probably went unnoticed by those earning more than $1 million, whose income increased 2,184 percent.[68]

Life in the United States has been especially good for the rich. In the 1980s the income of the richest 1 percent of families grew 62.9 percent, "representing 53 percent of the total income growth among all families," while the income of the bottom 60 percent of families actually experienced a decline.[69] The richest 1 percent of United States households also owns nearly 40 percent of the nation's wealth. These figures indicate that money for the literacy education and well-being of all children and their families exists in our society but has been traveling upward with the aid of new policies.

The extent to which money has been moving in one direction has led economist Lester Thurow to observe, "No country without a revolution or a military defeat and subsequent occupation has ever experienced such a sharp shift in the distribution of earnings as America has in the last generations."[70] In addition to working people earning less, money has also been redistributed to the wealthy through tax policies. For example, the tax breaks supplied during the Reagan-Bush administrations have garnered the top 1 percent of the income earners $860 billion.[71] In 1989, taxpayers earning $200,000 or more were charged at a 24.1 percent rate and paid $96 billion in federal taxes. Ten years earlier, however, people at this income level were charged an effective rate of 45.3 percent. Returning to that rate would now yield $82 billion more for federal spending each year.

Since tax laws are weighted ever more in favor of corporate America, over the past forty years the corporate sector has persistently decreased its contribution to the federal budget. In 1952, business paid 32 percent of the budget. That figure dropped to 23 percent in the 1960s and to 16 percent in the 1970s. From the 1980s until now it has been between 8 and 11 percent. Again, the U.S. version of capitalism falls short in an international comparison. Overall, the "U.S. tax system is among the least progressive in the industrial world, and the burden on business and the rich is among the lightest."[72]

Money for literacy education and children's well-being can also be found in "corporate welfare"—that is, those subsidies and tax breaks that aid major corporations. These include money to help promote U.S. products overseas, subsidies and tax breaks to corporate agribusiness, subsidies for corporate research, loans at below-market interest rates, and countless tax breaks and loopholes. Estimates of this corporate welfare range from $85 billion to over $150 billion a year.[73]

Another place to get money for children is the military budget, presently at about $255 billion, a figure that cloaks an array of other military costs that go indirectly to the Department of Defense. For example, military money that appears to be in civilian and quasi-military categories includes projects for NASA and the Department of Energy (for example, designing, testing, and producing new nuclear weapons), military retirement pay, veterans' benefits, and the military share of interest on the federal debt. When total military and military-related spending are added, the sum comes to nearly $500 billion per year![74] Administration and congressional plans call for more than $1.6 trillion in military spending between 1996 and 2002 (excluding the military-related categories just enumerated). Even if taken independently of the other hidden military costs, if the military spending were compared to $27 billion for education, $17 billion for housing, $24 billion for health, and so forth, the expenditures dwarf spending for programs dedicated to the education and well-being of children.

In 1996, when no more than $3.6 billion was spent on Head Start children, $3.3 billion was spent on antiballistic missile (ABM) defense research, a legacy of the "Star Wars" program launched by President Reagan in 1983. The money was spent even though the Joint Chiefs of Staff and the CIA both said they saw little if any need for the ABM system and also had doubts about its effectiveness. More than $70 billion has been spent on ABM research and weaponry over the first dozen years of the program, more than double the amount spent on Head Start during the same period of time.

A massive reduction of the military budget—certainly justified by the end of the Cold War—would yield extraordinary resources.[75] A cutback comparable to Japanese military spending, which is about 1 percent of its GNP, would bring the budget down to around $50 billion, freeing $200 billion or more for a real and essential peace dividend. Using the military budgets of other industrial nations as a model provides the elements for another cutback formula. For example, if the United States spent on its military a sum comparable to that of all of the European Community nations, the military budget could still be cut by $150 billion.

Why There Are Not More Resources

The deteriorating quality of life for such large numbers of people is sometimes interpreted in society as being caused by the very people who are suffering, through their failure to acquire the literacy, education, and skills necessary for work in the new global, high-tech economy. It is a pervasive explanation but a false one, and it helps cloak the real causes of economic inequities and the declining well-being of millions of Americans.

The 1993 survey *Adult Literacy in America*, published under the Clinton administration, advances the connection between education and the global economy by explaining that lower literacy skills, in the human capital model, mean "low earnings" and "lower quality of life." U.S. Secretary of Education Richard W. Riley commented, "This report underscores literacy's strong connection to economic status. It paints a picture of a society in which the vast majority of Americans do not have the skills they need to earn a living in our increasingly technological society and international marketplace."[76] The report, like its predecessors, placed a double burden on individuals. Not only were they co-responsible for whatever financial misery had befallen them; they also were co-responsible for the fate of corporate America, slugging it out in the international fray. Educators were told that "our current systems of education and training are inadequate to ensure individual opportunities, improve economic productivity, or strengthen our nation's competitiveness in the global marketplace."[77]

How much literacy and education does the economy "need"? Jared Bernstein, an economist with the Economic Policy Institute, observes that if the decline in wages and extensive job losses were a result of the need for highly educated workers in the new technological economy, one would expect increased job opportunities and higher salaries for highly educated, skilled white-collar workers. "Neither of those pieces of evidence is there," he said.[78] Nor can the decline in wages in the last decade be explained by the introduction of new technologies in the workplace requiring a more literate and highly skilled workforce:

> [M]any policy makers have cited a technology-driven increase in demand for "educated" or "skilled" workers as the significant force behind wage inequality. Yet there is evidence that the overall impact of technology on the wage and employment structure was no greater in the 1980s than in the 1970s. Technology has been and continues to be an important force; but there was no "technology shock" in the 1980s, and no ensuing demand for "skill" that could not be satisfied by the continuing expansion of the educational attainment of the workforce.[79]

Lower wages have less to do with education and skills and more to do with the decision of employers to pay people less and accrue more profit. The jobs that are "disappearing are those of higher-paid, white-collar workers, many at large corporations, women as well as men, many at the peak of their careers." Reversing previous trends, "workers with at least some college education make up the majority of people whose jobs were eliminated, outnumbering those with no more than high school education."[80]

The limits of seeing education as a solution to deteriorating well-being is evident in an Economic Policy Institute report showing that the U.S. economy does not have a problem in finding workers with sufficient skills for new jobs. The real problem is a halt in the growth in highly skilled jobs both now and for the foreseeable future.[81] An economist at the Bureau of Labor Statistics reached the related conclusion that the "value of a college degree is likely to decline, leading to a growing number of people working in jobs for which they are overqualified."[82] The declining value of a college degree is evident in the substantial increase in college graduates, since the 1980s, who work as salesclerks, secretaries, stenographers, typists, bartenders, waiters, and at similar jobs never before requiring a college degree. Increasingly, too, college graduates find themselves taking "contingent jobs"—part-time and temporary jobs or short-term contract work.[83]

Among the new jobs that will be created up to the year 2000, 30 percent will require at most a college degree; the rest will need almost no increase in skills already available in the workforce. As for workers needing more literacy, education, and skills, the millions of new jobs that have been created have mostly been low-tech, not high-tech, and about half of them have paid wages below the poverty level for a family of four. The Bureau of Labor Statistics forecasts that of the thirty occupations with the greatest projected growth between 1994 and 2005, the majority—cashiers, janitors and cleaners, retail salespersons, waiters and waitresses, home health aides, nursing aides, orderlies, truck drivers, etc.—do not require high levels of education. A small portion—about 13 percent—of the projected growth does entail jobs demanding new, highly technical skills, such as systems analysts and computer engineers. However, jobs such as secondary school teachers, lawyers, social workers, and registered nurses, are those for which people are already amply trained and more could be readily trained if access to higher education were possible for more people.[84]

Although much finger pointing is at the "global economy," this economy is not entirely new, as the long history of U.S. economic interests from Central America to the Philippines demonstrates.[85] One difference for U.S. workers is the relocation to other countries of factories and jobs formerly secure within United States borders. Globalization has produced a substantial decline in the ties "U.S." companies might have to the United States economy: "Between 1980 and 1990, American companies increased their overseas spending on new factories, equipment, and research and development at a higher rate than their investments in the United States."[86] The foreign operations of American corporations "account for more than $1 trillion in sales annually—about four times America's total exports. As a business writer for *The New York Times* noted: "Many American companies are shedding the banner of a national identity and proclaiming themselves to be global enterprises whose fortunes are no longer so dependent on the economy of the United States."[87] They are likely to go anywhere around the globe to reap the best profit—which usually includes, at the top of the list, hiring workers in other countries at the lowest wages.[88]

> With the more highly integrated world economy, where capital is highly mobile and labor is relatively immobile, the negative impacts in the United States were especially severe for low wage workers and workers in many manufacturing industries where production had been highly routinized and deskilled. International integration placed these workers in direct competition with poorly paid workers elsewhere in the world.[89]

This does not mean these corporations cannot pay good wages in the United States and abroad; rather, they often can pay low-skilled workers overseas abominable wages and reap more profits.

In *Who Needs the Negro?* sociologist Sidney Willhelm quotes Dr. Theodore Levit, marketing adviser to Standard Oil, from a speech before the Harvard Graduate School of Business: "Profit, not public welfare, is the goal of business," said Levit, who stressed that "the point is this: the businessman exists for only one purpose, to create and deliver value satisfactions at a profit to himself. The cultural, spiritual, social, and moral consequences are none of his personal concern."[90] And in more recent years, a representative of a major corporation said, "The United States does not have an automatic call on our resources. There is no mind-set that puts this country first."[91]

Why are there not more resources for the literacy education of all children? From the viewpoint of those who have power and control policy, there is no "advantage" to that. Corporate America does not require a fully literate and educated workforce now or in the future, any more than it did in the past.

CONCLUSION:

CHANGING THE LITERACY DEBATE

When surveyed by the International Reading Association about the "compelling questions" that preoccupied them, today's leading reading experts included the following:

- how teachers create and maintain classrooms
- how to assess reading outcomes
- how reading errors ("miscues" in reading jargon) provide a "window on the reading process"
- how to understand historical assumptions about reading instruction and how children learn
- how to merge skills with whole language
- how to ensure that teachers know how to teach readers through the literature immersion approach used in whole language
- how to bring about change in reading instruction in schools[1]

These worthwhile questions are overwhelmingly about instruction and the reading process, tend to focus on the psychology of literacy, are confined to the classroom, and disregard the many influences—especially those *outside* the classroom—that contribute to the creation of teaching and learning.

As I have been writing this book, the terms of the dominant debate have intensified through efforts to pass legislation at the state and federal levels that would mandate the direct instruction of skills in beginning literacy education. Aiding this intensification are ever growing media criticisms of whole language and calls for more phonics teaching. In October 1997, major U.S. magazines published articles on literacy, almost all using the popular "war" metaphor. A *Time* article began: "A war is on between supporters of phonics and those who believe in the whole-language method of learning to read; caught in the middle—the nation's schoolchildren." Phonics "must be systematic and explicit," the article advised, "if the full benefit is to be derived from it. To deprive children of that benefit is destructive."[2] The *U.S. News & World Report* article was headlined "The reading wars continue," and stressed the importance of first teaching "language sounds and the relationship of sounds to letters" before exposing children to good literature "to promote comprehension."[3] An article in *The Atlantic Monthly* on "the reading wars" observed: "No independent scientific researchers trumpet whole language's virtues" (implying that there existed independent scientific researchers who were trumpeting an attack on whole language).[4] *Newsweek* omitted the martial metaphor, but tendered an appraisal consistent with that in the other articles. "The reading instruction methods" beneficial to all children, the article explained, are known as "linguistics (sound to letters) and phonics (letters to sound)," methods that make "kids sound out words." Doing so makes the "association between symbol and sound virtually automatic," thereby enabling children to concentrate on the meaning of words.[5]

A few weeks after these articles appeared, the House of Representatives, with the support of President Clinton, passed a bill called the Reading Excellence Act (H.R. 2514).[6] Formulated in the Committee on Education and the Work Force, the bill provided grants to states for in-service training of teachers, after-school tutoring in schools with high numbers of poor children, and family literacy programs. Its potential impact on the future of literacy education lay in its explicit definitions of reading, reading instruction, and "reliable" research—all of which emphasized skills. At the forefront of the definitions was reading, said to be "the ability to use phonics skills, that is, knowledge of letters and sounds, to decode printed words quickly and effortlessly, both silently and aloud." Instructional practices were defined as those based on "replicable, reliable" research, a term that at first glance might seem reasonable. Upon examining who was asked to testify during the committee hearings and which research the committee thought "replicable and reliable," however, one can see that it refers only to research believed to demonstrate the need for early, direct instruction of skills.

Bob Sweet, who formally left his post as executive director of the politically conservative National Right to Read Foundation, which among other agendas promotes a narrow phonics approach, joined the committee's staff to help draft the legislation. In the *Right to Read Report*, describing the phonics advances and the possible significance of the Reading Excellence Act, he wrote with millennial exuberance:

> [T]he new legislation just passed in California that codifies systematic phonics training for teachers; the definitive research [emphasizing early skills instruction] coming out of the National Institute of Child Health and Human Development; the avalanche of state legislation requiring systematic phonics; the publishing companies gearing up to produce new phonics programs for school children; and the constant barrage of press accounts trumpeting the return of phonics as the first step in teaching children to read. Such is the situation less than three years before a new millennium dawns.
>
> Passage of the Reading Excellence Act can become a major catalyst in the national effort to restore sound reading teaching practices to our schools.[7]

As Sweet's appraisal suggests, the Reading Excellence Act, following Senate approval, might be less influential in the programs it funds than in its function as "catalyst." The act could become both a standard for instruction deemed valid by the federal government and, therefore, deserving of funds, and a model of educational definitions that could go into other federal legislation. If this particular act were not to pass through Congress with all its definitions intact, and if its ramifications did not extend to other legislation, it would nonetheless remain a measure of the power, single-mindedness, and simple-mindedness of the skills-first side to dictate the terms and outcome of the debate.

We must respond at several levels. The arguments and assumptions on behalf of the skills-first side must be met with reviews and critiques of its research. The evidence that already counters the skills-first approach must continue to grow.[8] At the same time, as I have argued throughout this book, the debate must change because it not only fails to provide an adequate understanding of literacy teaching and learning, and the reading process: it misconstrues these concerns.

In *The Learning Mystique* I discussed a theory of "interactivity" for understanding learning and reading problems. I introduced the term because I felt that neither interaction nor activity—terms common in educational and psychological theories—sufficiently accounted for the many influences that shape learning.[9]

The term "interaction" is commonly used to refer to relationships between or among individuals or between individuals and situations— say, between a parent and a child or between a student and classroom instruction. Another conception of interaction sees the reading process as an interaction between the reader and the information in the material being read. The term is also used to describe relationships inside an individual, as between emotions and cognition. Seldom included in examinations of "interaction," however, are interactions created by influences not readily evident within the interactions themselves.

Activity theory, as used by Soviet psychologist Lev Vygotsky and those who have used and attempted to build upon his work, stresses understanding thinking within various contexts and relationships. Generally, it appears to understand the "mind in society," but it seldom goes beyond social organization to include the societal sphere.[10] In activity theory, as well as in psychology in general, the words "societal" and "social" are often blurred, particularly when the latter is used for the former, as when the term "social relationships" refers to relationships at the societal level. It is essential to distinguish between the two: to use "societal" in referring to the broader organization of society— its classes, economic systems, and political organization—and to use "social" in referring to smaller units of organization, such as family and classroom groupings.

As has been evident throughout this book, and especially as my work with "Earl" illustrates, I advocate what I practice, a meticulous understanding of the individual learner. In addition, my conception of "interactivity" emphasizes the importance of societal organization and power for classroom teaching and learning, even when the influences of that organization and power are not readily apparent. This does not mean that societal influences determine smaller units of teaching and learning literacy. Rather, they contribute mightily to, and therefore are inseparable from, the interactivity that comprises literacy teaching and learning.

In applying this theory to the literacy debate, three interwoven categories can be useful. The first is the "act of literacy," including but extending beyond the prevailing psychological, interpersonal, and narrowly contextual meanings of instruction and the reading process. Other influences in this category are:

- children's literacy experiences outside of school
- children's overall well-being (their health, nutrition, housing, etc.)
- economic and policy needs of those in power that affect teaching and learning
- standards of literacy success and the extent to which they include developmental goals
- emotions that are fostered in literacy education
- assumptions about how children should think, feel, and act, and what kind of adults they should grow up to be

I do not mean to imply that the entire context must be accounted for every time the "act of literacy" is discussed and studied. Any individual part can be considered separately, but any one part by itself will not give us a full understanding of reading, learning, or teaching.

What constitutes teaching and learning is also determined by the second category, the "availability of literacy." Included in this second category of "interactivity" are the availability of the following influences for promoting or impairing literacy achievement:

- the ideas for children to consider, accept, or reject
- the activities or extensions of literacy
- physical classroom and school conditions
- children's fundamental well-being—such as housing, food, medical and child care
- financial resources for ensuring the best educational conditions for literacy achievement
- particular assumptions about children and their futures

This category aims to raise questions about whether the elements that should contribute to the "act of literacy" are in fact available and to encourage educators in particular to ask why they might or might not be.

The third category is the "uses of literacy" by individuals, organizations, institutions, social groups, and societal groups. It includes the ways in which

- uses of literacy education affect motivation, attention, and comprehension
- uses of literacy education relate to students' lives
- uses of literacy education constrain or foster thinking and emotions
- uses of literacy in the political economy influence teaching and learning in the classroom
- uses of literacy embody assumptions about children and their futures

Each of the categories has a certain meaning and organization of its own, but all contribute to the creation of each other, and none has an independent meaning and organization without the others. These categories emphasize the need to look beyond the classroom to understand both what is happening and what is possible in the classroom.

In stark contrast, those advocating a regimented skills approach behave as though the issues in these categories were outside their domain, as if they were focused strictly on literacy achievement to ensure that children learn to read and write. Their instructional method goes beyond these professed goals, however, and the kind of person that is likely to be nurtured in this education is revealed in those who have actively or tacitly supported legislation mandating skills instruction. They approve legislation that excludes the legitimacy of all views other than the one mandated. Under the banner of "scientifically correct," they dismiss as "unreliable" and "unreplicable" the research, theory, and instructional approaches of countless literacy scholars. They disregard other views, even when they have been published in established, "peer-reviewed" professional journals. They promote an authoritarian, conformist, top-down version of truth to which all literacy educators are required to adhere. They discourage critical thinking that originates beyond the postulates they regard as incontestable.

Those of us who advocate a different literacy education must continue to argue on behalf of instruction that promotes greater children's participation, puts a greater emphasis from the beginning on the purposes of written language, has greater concern in promoting children's motivation, engages children in the totality of written language, and encourages teacher initiatives and empowerment in formulating children's education. In this conclusion I have concentrated more on the skills-emphasis side of the debate because of its increasingly antidemocratic, authoritarian legislative tactics. At the same time, whole-language educators, who aspire to provide this kind of instruction, need to reflect on and change their own limitations.

In "keeping the faith" while working toward changing the debate and literacy education, the two favorite sayings in the dedication of this book—one from my mother, the other from my wife's mother—can be helpful. "Que sera, sera"—"what will be, will be"—is an old European saying made famous in a song sung by Doris Day, and constituted a philosophy for my mother, an avid listener of popular songs. She frequently quoted it in response to the hardships and disappointments of her life, usually to convey the idea that although we may have to accept the hardships and disappointments, we should never let them destroy us.

For literacy teaching and learning, this means that teachers will have to teach many children in unsatisfactory, often deplorable conditions and do their utmost to counter the effects of these conditions, but "Que sera, sera," must not mean demoralization and surrender.

The saying my mother-in-law frequently quoted, "Quando ti vuoi mozzicare il gomito, sarà troppo tardi," like other folk sayings, can convey many meanings. It can carry a bite that can shrivel a person or a dose of enlightenment to use over a lifetime, and sometimes both. The literal meaning of the saying is: "When you'll want to bite your elbow, it will be too late." It emphatically advises that we find ways to confront and transcend the setbacks, otherwise it might be too late. To do nothing, to ignore it, can only mean enduring more pain, more unhappiness, more disappointment, more limits.

NOTES

INTRODUCTION

1. Kathleen K. Manzo, "Study Stresses Role of Early Phonics Instruction," *Education Week*, March 12, 1997.
2. "Phonics Reading Method Best, Study Finds; Whole-Language Approach Significantly Less Effective, Houston Research Shows," Toronto *Globe & Mail*, February 20, 1997.
3. "Sound It Out: Phonics Works Better," *Arizona Republic*, February 19, 1997.
4. Gerald S. Coles, "Phonics Findings Discounted as Part of Flawed Research," *Education Week*, April 2, 1997.
5. Christina Duff, "ABCeething: How Whole Language Became a Hot Potato in and out of Academia; Reading Method Ditched Phonics, Won Adherents But Test Scores Tanked," *Wall Street Journal*, October 30, 1996.
6. John Silber, "Emergency Room Philosophy," *Right to Read Report*, March 1994, pp. 2–3. (Quotation on p. 2.)

1. THE DEBATE OVER READING

1. Marilyn Jager Adams, *Beginning to Read: Thinking and Learning about Print* (Cambridge, Mass.: MIT Press, 1990). (Quotation on p. 13.)
2. Robert Rothman, "From a 'Great Debate' to a Full-Scale War: Dispute over Teaching Reading Heats Up," *Education Week*, March 21, 1990, pp. 1–11.

3. Barbara Kantrowitz, "The Reading Wars," *Newsweek* (Special Edition: "How to Teach Our Kids"), September 1990, pp. 8–14.

4. Patrick Groff, "The Bicoastal Uprising Against Whole Language," *Right to Read Report*, January–February 1996, pp. 1–2.

5. Jeanne Chall, *Learning to Read: The Great Debate* (New York: McGraw-Hill, 1967).

6. Art Levine, "The Great Debate Revisited," *Atlantic Monthly*, December 1994, pp. 38–44.

7. Debra Viadero, "Opposed to Whole Language, Houston Schools Revert to Phonics," *Education Week*, November 20, 1991. Similar scenes were enacted throughout the country. In Aberdeen, Mississippi, for example, a town 75 percent black and poor, one third-grade teacher in 1990 praised a phonics program for accomplishing what a previous "look-say" program could not. Under the "look-say" approach, children's average reading test scores had been below the 30th percentile.

    As I have suggested, the "look-say" approach is not whole language, and whole-language advocates have long criticized the use of basal reading series. For this teacher, however, the presumed common emphasis on meaning was all that was needed to equate the two and thereby avoid addressing why whole language could not also have been chosen as an alternative. The new "phonics first" program, "Sing, Spell, Read, and Write," generated a "phonics phoenix": third-grade children who began the school year in the 27th percentile on the Stanford Achievement Test ended the year in the 57th! This transformation did not go unrecognized in a state noted as an abominable literacy and educational showplace. Barbara A. Rowe, "Phonics Phoenix: A Lesson in Literacy in Small-Town Mississippi," *Policy Review*, Winter 1990, pp. 74–77.

    The issue of whole language vs. phonics and skills also split parents and teachers in the town of Cortlandt Manor, New York. Parents supporting the whole-language curriculum talked of the excitement they felt seeing their young children read books instead of doing ditto sheets. But other parents complained that their children were not mastering basic skills and that without tests and work sheets the parents could not gauge their children's progress. In the end, the principal was fired. "Fighting over Reading: Principal and Methods Are Under Fire," *New York Times*, November 17, 1993.

8. "The Uprising Continues!," *Right to Read Report*, March–April 1996.

9. Jim Jacobson, "Ohio Mandates Intensive, Systematic Phonics Instruction," *Right to Read Report*, November–December 1993.

10. Karen Diegmueller, "A War of Words: Whole Language Under Siege," *Education Week*, March 20, 1996.

11. "California Leads Revival of Teaching by Phonics," *New York Times*, May 22, 1996.

12. Ken Goodman, "Forced Choices in a Non-crisis," *Education Week*, November 15, 1995.

13. George W. Bush, "Governor George W. Bush Speaks Out!" *Right to Read Report*, March–April 1996. (Quotations on pp. 1 and 2.)

14. Diegmueller, "A War of Words." (Quotation on p. 14.)

15. U.S. Senate Republican Policy Committee, *Illiteracy: An Incurable Disease or Education Malpractice?* (Washington, D.C.: U.S. Senate Republican Policy Committee, 1989).

16. Rothman, "From a 'Great Debate.'" (Quotation on p. 11.)

17. "An Injustice to Juveniles," *Boston Sunday Globe*, February 25, 1990.

18. Robert Sweet, "Outlaw Phonics?" *Right to Read Report*, April–May 1994. (Quotation on p. 7.)

19. Sweet, "Outlaw Phonics?" (Quotation on p. 7.)

20. "Major Victory for Phonics!" *Right to Read Report*, November–December 1994. (Quotation on p. 4.)

21. John Silber, "Emergency Room Philosophy," *Right to Read Report*, March 1994. (Quotations on pp. 2 and 3.)

22. Elizabeth McPike, "Learning to Read: Schooling's First Mission," *American Educator*, 19, Summer 1995. (Quotation on p. 3.)

23. Louisa Cook Moats, "The Missing Foundation in Teacher Education," *American Educator*, 19, Summer 1995, 9–51.

24. Marilyn J. Adams and Maggie Bruck, citing what they believed was compelling research for "Resolving the 'Great Debate,'" dismissed the whole-language theory of how normal reading develops. Underscoring the necessity of learning phonemes in early reading, the authors emphasized that "scientific research converges on the point that the association of spellings with sounds is a fundamental step in the early stages of literacy instruction." Marilyn J. Adams and Maggie Bruck, "Resolving the 'Great Debate,'" *American Educator*, 19, Summer 1995, 7–20.

   Similarly, Isabel L. Beck and Connie Juel insisted on the importance of the "early attainment of decoding skill" for ensuring that "children gain reading independence early." Isabel L. Beck and Connie Juel, "The Role of Decoding in Learning to Read," *American Educator*, 19, Summer 1995, 8–42.

25. Marie Carbo, "Debunking the Great Phonics Myth," *Phi Delta Kappan*, 70, November 1988, 226–240.

26. Richard L. Turner, "The 'Great' Debate—Can Both Carbo and Chall Be Right?" *Phi Delta Kappan*, 71, December 1989, 276–283; Denny Taylor, "Toward a Unified Theory of Literacy Learning and Instructional Practices," *Phi Delta Kappan*, 71, November 1989, 184–193.

27. Frank Smith, "Learning to Read: The Never-Ending Debate," *Phi Delta Kappan*, 73, February 1992, 432–441.

   Because "learning is continuous, spontaneous, and effortless, requiring no particular attention, conscious motivation, or specific reinforcement," Smith contends, teachers needed to facilitate, not "teach," learning to read. His position on facilitating, not teaching, literacy is not shared by all whole-language proponents, but does seem to be an interpretation of whole language that has influenced many whole-language teachers, to one degree or another, even though most do actively "teach."

28. Kenneth J. Smith, Valerie F. Reyna, and Charles J. Brainerd, "The Debate Continues," *Phi Delta Kappan*, 74, January 1993, 407–410.

29. Frank Smith, "The Never-Ending Confrontation," *Phi Delta Kappan*, 74, January 1993, 411–412.

30. Adams, *Beginning to Read*. (See Chapter 15 especially.)

31. U.S. Department of Education, *Reading Report Card, 1971–1988* (Princeton, N.J.: National Assessment of Educational Progress, 1989); U.S. Department of Education, *NAEP 1994 Reading Report Card for the Nation and the States* (Washington, D.C.: Office of Educational Research and Improvement, 1996).

32. U.S. Department of Education, *The Writing Report Card: Writing Achievement in American Schools* (Princeton, N.J.: National Assessment of Educational Progress, 1986).

33. U.S. Department of Education, *NAEP 1994 Reading Report Card*.

34. *Literacy: Profiles of America's Young Adults* (Princeton, N.J.: National Assessment of Educational Progress, 1986).

35. National Center for Education Statistics, *Adult Literacy in America: A First Look at the Results of the National Adult Literacy Survey* (Washington, D.C.: U.S. Government Printing Office, 1993).

36. David LeBerge and S. Jay Samuels, "Toward a Theory of Automatic Information Processing in Reading," *Cognitive Psychology*, 6, 1974, 193–323.

37. S. Jay Samuels and Michael L. Kamil, "Models of the Reading Process," in P. David Pearson (ed.), *Handbook of Reading Research* (White Plains, N.Y.: Longman, 1984).

38. Yetta M. Goodman and Kenneth S. Goodman, "To Err Is Human: Learning about Language Processes by Analyzing Miscues," in Robert B. Ruddell, Martha R. Ruddell, and Harry Singer (eds.), *Theoretical Models and Processes of Reading* (4th ed.; Newark, Del.: International Reading Association, 1994), pp. 104–123. (Quotation on p. 115.)

39. Ken Goodman, *On Reading* (Portsmouth, N.H.: Heinemann, 1996).

40. Adams, *Beginning to Read*. (Quotation on p. 42.) Also "My Purpose in Writing This Book," *Reading Teacher*, 44, February 1991, 386–395.

41. Biographical note accompanying Adams and Bruck, "Resolving the 'Great Debate.'" (Quotation on p. 7.)

42. Harry Singer and Robert B. Ruddell (eds.), *Theoretical Models and Processes of Reading* (3rd ed.; Newark, Del.: International Reading Association, 1985).

43. Some sense of the almost exclusive emphasis in this volume on cognition can be gleaned from models of the reading process that describe the route to reading as one that "begins with an eye fixation," interactive semantic, syntactic, lexical, and letter information, and continues on to comprehension. See Philip B. Gough, "One Second of Reading," in Singer and Ruddell (eds.), *Theoretical Models and Processes of Reading*, pp. 661–686.

44. Robert B. Ruddell and Robert Speaker, "The Interactive Reading Process: A Model," in Singer and Ruddell (eds.), *Theoretical Models and Processes of Reading*, pp. 751–793.

45. The 1994 edition gives more attention to learning interactions in the classroom, community characteristics and influences, and various cultural dimensions. But the analyses continue to concentrate overwhelmingly on cognition and the reading process.

   A comparable focus is found in *Handbook of Reading Research*, a primary resource in literacy studies. All discussions in the first volume (1984) on the "state of the art" revolved around the "reading process" and its centrality in designing instruction. This range broadened in the second volume (1991), with an essay on politics, another on social class, and a few others that diverged from the dominant debate. Overall, however, the divergences, even when sharp, adjoined but did not reframe the primary stress in the first volume. (See P. David Pearson (ed.), *Handbook of Reading Research*, Vol. 1 (White Plains, N.Y.: Longman, 1984); P. David Pearson, Rebecca Barr, Michael L. Kamil, and Peter Mosenthal (eds.), *Handbook of Reading Research*, Vol. 2 (White Plains, N.Y.: Longman, 1991).

   A similar emphasis is common in professional journals. For instance, in a special issue on teaching poor readers in *The Reading Teacher* (1988), the editor emphasized that successful classroom teaching was grounded in the "reading process." This grounding greatly influenced her work, said the editor, because she recognized that "the way I defined reading determined the way I taught reading." Irene W. Gaskins, "A Special Issue on Poor Readers in the Classroom," *The Reading Teacher*, 1988, 41, 748–749.

46. Commission on Reading, National Academy of Education, *Becoming a Nation of Readers* (Washington, D.C.: National Institute of Education, 1985).

47. Commission on Reading, *Becoming a Nation of Readers*. (Quotations on pp. 57, 85–87.)

48. William J. Bennett, *First Lessons: A Report on Elementary Education in America* (Washington, D.C.: U.S. Department of Education, 1986). (Quotations on pp. 21–22.)

49. Jane L. Davidson (ed.), *Counterpoint and Beyond: A Response to Becoming a Nation of Readers* (Urbana, Ill.: National Council of Teachers of English, 1988).

50. Connie A. Bridge, "Focusing on Meaning in Beginning Reading Instruction," in Davidson (ed.), *Counterpoint and Beyond*, pp. 51–62.

51. David Bloome, Cheryl Cassidy, Marsha Chapman, and David Schaafsma, "Reading Instruction and Underlying Metaphors in *Becoming a Nation of Readers*," in Davidson (ed.), *Counterpoint and Beyond*, pp. 5–16.

52. Rudine Sims Bishop, "The Treatment of Literature and Minorities in *Becoming a Nation of Readers*," in Davidson (ed.), *Counterpoint and Beyond*, pp. 63–68.

53. Denise Schmandt-Besserat, "The Earliest Precursor of Writing," *Scientific American*, 238, June 1978, 50–59.

54. Sylvia Scribner and Michael Cole, *The Psychology of Literacy* (Cambridge, Mass.: Harvard University Press, 1981).

55. Scribner and Cole, *The Psychology of Literacy*. (Quotation on pp. 131–132.)

56. Scribner and Cole, *The Psychology of Literacy*. (Quotation on pp. 131–132.)

57. J. Gus Liebenow, *Liberia: The Quest for Democracy* (Bloomington: Indiana University Press, 1987). (Quotation on p. 2.)

58. Liebenow, *Liberia*. (Quotations on pp. 4, 48, 170.)

59. Liebenow, *Liberia*. (Quotation on p. 69.)

2. THE "NATURAL" ROAD TO READING

1. William Blake, "The Schoolboy," *The Poetical Works of William Blake* (London: Oxford University Press, 1956). (Quotation on p. 100.)

2. Friedrich Gedike, *Kinderbuch* (Berlin, 1791), quoted in Mitford M. Matthews, *Teaching to Read, Historically Considered* (Chicago: University of Chicago Press, 1966). (Quotation on p. 39.)

3. Matthews, *Teaching to Read*. (Quotation on p. 43.)

4. Matthews, *Teaching to Read*. (Quotation on p. 68.)

5. Matthews, *Teaching to Read*. (Quotation on p. 69.)

6. Matthews, *Teaching to Read*. (Quotation on p. 20.)

7. Cyrus Pierce, 1840s, quoted by Matthews, *Teaching to Read*. (Quotation on p. 11.)

8. Josiah Bumstead, author of *My First School Book* (1840), quoted in Nila B. Smith, *American Reading Instruction* (Newark, Del.: International Reading Association, 1965). (Quotation on p. 88.)

9. Barbara Finkelstein, *Governing the Young: Teacher Behavior in Popular Primary Schools in 19th Century United States* (New York: Falmer Press, 1989). (Quotation on p. 16.)

10. Larry Cuban, *How Teachers Taught: Constancy and Change in American Classrooms, 1890–1980* (White Plains, N.Y.: Longman, 1984).

11. Jack K. Campbell, *Colonel Francis W. Parker: The Children's Crusader* (New York: Teachers College Press, 1965). (Quotation on p. 79.)

12. Merle Curti, *The Social Ideas of American Educators*. (New York: Charles Scribner's Sons, 1935). (Quotation on p. 381.)

13. Charles F. Adams, Jr., *The New Departure in the Common Schools of Quincy and Other Papers on Educational Topics* (Boston: Estes & Lauriat, 1879, pp. 31–51).

14. Francis Parker, "The Quincy Method," *American Journal of Sociology*, 6, July 1900, quoted in Campbell, *Colonel Francis W. Parker*. (Quotation on p. 88.)

15. "The children who had been in school roughly four years, that is, those who had been in schools under Parker's supervision for three-fourths of their school life, outdistanced children in rival communities by considerably more than did the children who had been in the school for eight years, ones who had been affected by reform for less than half of their educational careers." Michael Katz, "The 'New Departure' in Quincy, 1873–1881: The Nature of

Nineteenth Century Educational Reform," *New England Quarterly*, 40, March 1967, 3–30. (Quotation on p. 24.)

16. Charles Francis Adams, Jr., the committee member who was Parker's strongest supporter, wrote in his diary three years after Parker had come to Quincy that an examination of children in one school found that not one in six could read a common book. Parker himself, several years after leaving Quincy, said that the changes in the primary grades were "fairly a success" and that of the grammar grades "by no means a failure." Francis W. Parker, "A Sketch of the Work in the Quincy Schools from 1875 to 1880," *School Journal*, 30, August 1, 1885, quoted in Campbell, *Colonel Francis W. Parker*. (Quotations on pp. 91, 92.)

17. Edmund B. Huey, *Psychology and Pedagogy of Reading* (Cambridge, Mass.: MIT Press, 1968 [1908]).

18. Huey, *Psychology and Pedagogy*. (Quotations on pp. 272, 274, 281.)

19. William S. Gray, *On Their Own in Reading* (New York: Scott, Foresman, 1948). (See especially Chapter 1.)

20. Herbert M. Kliebard, *The Struggle for the American Curriculum, 1893–1958* (New York: Routledge, 1987).

Spearheaded by William Heard Kilpatrick, the method was to have meaning to children in the present, not to be information and skills stored for later life. Kilpatrick saw subject matter and knowledge as functioning to solve problems in, and to advance the work in, a project. Examples of a project are a study of city life or a study of feudal life. Children constructed models appropriate to the project (e.g., buildings) and did "subject" work appropriate to the project (e.g., reading about the subjects in order to advance the project). Reading would be spurred by the need to finish the project.

21. Advocates of the activity method formed the Progressive Education Association, an organization made up mostly of educators associated with private, experimental schools that emphasized natural development of children as fundamental to curriculum and used the activity method in varying degrees up through the 1940s and 1950s. Patrick Shannon, *The Struggle to Continue: Progressive Reading Instruction in the United States* (Portsmouth, N.H.: Heinemann, 1990). (See pp. 116–123.)

22. John Holt, *How Children Learn* (New York: Pitman, 1967). (Quotation on p. 107.)

23. Charles H. Rathbone, "The Implicit Rationale of the Open Education Classroom," in Charles H. Rathbone (ed.), *Open Education: The Informal Classroom* (New York: Citation Press, 1971). (Quotation on p. 107.)

24. Roland Barth, *Open Education and the American School* (New York: Agathon, 1972). (Quotation on p. 37.)

"The curriculum is open to choices by adults and children as a function of the interests of children. The curriculum is the dependent variable, dependent on the child, rather than the independent variable upon which the child must depend. . . . [T]he role of the teacher in an open school is to facilitate learning—to provide conditions which will encourage children to learn for

themselves and to fulfill themselves, personally, socially, and intellectually."
(Quotations on pp. 55–56, 106.)

25. Cuban, *How Teachers Taught*, pp. 166–171.
26. Cuban, *How Teachers Taught*. (Quotations on pp. 193, 195.)
27. James Rothenberg, "The Open Classroom Reconsidered," *Elementary School Journal*, 90, 1989, 69–86. (Quotation on p. 76.)
28. Rothenberg, "The Open Classroom Reconsidered." (Quotation on p. 78.)
29. Smith, *American Reading Instruction*. (See Chapter 6.)
30. Jeanne S. Chall, *Stages of Reading Development* (New York: McGraw-Hill, 1983). (Quotations on pp. 1, 11.)
31. Chall, *Stages*. (Quotation on p. 20.)
32. Chall, *Stages*. (Quotations on p. 120.)
33. Chall, *Stages*. (Quotations on p. 13, 20, 22.)
34. Chall, *Stages*. (Quotation on p. 10.)
35. Chall, *Stages*. (Quotation on p. 39.)
36. Chall, *Stages*. (Quotation on p. 65.)
37. Emilia Ferreiro, "Literacy Development: Psychogenesis," in Yetta M. Goodman (ed.), *How Children Construct Literacy: Piagetian Perspectives* (Newark, Del.: International Reading Association, 1990). (Quotation on p. 24.)
38. Nigel Hall, *The Emergence of Literacy* (Portsmouth, N.H.: Heinemann,1987). (Quotations on p. 9.)
39. Hall, *The Emergence of Literacy*. (Quotation on p. 9.)
   Hall defines natural as a propensity children have for learning language in social situations in which language is used to communicate meaning and to generate and accompany actions. Within these settings children do not have to be taught to be literate—that is, taught by formal instruction. They will figure out reading and writing for themselves.
40. Claire F. Staab, "Teacher Mediation in One Whole Literacy Classroom," *The Reading Teacher*, 43, April 1990, 548–552.
41. Staab, "Teacher Mediation." (Quotation on p. 550.)
42. Staab, "Teacher Mediation." (Quotation on p. 549.)
43. Linda Christensen, "Writing the Word and the World," *Rethinking Schools*, 3, 1988, pp. 1–10. (Quotation on p. 10.)
44. Denny Taylor, "Toward a Unified Theory of Literacy Learning and Instructional Practices," *Phi Delta Kappan*, 71, November 1989, 184–193. (Quotation on p. 187.)
45. Judith M. Newman, "Insights from Recent Reading and Writing Research and Their Implications for Developing a Whole Language Curriculum," in Judith M. Newman (ed.), *Whole Language: Theory in Use* (Portsmouth, N.H.: Heinemann, 1985).
46. Dorothy J. Watson, "Whole Language: Why Bother?" *The Reading Teacher*, 47, May 1994, 600–607.
47. Carol Edelsky, *With Literacy and Justice for All: Rethinking the Social in Language and Education* (New York: Falmer Press, 1991). (Quotation on p. 164.)

48. Harvey Daniels, "Whole Language: What's the Fuss?" *Rethinking Schools*, 8, Winter 1993, 4–7. (Quotation on p. 4.)

49. Rexford G. Brown, *Schools of Thought: How the Politics of Literacy Shape Thinking in the Classroom* (San Francisco: Jossey-Bass, 1991). (Quotation on p. 135.)

50. Brown, *Schools of Thought*. (Quotation on p. 235.)

51. Susan M. Church, "Rethinking Whole Language: The Politics of Educational Change," in Patrick Shannon (ed.), *Becoming Political: Readings and Writing in the Politics of Literacy Education* (Portsmouth, N.H.: Heinemann, 1991). (Quotation on p. 240.)

52. "It is possible to speak of the 'natural' process of written language acquisition in the same way we speak about the 'natural' spoken language acquisition." Liliana T. Landsmann, "Literacy Development and Pedagogical Implications: Evidence from the Hebrew System of Writing," in Goodman (ed.), *How Children Construct Literacy*, pp. 26–44. (Quotation on p. 42.)

   "Words are learned by reading," says Frank Smith, a leader in whole-language education, "just as speech is learned through an active involvement in spoken language. No formal exercises are required, simply the opportunity to make sense of language in meaningful circumstances." Frank Smith, *Reading Without Nonsense* (2nd ed.; New York: Teachers College Press, 1985). (Quotation on p. 64.)

53. Courtney B. Cazden, *Child Language and Education* (New York: Holt, Rinehart and Winston, 1972), quoted in Dina Feitelson, *Facts and Fads in Beginning Reading: A Cross-Language Perspective* (Norwood, N.J.: Ablex, 1988). (Quotation on p. 30.)

54. Michael C. McKenna, Richard D. Robinson, and John W. Miller, "Whole Language: A Research Agenda for the Nineties," *Educational Researcher*, 19, November 1990, pp. 3–6.

3. ALPHABET SOUNDS AND LEARNING TO READ

1. Keith E. Stanovich, "Romance and Reality," *The Reading Teacher*, 47, December 1993–January 1994, 280–291. (Quotation on p. 283.)

2. Richard K. Wagner and Joseph K. Torgesen, "The Nature of Phonological Processing and Its Causal Role in the Acquisition of Reading Skills," *Psychological Bulletin*, 101, 1987, 192–212. (Quotations on pp. 208, 209.)

3. Stanovich, "Romance and Reality." (Quotation on p. 283.)

4. Charles Read, Zhang Yun-Fei, Nie Hong-Yin, and Ding Bao-Qing, "The Ability to Manipulate Speech Sounds Depends on Knowing Alphabetic Writing," in Paul Bertelson (ed.), *The Onset of Literacy: Cognitive Processes in Reading Acquisition* (Cambridge, Mass.: MIT Press, 1987). (Quotation on p. 31.)

5. Keith E. Stanovich, Anne E. Cunningham, and Dorothy J. Feeman, "Intelligence, Cognitive Skills, and Early Reading Progress," *Reading Research*

Quarterly, 29, 1984, 278–303; Keith E. Stanovich, Anne E. Cunningham, and Barbara B. Cramer, "Assessing Phonological Awareness in Kindergarten Children: Issues of Task Comparability," *Journal of Experimental Child Psychology*, 38, 1984, 175–190; Virginia A. Mann, "Phoneme Awareness and Future Reading Ability," *Journal of Learning Disabilities*, 26, 1993, 259–269; Benita A. Blachman, "Phonological Awareness: Implications for Prereading and Early Reading Instruction," in Susan A. Brady and Donald P. Shankweiler (eds.), *Phonological Processes in Literacy* (Hillsdale, N.J.: Lawrence Erlbaum, 1991), pp. 29–36; Diane J. Sawyer, "Inquiry into the Nature and Function of Auditory Segmentation Abilities: In Search of the Roots of Reading," in Diane J. Sawyer and Barbara J. Fox (eds.), *Phonological Awareness in Reading* (New York: Springer-Verlag, 1991), pp. 97–126; William E. Tunmer and Mary Rohl, "Phonological Awareness and Reading Acquisition," in Sawyer and Fox (eds.), *Phonological Awareness in Reading*, pp. 1–30.

6. Stanovich, "Romance and Reality." (Quotation on p. 284.)
7. Stanovich, "Romance and Reality." (Quotation on p. 284.)
8. L. Bradley and P. E. Bryant, "Categorizing Sounds and Learning to Read—A Causal Connection," *Nature*, 301, 1983, 419–21; Lynette Bradley and Peter Bryant, "Phonological Skills Before and After Learning to Read," in Brady and Shankweiler (eds.), *Phonological Processes in Literacy*, pp. 37–45.
9. Ingvar Lundberg, "Phonemic Awareness Can Be Developed Without Reading Instruction," in Brady and Shankweiler (eds.), *Phonological Processes in Literacy*, pp. 47–53; also see Ingvar Lundberg and Torliev Hoien, "Initial Enabling Knowledge and Skills in Reading Acquisition: Print Awareness and Phonological Segmentation," in Sawyer and Fox (eds.), *Phonological Awareness in Reading*, pp. 73–96.
10. Lundberg, "Phonemic Awareness." (Quotation on p. 50.)
11. Eileen W. Ball and Benita A. Blachman, "Does Phoneme Awareness Training in Kindergarten Make a Difference in Early Word Recognition and Developmental Spelling?" *Reading Research Quarterly*, 26, 1991, 49–66; Anne E. Cunningham, "Phonemic Awareness: The Development of Early Reading Competency," *Reading Research Quarterly*, 24, 1989, 471–472; D. M. Goldstein, "Cognitive-Linguistic Functioning and Learning to Read in Preschoolers," *Journal of Educational Psychology*, 68, 1976, 680–688; Connie Juel, Priscilla L. Griffith, and Philip B. Gough, "Acquisition of Literacy: A Longitudinal Study of Children in First and Second Grade," *Journal of Educational Psychology*, 78, 1986, 243–255; A. Olofsson and I. Lundberg, "Can Phonemic Awareness Be Trained in Kindergarten?" *Scandinavian Journal of Psychology*, 24, 1983, 35–44; R. Treiman and J. Baron, "Phonemic-Analysis Training Helps Children Benefit from Spelling-Sound Rules," *Memory and Cognition*, 4, 1983, 382–389.
12. Charles A. Perfetti, Isabel Beck, Laura C. Bell, and Carol Hughes, "Phonemic Knowledge and Learning to Read Are Reciprocal: A Longitudinal Study

of First Grade Children," *Merrill-Palmer Quarterly*, 33, 1987, 283–319; Margaret Snowling, "Learning to Read and Making Connections," *Educational Researcher* 22, 1993, 30–32; William E. Tunmer and Andrew R. Nesdale, "Phonemic Segmentation Skill and Beginning Reading," *Journal of Educational Psychology*, 77, 1985, 417–427.

13. Brian Byrne, "Studies in the Acquisition Procedure for Reading: Rationale, Hypotheses, and Data," in Philip B. Gough, Linnea C. Ehri, and Rebecca Treiman (eds.), *Reading Acquisition* (Hillsdale, N.J.: Lawrence Erlbaum, 1992), pp. 1–34.

14. Usha Goswami and Peter Bryant, *Phonological Skills and Learning to Read* (Hillsdale, N.J.: Lawrence Erlbaum, 1990), p. 46.

15. Usha Goswami and Peter Bryant, "Rhyme, Analogy, and Children's Reading," in Gough, Ehri, and Treiman (eds.), *Reading Acquisition*, pp. 49–63. (Quotation on p. 50.)

16. Goswami and Bryant, *Phonological Skills*.

17. In simple words, onsets might be /p/, /s/, or /b/ and a rime might be /it/. Similarly, the onset and rime for "string" are "str" and "ing." This level of phonological awareness enables children to make "strong" and "consistent" relationships between these units and sequences of letters like "str-," "-and," and "-ing." Goswami and Bryant, *Phonological Skills*. (Quotation on p. 47.) Also see Rebecca Treiman, "Onsets and Rimes as Units of Spoken Syllables: Evidence from Children," *Journal of Experimental Child Psychology*, 39, 1985, 161–181; Rebecca Treiman, "Phonological Awareness and Its Roles in Learning to Read and Spell," in Sawyer and Fox (eds.), *Phonological Awareness in Reading*, pp. 159–90; Rebecca Treiman and Andreas Zukowski, "Levels of Phonological Awareness," in Brady and Shankweiler (eds.), *Phonological Processes in Literacy*, pp. 47–53; Rebecca Treiman, "The Role of Intrasyllabic Units in Learning to Read and Spell," in Gough, Ehri, and Treiman (eds.), *Reading Acquisition*, pp. 65–106.

18. Beginning readers use analogies "spontaneously and naturally," more than they use grapheme-phoneme correspondences. Continued recognition that "words which have sounds in common often share spelling sequences as well" gives beginning readers "a powerful way to work out how to read and spell new words. They can use the spelling pattern in one word to work out the sound of another word with the same spelling sequence, and to decide how to spell a word which rhymes with a word that they know how to spell already." Goswami and Bryant, *Phonological Skills*. (Quotations on pp. 63–64, 68, 77–78.) When children are learning to read, "they become adept at recognizing when words have common rimes or common onsets. So they form categories of words and when they begin to read they soon recognize that words in the same categories often have spelling patterns in common and that this spelling sequence represents the common sound. As soon as they realize this, they can make inferences about new words, and they do." Goswami and Bryant, *Phonological Skills*. (Quotation on p. 147.)

19. Goswami and Bryant, *Phonological Skills*. (Quotation on p. 26.)
20. Steven A. Stahl and Bruce A. Murray, "Defining Phonological Awareness and Its Relationship to Early Reading," *Journal of Educational Psychology*, 86, 1994, 221–234.
21. Wagner and Torgesen, "The Nature of Phonological Processing." (Quotation on p. 208.)
22. Perfetti, Beck, Bell, and Hughes, "Phonemic Knowledge." (Quotation on p. 315.)
23. Joseph K. Torgesen, Sharon T. Morgan, and Charlotte Davis, "Effects of Two Types of Phonological Awareness Training on Word Learning in Kindergarten Children," *Journal of Educational Psychology*, 84, 1992, 364–370.
24. Stahl and Murray, "Defining Phonological Awareness." (Quotation on p. 243.)
25. Marie M. Clay, *Becoming Literate: The Construction of Inner Control* (Portsmouth, N.H.: Heinemann, 1991).
26. Clay, *Becoming Literate*. (Quotation on p. 86.)
27. Emilia Ferreiro and Ana Teberosky, *Literacy Before Schooling* (Portsmouth, N.H.: Heinemann, 1982).
28. Donald H. Graves, *Writing: Teachers and Children at Work* (Portsmouth, N.H.: Heinemann, 1983). (Quotation on p. 184.)
29. Graves, *Writing*. (Quotation on p. 184.)
30. Ferreiro and Teberosky, *Literacy Before Schooling*. (Quotation on p. 41.) Also see Margaret M. Clark, "Literacy at Home and at School: Insights from a Study of Young Fluent Readers," in Hillel Goelman, Antoinette Oberg, and Frank Smith (eds.), *Awakening to Literacy* (Portsmouth, N.H.: Heinemann, 1984), pp. 122–130; Elizabeth Sulzby, William H. Teale, and George Kamberelis, "Emergent Writing in the Classroom: Home and School Connections," in Dorothy S. Strickland and Lesley Mandel Morrow (eds.), *Emerging Literacy: Young Children Learn to Read and Write* (Newark, Del.: International Reading Association, 1989), pp. 63–79.
31. Graves, *Writing*. (Quotations on pp. 187, 188.)
32. Sandra Iversen and William E. Tunmer, "Phonological Processing Skills and the Reading Recovery Program," *Journal of Educational Psychology*, 85, 1993, 112–126.
33. William E. Tunmer and Wesley A. Hoover, "Phonological Recoding Skill and Beginning Reading," *Reading and Writing*, 5, 1993, 161–179. (Quotation on p. 176.)
34. Gay Su Pinnell, Carol A. Lyons, Diane E. DeFord, Anthony S. Bryk, and Michael Seltzer, "Comparing Instructional Models for the Literacy Education of High-Risk First Graders," *Reading Research Quarterly*, 29, January–March 1994, 8–39.
35. Curt Dudley-Marling and Sharon Murphy, "A Political Critique of Remedial Reading Programs: The Example of Reading Recovery," *The Reading Teacher*, 50, 1997, 460–468.

36. At times, the effort to bash whole language in favor of a skills approach is evident in distorted research conclusions. For example, a study entitled "Effect of Phonological Training on Reading and Writing Acquisition" offered the following judgment: "Our results also throw some light on the longstanding controversy concerning methods for teaching children to read. Reviews on this issue have generally favored the phonetic over the global methods. In our experiment the comparison of groups [using sounds plus letters vs. categorizing words conceptually] shows a clear advantage of the phonetic approach. The acquisition of reading (and writing) during the first school year was better for children trained to discriminate phonemes with the aid of plastic letters, than for children trained to discriminate concepts with the aid of written words." Sylvia Defior and Pio Tudela, "Effect of Phonological Training on Reading and Writing Acquisition," *Reading and Writing*, 6, 1994, 299–320. (Quotation on p. 316.)

    In other words, the alternative to the "phonetic approach" was a "global method" in which children were trained to categorize words conceptually, as though whole language could be reduced to this method. Clearly, only a desire to critique "global" instruction like whole language at all costs could explain this ersatz definition and lead to conclusions about the comparative superiority of "phonetic" teaching.

    Another example is the conclusion that "teachers who dismiss the phonological awareness theory and take the so-called 'holistic' approach" (that is, whole language) are misguided when they "claim that vocabulary size and the ability to comprehend and manipulate text are more important factors for reading acquisition than phonological awareness." Shlomo Bentin, "On the Interaction Between Phonological Awareness and Reading Acquisition: It's a Two-Way Street," *Annals of Dyslexia*, 43, 125–148. (Quotation on p. 132.)

    Ignored in this cudgel is the fact that whole-language theory and practice includes the need for children to develop phonological awareness. By ignoring this fact, whole language can be inaccurately interpreted as a method bent solely on increasing vocabulary size and comprehension.

37. Gordon Wells, "Preschool Literacy-Related Activities and Success in School," in David R. Olson, Nancy Torrance, and Angela Hildyard (eds.), *Literacy, Language, and Learning* (New York: Cambridge University Press, 1985), pp. 229–255. Also Elizabeth Sulzby, "Children's Emergent Reading of Favorite Storybooks: A Developmental Study," *Reading Research Quarterly*, 20, 1985, 458–481.

38. Wells, "Preschool Literacy-Related Activities." (Quotation on pp. 250–251.)

39. Victoria Purcell-Gates, "Lexical and Syntactic Knowledge of Written Narrative Held by Well-Read-To Kindergartners and Second Graders," *Research in the Teaching of English*, 22, 1988, 128–160.

40. William H. Teale, "Reading to Young Children: Its Significance for Literacy Development," in Goelman, Oberg, and Smith (eds.), *Awakening to Literacy*. (Quotation on p. 117.)

41. Stahl and Murray, "Defining Phonological Awareness." (Quotation on p. 231.)
42. Denny Taylor and Dorothy S. Strickland, *Family Storybook Reading* (Portsmouth, N.H.: Heinemann, 1986); Joan Brooks McLane and Gillian Dowley, *Early Literacy* (Cambridge, Mass.: Harvard University Press, 1990).
43. Jana M. Mason, "Reading Stories in Preliterate Children: A Proposed Connection to Reading," in Gough, Ehri, and Treiman (eds.), *Reading Acquisition*, pp. 215–241; Catherine E. Snow, Wendy S. Barnes, Jean Chandler, Irene F. Goodman, and Lowry Hemphill, *Unfulfilled Expectations: Home and School Influences on Literacy* (Cambridge, Mass.: Harvard University Press, 1991); Elizabeth Sulzby and William Teale, "Emergent Literacy," in P. David Pearson, Rebecca Barr, Michael L. Kamil, and Peter Mosenthal (eds.), *Handbook of Reading Research*, Vol. 2 (White Plains, N.Y.: Longman, 1991), pp. 727–758; William H. Teale, Miriam G. Martinez, and Wanda L. Glass, "Describing Classroom Storybook Reading," in David Bloome (ed.), *Classrooms and Literacy* (Norwood, N.J.: Ablex, 1989); Allan Wigfield and Steven R. Asher, "Social and Motivational Influences on Reading," in Pearson (ed.), *Handbook of Reading Research*, Vol. 1, pp. 423–452.
44. Eileen W. Ball, "Phonological Awareness: What's Important and to Whom?" *Reading and Writing*, 5, 1993, 141–159. (Quotation on p. 150.)
45. Reginald M. Clark, *Family Life and School Achievement: Why Poor Black Children Succeed or Fail* (Chicago: University of Chicago Press, 1983).
46. Gerald Coles, *The Learning Mystique: A Critical Look at "Learning Disabilities"* (New York: Pantheon, 1987). (See Chapter 7.)

4. EMOTIONS AND LEARNING TO READ

1. Lev S. Vygotsky, *The Collected Works of L. S. Vygotsky*, Vol. 1 (New York: Plenum Press, 1987). (Quotation on p. 50.)
2. Richard J. Davidson and John T. Cacioppo, "New Developments in the Scientific Study of Emotion: An Introduction to the Special Section," *Psychological Science*, 3, January 1992, 21–22. (Quotation on p. 21.)
3. Joseph LeDoux, *The Emotional Brain: The Mysterious Underpinnings of Emotional Life* (New York: Simon & Schuster, 1996). (Quotation on p. 25.)
4. American Psychiatric Association, *Diagnostic and Statistical Manual of Mental Disorders*, 4th ed. (DSM IV). (Washington, D.C.: American Psychiatric Association, 1994). (See pp. 78–85.)
5. James A. Beane, *Affect in the Curriculum: Toward Democracy, Dignity, and Diversity* (New York: Teachers College Press, 1990). (Quotations on pp. 42, 138.)
6. Irene Athey, "Reading Research in the Affective Domain," in Harry Singer and Robert B. Ruddell (eds.), *Theoretical Models and Processes of Reading* (Newark, Del.: International Reading Association, 1985), pp. 527–557. (Quotation on p. 527.)
7. John I. Goodlad, *A Place Called School* (New York: McGraw-Hill, 1984). (Quotation on p. 124.)

8. Michael Lewis, Margaret W. Sullivan, and Linda Michalson, "The Cognitive-Emotional Fugue," in Carroll E. Izard, Jerome Kagan, and Robert B. Zajonc (eds.), *Emotions, Cognition, and Behavior* (New York: Cambridge University Press, 1984), pp. 264–288.

9. Aleksei N. Leontiev, "The Present Tasks of Soviet Psychology," in *Soviet Psychology: A Symposium* (Westport, Conn.: Greenwood Press, 1973), pp. 44–45.

10. Bernard Weiner and Sandra Graham, "An Attributional Approach to Emotional Development," in Izard, Kagan, and Zajonc (eds.), *Emotions, Cognition, and Behavior,* pp. 167–191.

11. Claude Brown, *Manchild in the Promised Land* (New York: New American Library, 1965). (Quotation on p. 174.)

12. Jonathan Kozol, *Children of the Revolution: A Yankee Teacher in the Cuban Schools* (New York: Dell, 1978). (Quotation on p. 36.)

13. Lev S. Vygotsky, *Mind in Society: The Development of Higher Psychological Processes* (Cambridge, Mass.: Harvard University Press, 1978). (Quotations on pp. 85–86.)

14. Paulo Freire, *Pedagogy of the Oppressed* (New York: Herder and Herder, 1971).

15. Carroll Izard, "Emotion-Cognition Relationships and Human Development," in Izard, Kagan, and Zajonc (eds.), *Emotions, Cognition, and Behavior,* pp. 17–37.

16. John C. Masters, R. Christopher Barden, and Martin E. Ford, "Affective States, Expressive Behavior, and Learning in Children," *Journal of Personality and Social Psychology,* 37, 1979, 380–390.

17. W. Nasby and R. Yando, "Selective Encoding and Retrieval of Affectively Valent Information," *Journal of Personality and Social Psychology,* 43, 1982, 1244–1255.

18. R. Potts, M. Morse, E. Felleman, and J. C. Masters, "Children's Emotions and Memory for Affective Narrative Content," *Motivation and Emotion,* 10, 1986, 39–57.

19. Bettina Seipp, "Anxiety and Academic Performance: A Meta-analysis of Findings," *Anxiety Research,* 4, 1991, 27–41.

20. Tanis Bryan and James Bryan, "Positive Mood and Math Performance," *Journal of Learning Disabilities,* 24, October 1991, 490–494.

21. Bertolt Brecht, *The Mother* (New York: Grove Press, 1965). (Quotation on pp. 76–77.)

22. B. K. Eakman, "It's about Mental Health, Stupid!" *Education Week,* October 20, 1993, pp. 40–43.

23. Chester E. Finn, Jr., *We Must Take Charge: Our Schools and Our Future* (New York: Free Press, 1991). (Quotation on p. 216.)

24. We can also see from Earl's work and literacy development that his transformations were not unidirectional but continuous interactive transformations between the (objective) social world and the (subjective) person. In these "transformations" the objective is transformed into the subjective: the person appropriates and interprets the objective world. At the same time, the sub-

ject's activity is converted into objective results and products: therefore, subjective activity produces objective conditions. These subjective changes do not occur at the cognitive and emotional level alone. For changes in thinking and emotion to occur, there must be a change in activity. The subject has to act in and upon the world in a different way, which in turn will produce changes in thinking, emotions, and learning.

Understanding cognition and emotions and literacy progress requires looking at them not at a fixed moment in time or as fixed entities, but "historically," within the course of their development and transformations. In Earl's case, his cognitive and emotional processes had to be understood in two ways: as they had developed and as they were developing. To have looked simply at Earl's case ahistorically, without attempting to understand how his emotions and cognition developed through past experiences, would have led to erroneous conclusions. These past experiences were living "phantoms of the past" containing emotional associations that could impede his learning and had to be dealt with if learning were to proceed.

25. Antonio R. Damasio, *Descartes' Error: Emotion, Reason, and the Human Brain* (New York: G. P. Putnam's Sons, 1994).

Thinking "depends on several brain systems, working in concert across many levels of neuronal organization, rather than on a single brain center. Both 'high-level' and 'low-level' brain centers, from the prefrontal cortices to the hypothalamus and brain stem, cooperate in the making of reason." (Quotation on p. xiii.)

26. Parts of the brain activated in emotions are the prefrontal cortex and the amygdala.

27. Joseph E. LeDoux, "Emotion, Memory and the Brain," *Scientific American,* 270, June 1994, 50–57. (Quotation on p. 55.)

28. LeDoux, "Emotion." (Quotation on p. 56.)

29. Quoted in Daniel Goleman, *Emotional Intelligence* (New York: Bantam, 1995). (Quotation on p. 18.)

30. LeDoux, "Emotion." (Quotation on p. 57.)

31. LeDoux, "Emotion." (Quotation on p. 57.)

32. LeDoux, *The Emotional Brain.* (See Chapter 9.)

33. Goleman, *Emotional Intelligence.* (Quotation on p. 27.)

34. Peter Applebome, "School District Elevates Status of Black English," *New York Times,* December 19, 1996.

35. Charles Dickens, *Hard Times* (New York: Methuen, 1987 [1845]). (Quotations on pp. 26–28.)

36. When Earl found he could talk with people outside the program about what he had read—he could use his knowledge and add to their knowledge and understanding—this too was a new experience for him. Previously, he always felt himself to be only the recipient of information. An example of this change occurred when he was reading the biography of Phillis Wheatley. He was talking with a college student one day and began telling her about Wheatley

and her poetry. The student confessed never having heard of her and asked Earl if she could read his book when he was done: "When I told that college student about Phillis Wheatley, it made me feel important because she was a sophomore and didn't know about her."

37. Beane, *Affect in the Curriculum.* (Quotation on p. 19.)

5. MEANING, COMPREHENSION, AND READING SUCCESS

1. Harvey J. Graff, "The Legacies of Literacy: Continuities and Contradictions in Western Society and Culture," in Suzanne de Castell, Allan Luke, and Kiera Egan (eds.), *Literacy, Society, and Schooling* (New York: Cambridge University Press, 1986). (Quotation on p. 79.)
2. Nila B. Smith, *American Reading Instruction* (Newark, Del.: International Reading Association, 1965). (Quotation on p. 20.)
3. Smith, *American Reading Instruction.* (Quotation on p. 40.)
4. David Nasaw, *Schooled to Order: A Social History of Public Schooling in the United States* (New York: Oxford University Press, 1979). (Quotation on p. 40.)
5. Michael B. Katz, *Reconstructing American Education* (Cambridge, Mass.: Harvard University Press, 1987). (Quotation on pp. 22–23.)
6. Charles W. Sanders, *The School Reader: Second Book* (New York: Ivison & Phinney, 1840). (Quotation on p. 13.)
7. Richard Edwards and J. Russell Webb, *Analytical Second Reader* (New York: Taintor & Co., 1866). (Quotation on p. 65.) The book remains filled with insipid stories, but these are interspersed with stories criticizing boys who are mean and who steal, girls who are proud and vain, and children who lie. Stories about God are interspersed throughout the book, which ends with a prayer asking, "O, who would not love Jesus, and dwell with Him above?"
8. Edwards and Webb, *Analytical Second Reader.* (Quotations on pp. 32–33.)
9. Sarah L. Arnold and Charles B. Gilbert, *Stepping Stones to Literature, a First Reader* (New York: Silver, Burdett and Co., 1897). (Quotation on p. 40.)
10. Clara Murray, *Wide Awake Junior, an Easy Primer* (New York: Little, Brown, 1916). (Quotation on p. 102.)
11. Kenneth S. Goodman, Patrick Shannon, Yvonne S. Freeman, and Sharon Murphy, *Report Card on Basal Readers* (Katonah, N.Y.: Richard C. Owen, 1988). (Quotation on p. 59.)
12. Tom Engelhardt, "Reading May Be Harmful to Your Kids," *Harper's,* June 1991, pp. 55–62. (Quotation on p. 56.)
13. Kathy G. Short and Kathryn M. Pierce, "Children's Books: Living in Harmony," *The Reading Teacher,* 48, 1995, 422–430. (Quotation on p. 422.)
14. Patrick Shannon, "Overt and Covert Censorship of Children's Books," in Patrick Shannon (ed.), *Becoming Political: Readings and Writings in the Politics of Literacy Education* (Portsmouth, N.H.: Heinemann, 1992), pp. 65–71. (Quotation on p. 69.)

15. Herbert Kohl, *Should We Burn Babar?: Essays on Children's Literature and the Power of Stories* (New York: New Press, 1995). (Quotation on p. 2.)
16. Mem Fox, "Politics and Literature: Chasing the "Isms" from Children's Books," *The Reading Teacher*, 46, 1993, 654–658. (Quotation on p. 656.)
17. Linda B. Gambrell and Paula B. Jawitz, "Mental Imagery, Text Illustrations, and Children's Story Comprehension and Recall," *Reading Research Quarterly*, 28, 1993, 265–276; Victoria C. Hare, Mitchell Rabinowitz, and Karen M. Schieble, "Text Effects on Main Idea Comprehension," *Reading Research Quarterly*, 24, Winter 1989, 72–88; Jeffrey J. Walczyk and Laura J. Raska, "The Relation Between Low- and High-Level Reading Skills in Children," *Contemporary Educational Psychology*, 17, January 1992, 38–46.
18. R. Scott Baldwin, Ziva Peleg-Bruckner, and Ann H. McClintock, "Effects of Topic Interest and Prior Knowledge on Reading Comprehension," *Reading Research Quarterly*, 20, Summer 1985, 497–504; Barbara Erwin, "The Relationship Between Background Experience and Students' Comprehension: A Cross-cultural Study," *Reading Psychology*, 12, January–March 1991, p. 43–61; Paul T. Wilson and Richard C. Anderson, "What They Don't Know Will Hurt Them: The Role of Prior Knowledge in Comprehension," in Judith Orasanu (ed.), *Reading Comprehension: From Research to Practice* (Hillsdale, N.J.: Lawrence Erlbaum, 1986).
19. Sharon B. Kleitzien, "Proficient and Less Proficient Comprehenders' Strategy Use for Different Top-Level Structures," *Journal of Reading Behavior*, 24, June 1992, 191–215.
20. Janice A. Dole, Gerald G. Duffy, Laura R. Roehler, and P. David Pearson, "Moving from the Old to the New: Research on Reading Comprehension Instruction," *Review of Educational Research*, 61, Summer 1991, 239–264.
21. Marilyn Jager Adams, *Beginning to Read: Thinking and Learning about Print* (Cambridge, Mass.: MIT Press, 1990). (Quotation on p. 140.)
22. Ana Teberosky, "The Language Young Children Write: Reflections on a Learning Situation," in Yetta M. Goodman (ed.), *How Children Construct Literacy: Piagetian Perspectives* (Newark, Del.: International Reading Association, 1990), 45–58.
23. Marie M. Clay, *Becoming Literate: The Construction of Inner Control* (Portsmouth, N.H.: Heinemann, 1991). (Quotation on p. 63.)
24. Paulo Freire proposes that no matter how rudimentary the reading material, it contains a particular view of the world. Freire urges educators to be explicit about particular views they want to advance and to be sure literacy education is "laden with the meaning of the [student's] existential experience." (Paulo Freire and Donaldo Macedo, *Literacy: Reading the Word and the World* (South Hadley, Mass.: Bergin & Garvey, 1987). (Quotation on p. 35.)
25. Robert Swartz and Sandra Parks, *Infusing the Teaching of Critical and Creative Thinking into Secondary Instruction: A Lesson Design Handbook for Secondary Education* (Pacific Grove, Calif.: Critical Thinking Press & Software, 1992). (Quotation on p. 6.)

26. See Martin J. Sherwin, *A World Destroyed: Hiroshima and the Origins of the Arms Race* (New York: Vintage, 1987); Robert J. C. Butow, *Japan's Decision to Surrender* (Stanford, Calif.: Stanford University Press, 1954); Gar Alperovitz, *Atomic Diplomacy: Hiroshima and Potsdam: The Use of the Atomic Bomb and the American Confrontation with Soviet Power* (Boulder, Colo.: Pluto Press, 1994).

27. Jay L. Lemke, "Social Semiotics: A New Model for Literacy Education," in David Bloome (ed.), *Classrooms and Literacy* (Norwood, N.J.: Ablex, 1989), 289–309. (Quotation on p. 295.)

28. S. Jay Samuels and Michael Kamil, "Models of the Reading Process," in P. David Pearson (ed.), *Handbook of Reading Research*, Vol. 1 (White Plains, N.Y.: Longman, 1984), 185–224. (Quotation on pp. 205–206.)

29. Richard C. Anderson and P. David Pearson, "A Schema-Theoretic View of Basic Processes in Reading Comprehension," in Pearson (ed.), *Handbook of Reading Research*, 255–292. (Quotation on p. 258.)

30. Anderson and Pearson, "A Schema-Theoretic View." (Quotation on pp. 259–260.)

31. Anderson and Pearson, "A Schema-Theoretic View." (Quotation on p. 260.)

32. Anderson and Pearson, "A Schema-Theoretic View." (Quotation on p. 261.)

33. E. D. Hirsch, Jr., *Cultural Literacy: What Every American Needs to Know* (New York: Random House, 1987). (Quotation on p. 24.)

34. Another illustration of the miscomprehension that "facts" and "information" can promote is a 1987 report, *What Do Our 17-Year-Olds Know?*, documenting the sizable lack of historical and literary knowledge high school students possess. However, there is another side to the survey: what knowledge do the authors, Diane Ravitch and Chester Finn, think these students should know? While it is true that the survey tried to keep to minimal events and facts, the "bare outline" was created within a point of view, within a vision that arguably promotes one kind of understanding of history. Ravitch and Finn make clear that right answers are guided by a view that American history "belongs to all of us": "It is possible to define American history, with all its complexity, controversy, and variety, as the story of a people forged from many different pasts but joined together under a common political system. There is, in short, an American people, not just a mosaic of unrelated groups, each with its own story, disconnected from the whole." Diane Ravitch and Chester E. Finn, Jr., *What Do Our 17-Year-Olds Know?* (New York: Harper & Row, 1987). (Quotation on p. 35.)
    Omitted in the interpretation is another array of facts that merge into an altogether different assessment of the country. This interpretation sees Americans "joined together" but not equally, not for each other's good, not for the common good. It is an interpretation of a history of people joined together within a system, but some groups—labor, slaves, poor, ethnic groups, to name a few—have been joined under, not with, those of wealth and power. It is a view of irreconcilable differences between haves and have-nots and of power-

ful and powerless. See Noam Chomsky, *Year 501: The Conquest Continues* (Boston: South End Press, 1993); Sidney Lens, *Radicalism in America* (New York: Crowell, 1966); John Marciano, *Civic Illiteracy and Education: The Battle for the Hearts and Minds of American Youth* (New York: Peter Lang, 1997); Michael Parenti, *Against Empire* (San Francisco: City Lights Books, 1995); William A. Williams, *The Contours of American History* (Chicago: Quadrangle, 1966); Howard Zinn, *A People's History of the United States* (New York: HarperCollins, 1990).

35. Bob Peterson, "What Should Kids Learn?: A Teacher Looks at E. D. Hirsch's Work on 'Cultural Literacy,'" *Rethinking Schools*, Winter 1993. (Quotation on p. 8.)

High school teacher Bill Bigelow argues that children's biographies of Christopher Columbus "function as primers on racism and colonialism, teach youngsters to accept the right of white people to rule over people of color, and of powerful nations to dominate weaker nations." Absent from these biographies is Columbus's slave trading, his murder and mutilation of indigenous people who resisted him, and the gold quotas he forced from every Indian fourteen and over. Acknowledging that he wanted "gold and spices," a second-grade biography asks, "Of course he wanted a lot! What was wrong with that?" According to these biographies, Columbus believed he was doing God's work, especially, in the words of one book, by "carrying the Christian faith to heathens." The latter term is used without the slightest criticism and overshadows any discussion of either Columbus's desire for wealth or the economic desires of the Spanish monarchs. Bigelow notes that none of the biographies dispute outright the "ugly facts about Columbus" but "every one of them encourages children to root for Columbus." These stories, Bigelow emphasizes, influence children's thinking as much about the present as the past: "The message to children is that white people in developed societies have consciousness and voice, but Third World people are thoughtless and voiceless objects. The text and images rehearse students in a way of looking at the world that begins from the assumption: they are not like us. A corollary is that we are more competent than they in determining the conditions of their lives, their social and economic systems, their political alliances and so on." Bill Bigelow, "Once upon a Genocide: A Review of Christopher Columbus in Children's Literature," *Rethinking Schools*, 5, 1990. (Quotations on pp. 1, 7, 8.)

36. For example: Harry Singer and Robert B. Ruddell, *Theoretical Models of Reading* (3rd ed.: Newark, Del.: International Reading Association, 1985); Marilyn Jager Adams, *Beginning to Read: Thinking and Learning about Print* (Cambridge, Mass.: MIT Press, 1990); P. David Pearson, Rebecca Barr, Michael Kamil, and Peter Mosenthal (eds.), *Handbook of Reading Research*, Vol. 2 (White Plains, N.Y.: Longman, 1991); Frank Smith, *Insult to Intelligence: The Bureaucratic Invasion of Our Classrooms* (Portsmouth, N.H.: Heinemann, 1986); Don Holdaway, *The Foundations of Literacy* (New York: Ashton Scholastic, 1979).

37. Lillian R. Putnam, "An Interview with Noam Chomsky," *The Reading Teacher*, 48, December 1994–January 1995, 328–333. (Quotation on p. 333.)
38. Noam Chomsky, *Syntactic Structures* (The Hague: Mouton, 1957).
39. Noam Chomsky, *Aspects of the Theory of Syntax* (Cambridge, Mass.: MIT Press, 1965).
40. Edward S. Herman and Noam Chomsky, *Manufacturing Consent: The Political Economy of the Mass Media* (New York: Pantheon, 1988).
41. Noam Chomsky, *Necessary Illusions: Thought Control in Democratic Societies* (Boston: South End Press, 1989). (Quotation on p. vii.)
42. For example, see Chomsky's *Power and Prospects: Reflections on Human Nature and the Social Order* (Boston: South End Press, 1996); *Chronicles of Dissent* (Monroe, Me.: Common Courage Press, 1992); *Keeping the Rabble in Line* (Monroe, Me.: Common Courage Press, 1994); *Secrets, Lies and Democracy* (Tucson, Ariz.: Odonian Press, 1994); *Deterring Democracy* (New York: Hill and Wang, 1992); *The Prosperous Few and the Restless Many* (Tucson, Ariz.: Odonian Press, 1993).

Chomsky's critique of print and other media is based on a "propaganda model" claiming that these media "inculcate and defend the economic, social, and political agenda of privileged groups that dominate the domestic society and the state. The media serve this purpose in many ways: through selection of topics, distribution of concerns, framing of issues, filtering of information, emphasis and tone, and by keeping debate within the bounds of acceptable premises." Herman and Chomsky, *Manufacturing Consent*. (Quotation on p. 298.). Chomsky's interpretation of miscomprehension recognizes that correct information does appear in print and other media, but the deck is often stacked against accurate comprehension of it: "That a careful reader looking for [information] can sometimes find it with diligence and a skeptical eye tells us nothing about whether the [information] received the attention and context it deserved, whether it was intelligible to the reader or effectively distorted or suppressed. [T]here is no merit to the pretense that because certain [information] may be found in the media by a diligent and skeptical researcher, the absence of radical bias and de facto suppression is thereby demonstrated." Herman and Chomsky, *Manufacturing Consent*. (Quotation on p. xv.)

6. LEARNING CAPACITY, CHILDREN'S FUTURES, AND READING ACHIEVEMENT

1. Herbert M. Kliebard, *The Struggle for the American Curriculum, 1893–1958* (New York: Routledge, 1986). (See pp. 42–51.)
2. G. Stanley Hall, *Adolescence: Its Psychology and Its Relations to Physiology, Anthropology, Sociology, Sex, Crime, Religion and Education*, Vol. 1 (New York: Appleton, 1904). Quoted in Kliebard, *Struggle*, p. 14.
3. Lewis M. Terman, *The Intelligence of School Children* (Boston: Houghton Mifflin, 1919). (Quotation on p. 10.)

4. Paul D. Chapman, *Schools as Sorters: Lewis M. Terman, Applied Psychology, and the Intelligence Movement, 1890–1930* (New York: New York University Press, 1988). (Quotation on p. 85.)

5. Terman, *Intelligence of School Children*. (Quotation on p. 115.)

6. Terman, *Intelligence of School Children*. (Quotation on p. 116.)

7. Lewis M. Terman, *The Measurement of Intelligence* (Boston: Houghton Mifflin, 1916), pp. 91–92. Quoted in Leon J. Kamin, *The Science and Politics of I.Q.* (New York: John Wiley & Sons, 1974), p. 6.

   In a similar vein, Ellwood P. Cubberley, dean of the Stanford School of Education, lamented over the mental capacity of the "many children of the foreign-born, who have no aptitude for book learning, and many children of inferior mental qualities who do not profit by ordinary classroom procedure." Ellwood P. Cubberley, *Public Education in the United States: A Study of and Interpretation of American Educational History* (Boston: Houghton Mifflin, 1919). (Quotation on p. 381.)

8. Chapman, *Schools as Sorters*. (Quotation on p. 35.)

9. David B. Tyack, *The One Best System: A History of American Urban Education* (Cambridge, Mass.: Harvard University Press, 1974). (Quotation on p. 209.)

10. Tyack, *The One Best System*. (Quotation on pp. 210–211.)

11. Leonard P. Ayres, *Laggards in Our Schools: A Study of Retardation and Elimination in City School Systems* (New York: Charities Publication Committee, 1909).

12. Scott Nearing, *The New Education* (New York: Row, Peterson, 1915). (Quotation on pp. 53–54.)

13. The testing movement's assumptions about natural capacity reached deep into the society. As David Tyack has said: "Perhaps the most significant result of the testing movement was that the notion of great and measurable differences in intellectual capacity became part of the conventional wisdom not only of school people but of the public—a development so pervasive in its influence that it is exceedingly difficult to perceive today how people conceived of differences in cognitive performance before scientists taught us to think of this as a function of 'intelligence.' [Testing] influenced the behavior of professionals and the self-concept of the children who lived in classrooms." Tyack, *The One Best System*. (Quotation on p. 216.)

14. Achievement and IQ tests were but a part of the enthusiasm for testing that gripped psychology and education. In the early 1920s approximately 65 percent of investigations by members of the American Psychological Association was devoted to testing research. Chapman, *Schools as Sorters*. (Quotation on p. 106.)

15. James Collins, "Differential Instruction in Reading Groups," in Jenny Cook-Gumperz (ed.), *The Social Construction of Literacy* (New York: Cambridge University Press, 1986), pp. 117–137. (Quotation on p. 121.)

16. Richard L. Allington, "Teacher Interruption Behaviors During Primary-Grade Oral Reading," *Journal of Education Psychology*, 72, 1982, 371–377. (Quotation on p. 374.)

17. Hilda Borko and Margaret Eisenhart, "Reading Ability Groups as Literacy Communities," in David Bloome (ed.), *Classrooms and Literacy* (Norwood, N.J.: Ablex, 1989), pp. 107–134.
18. Collins, "Differential Instruction in Reading Groups."
19. Richard L. Allington, "Poor Readers Don't Get to Read Much in Reading Groups," *Language Arts*, 57, November–December 1980, 872–876. (Quotation on p. 874.) Also see Richard Allington, "If They Don't Read Much, How They Ever Gonna Get Good?" *Journal of Reading*, 21, 1977, 57–61.
20. D. Felmee and D. Eder, "Contextual Effects in the Classroom: The Impact of Ability Groups on Student Attention," *Sociology of Education*, 56, 1983, 77–87.
21. Richard L. Allington, "The Reading Instruction Provided Readers of Differing Abilities," *Elementary School Journal*, 83, 1983, 548–559.
22. Adam Gamoran, "Rank, Performance, and Mobility in Elementary School Grouping," *Sociological Quarterly*, 30, 1989, 109–123. (Quotation on p. 112.)
23. Jo Michaelle Beld Fraatz, *The Politics of Reading: Power, Opportunity, and Prospects for Change in America's Public Schools* (New York: Teachers College Press, 1987). (Quotation on p. 10.)
24. Frances Schwartz, "Supporting or Subverting Learning: Peer Group Patterns in Four Tracked Schools," *Anthropology and Education Quarterly*, 14, 1981, 99–121.
25. Jeannie Oakes, "Can Tracking Research Inform Practice?: Technical, Normative, and Political Considerations," *Educational Researcher*, 21, May 1992, 12–22. (Quotation on p. 13.)
26. Oakes, "Tracking Research." (Quotation on p. 13.)
27. Jeannie Oakes and Martin Lipton, "Detracking Schools: Early Lessons from the Field," *Phi Delta Kappan*, 73, February 1992, 448–454. (Quotation on p. 449.)
28. Michael Parenti, *Dirty Truths* (San Francisco: City Lights Books, 1996). (Quotation on p. 18.)
29. Martin Carnoy, *Faded Dreams: The Politics and Economics of Race in America* (New York: Cambridge University Press, 1994). (Quotation on p. 58.)
30. Richard H. deLone, *Small Futures: Children, Inequality, and the Limits of Liberal Reform* (New York: Harcourt Brace Jovanovich, 1979). (Quotation on p. 110.)
31. Lawrence Mishel, Jared Bernstein, and John Schmitt, *The State of Working America, 1996–97* (Armonk, N.Y.: M. E. Sharpe, 1997). (See especially pp. 97–100.)
32. Deborah L. Cohen, "Silver Ribbon Panel Calls for Upgrading 25-Year-Old Head Start," *Education Week*, May 23, 1990.
33. Deborah L. Cohen, "Perry Preschool Graduates Show Dramatic New Social Gains at 27," *Education Week*, April 21, 1993.
34. Susan Chira, "New Head Start Studies Raise Question on Help: Should Fewer Get More?" *New York Times*, March 4, 1992.

35. Steve Barnett, "Does Head Start Fade Out?" *Education Week*, May 4, 1993.
36. Debra Viadero, "'Fade-out' in Head Start Gains Linked to Later Schooling," *Education Week*, April 20, 1994.
37. Edward Zigler and Susan Muenchow, *Head Start: The Inside Story of America's Most Successful Educational Experiment* (New York: Basic Books, 1992). (Quotation on p. 45.)
38. Zigler and Muenchow, *Head Start*. (Quotation on p. 194.)
39. Edward Zigler, "Head Start Falls Behind," *New York Times*, May 27, 1992.
40. Successful programs have about one teacher to five students, compared to 1:8 or 1:10 or higher ratios for most Head Start programs.
41. Deborah L. Cohen, "Head Start Advocates Say Funding Plan Favors Program Growth over Quality," *Education Week*, April 3, 1991.
42. Zigler and Muenchow, *Head Start*. (Quotation on p. 218.)
43. Mark Pitsch, "HHS Proposes Regulatory Overhaul of Head Start," *Education Week*, May 1, 1996.
44. Hood works for the John Locke Foundation.
45. "Study Suggests Head Start Helps Beyond School," *New York Times*, April 20, 1993.
46. Zigler and Muenchow, *Head Start*. (Quotation on p. 206.)

7. READING DISABILITIES AND LEARNING TO READ

1. A National Institutes of Health guide for researchers stated: "Converging evidence derived from anatomical microstructure studies, gross morphology studies, and neuroimaging studies suggests that the phenotypic expression in dyslexia is related to anomalous organization of brain structures and processing systems within the posterior left hemisphere." Figures from the National Institutes of Health, said to be based on longitudinal, epidemiological studies, maintain that reading disabilities (again, synonymous with "dyslexia") affect at least 10 million children, or approximately one child in five. "Learning Disabilities: Multidisciplinary Research Centers," *NIH Guide*, Vol. 23, No. 37, October 21, 1994. (Quotation on p. 5.)
2. Sally E. Shaywitz, "Dyslexia," *Scientific American*, November 1996, pp. 98–104. (Quotation on p. 103.)
3. Linda S. Siegel, "An Evaluation of the Discrepancy Definition of Dyslexia," *Journal of Learning Disabilities*, 25, December 1992, 618–628.
4. Franklin R. Manis, Rebecca Custodio, and Patricia A. Szeszulski, "Development of Phonological and Orthographic Skill: A 2-Year Longitudinal Study of Dyslexic Children," *Journal of Experimental Child Psychology*, 56, 1993, 64–86. (Quotation on p. 67.)
5. Regina Yap and Aryan V. Leij, "Word Processing in Dyslexics: An Automatic Decoding Deficit?" *Reading and Writing*, 5, 1993, 261–279. (Quotation on p. 266.)
6. Sally E. Shaywitz, , Bennett A. Shaywitz, Jack M. Fletcher, and Michael D. Escobar, "Prevalence of Reading Disabilities in Boys and Girls: Results of the

Connecticut Longitudinal Study," *Journal of the American Medical Association*, 264, 1990, 998–1002.

7. Mary Poplin, "Reductionism from the Medical Model to the Classroom: The Past, Present and Future of Learning Disabilities," *Research Communications in Psychology, Psychiatry and Behavior*, 10, 1985, 37–70.

8. Maryanne Wolf and Mateo Obregon, "Early Naming Deficits, Developmental Dyslexia, and a Specific Deficit Hypothesis," *Brain and Language*, 42, 1992, 219–247. (Quotation on p. 239.)

9. Wolf and Obregon, "Early Naming Deficits." (Quotation on p. 234, emphasis in original.)

10. Wolf and Obregon, "Early Naming Deficits." (Quotation on p. 235.)

11. Wolf and Obregon, "Early Naming Deficits." (Quotations on pp. 219, 241–242.)

12. D. Galin, J. Raz, G. Fein, J. Johnstone, J. Herron, and C. Yingling, "EEG Spectra in Dyslexic and Normal Readers During Oral and Silent Reading," *Electroencephalography and Clinical Neurophysiology*, 82, 1992, 87–101. (Quotation on p. 98.)

13. "Learning Disabilities: Multidisciplinary Research Centers," *NIH Guide*. (Quotations on pp. 5, 7.)

14. Shaywitz, "Dyslexia." (Quotation on p. 99.)

15. Measured in millimicrometers squared.

16. Albert M. Galaburda, Matthew T. Menard, and Glenn D. Rosen, "Evidence for Aberrant Auditory Anatomy in Developmental Dyslexia," *Proceedings of the National Academy of Science*, 91, August 1994, 8010–8013. (Quotation on p. 8010.)

17. Gerald Coles, *The Learning Mystique: A Critical Look at "Learning Disabilities"* (New York: Pantheon, 1987). (See pp. 86–90.)

18. Michael Posner and Marcus E. Raichle, *Images of Mind* (New York: Scientific American Library, 1994).

These technologies are not without potential dangers. Researchers emphasize that radioactive isotopes decay into a nonradioactive form very rapidly, but the "relatively short time" in which this happens is approximately ten minutes. Researchers are aware that isotopes have potential dangers but stress that the short decaying time "substantially reduces the exposure of subjects to the potentially harmful effects of ionizing radiation." (Quotation on p. 61.) "Substantially reduces" in this assurance still does not equate with "eliminates."

19. Judith M. Rumsey, Paul Andreason, Alan J. Zametkin, Tracy Acquino, Catherine King, Susan D. Hamburger, Anita Pikus, Judith L. Rapoport, and Robert M. Cohen, "Failure to Activate the Left Temporoparietal Cortex in Dyslexia," *Archives of Neurology*, 49, May 1992, 527–534.

20. D. Lynn Flowers, Frank B. Wood, and Cecile E. Naylor, "Regional Cerebral Blood Flow Correlates of Language Processes in Reading Disability," *Archives of Neurology*, 48, June 1991, 637–643.

21. Another study concluded that the "brain metabolism in dyslexic adults differs from that in normal adults when performing the same auditory discrimination

task." (The dyslexics made more mistakes in identifying syllables.) However, despite the implication of a "deficit," this finding reveals nothing about the cause of the difference. Jennifer O. Hagman, Frank Wood, Monte S. Buchsbaum, Paula Tallal, Lynn Flowers, and William Katz, "Cerebral Brain Metabolism in Adult Dyslexic Subjects Assessed with Positron Emission Tomography During Performance of an Auditory Task," *Archives of Neurology*, 49, 1992, 734–739.

22. The results of the line orientation task, said the researchers, "may indicate a tendency toward inadequate bihemispheric integration or inefficient simultaneous allocation of resources." Judith M. Rumsey, Karen F. Berman, Martha B. Denckla, Susan D. Hamburger, Markus J. Kruesi, and Daniel R. Weinberger, "Regional Cerebral Blood Flow in Severe Developmental Dyslexia," *Archives of Neurology*, 44, 1987, 1144–1150. (Quotation on p. 1149.)

23. I will only highlight some of the more salient findings.

1. In the temporal lobes, activation was symmetrical for the reading disabled but slightly *higher in the right lobes of the normal readers*. These findings were contrary to the long-standing "explanation" that a normal asymmetry in the brain hemispheres is one of activation larger in the left than the right, and that lower left than right activation may be the cause of reading disabilities. Here, in the temporal lobe—critical in reading—the normal readers showed the reverse pattern.

2. The middle temporal lobe showed asymmetry slightly favoring the *right* for normal readers and slightly favoring the *left* for reading disabled. The researchers simply reported the data but did not attempt to relate it to any aspect of long-standing reading disabilities theory, which would have expected the opposite results.

3. The parietal lobe showed equal activation in both hemispheres for both groups.

4. In the frontal lobe, activation was higher in the right side for both groups, but slightly higher for the normal readers.

The differences in the occipital lobe were another story. One portion of the lobe, the lingual lobe—part of the visual pathway—showed the same asymmetry pattern for both groups: higher left over right. Here, however, the blood flow was greater for the reading disabled in both hemispheres. When both groups had similar symmetry patterns for the frontal lobe, the higher metabolic rates for normal readers seemed to represent better brain functioning. Here, the opposite was true. Greater activation of the visual pathway could not possibly represent greater visual attention to the written language task. Rather, it was a bad sign because it suggested "inefficient visual word-form processing," presumed to be caused by a biological deficit.

There is no way a brief summary can provide an adequate picture of the overriding drive in this study to identify deficits in reading disabled. As I said, the results showed no differences in most of the brain areas studied. Karen Gross-Glenn, Ranjan Duara, Warren W. Barker, David Loewenstein, J. Y.

Chang, F. Yoshii, Anthony M. Apicella, Shlomo Pascal, Thomas Boothe, Steven Sevush, Bonnie J. Jallad, Loriana Novoa, and Herbert A. Lubs, "Positron Emission Tomographic Studies During Serial Word-Reading by Normal and Dyslexic Adults," *Journal of Clinical and Experimental Neuropsychology*, 13, 1991, 531–544.

24. Jan P. Larsen, Torleiv Hoien, Ingvar Lundberg, and Helge Odegaard, "MRI Evaluation of the Size and Symmetry of the Planum Temporale in Adolescents with Developmental Dyslexia," *Brain and Language*, 39, 1990, 289–301.

25. Norman Geschwind and Walter Levitsky, "Human Brain: Left-Right Asymmetries in Temporal Speech Region," *Science*, 161, 1968, 186–187.

26. Larsen, Hoien, Lundberg, and Odegaard, "MRI Evaluation." (Quotation on p. 299.)
    This note of caution is important because there is a precedent of failed reading disabilities research on brain symmetry that used computerized tomography (CT) scans (a method that provides images of the brain by determining the extent to which tissues absorb X-rays). Research using CT scans initially reported finding differences in brain symmetries between reading disabled and normal readers, but later research—some by the original researchers—subsequently criticized the measuring method and rejected the initial findings. See Coles, *The Learning Mystique*, pp. 83–85.)

27. "The division of the anterior from posterior is purely arbitrary and the relation of the posterior superior surface of the superior surface of the temporal lobe to the planum temporale is unknown." (Alexander Kushch, Karen Gross-Glenn, Bonnie Jallad, Herbert Lubs, Mark Rabin, Esther Feldman, and Ranjan Duara, "Temporal Lobe Surface Area Measurements on MRI in Normal and Dyslexic Readers," *Neuropsychologia*, 31, 1993, 811–821. (Quotation on p. 819.) Also see Larsen, Hoien, Lundberg, and Odegaard, "MRI Evaluation."

28. For example, a study by Galaburda and associates posited a relationship between planum size and lateralization for auditory processing. Albert M. Galaburda, Friedrich Sanides, and Norman Geschwind, "Human Brain: Cytoarchitectonic Left-Right Asymmetries in the Temporal Speech Region," *Archives of Neurology*, 35, 1978, 812–817. A subsequent review of the research—one that used the rear areas of the planum temporale as part of its measurements—questioned how the reported asymmetry could have been found in the Galaburda study. Helmuth Steinmetz, Jorg Rademacher, Lutz Jancke, Yanxiong Huang, Armin Thron, and Karl Zillis, "Total Surface of Temporoparietal Intrasylvian Cortex: Diverging Left-Right Asymmetries," *Brain and Language*, 39, 1990, 357–372. Another study, with its own definition of the planum temporale, not only found no correlation between the degree of anatomical asymmetry of the planum temporale and asymmetry of auditory functioning; it also concluded that the "language-related superior temporal cortex [where the planum temporale is] may not form an integral part of the anatomo-functional system subserving auditory lateralization."

Lutz Jancke and Helmuth Steinmetz, "Auditory Lateralization and Planum Temporale Asymmetry," *NeuroReport*, 5, 1993, 169–172.

29. Robert T. Schultz, Nam K. Cho, Lawrence H. Staib, Leon E. Kier, Jack M. Fletcher, Sally E. Shaywitz, Donald P. Shankweiler, Len Katz, John C. Gore, James S. Duncan, and Bennett A. Shaywitz, "Brain Morphology in Normal and Dyslexic Children: The Influence of Sex and Age," *Annals of Neurology*, 35, June 1994, 732–742. (Quotation on p. 741.)

30. Sandra Smith, "Family Patterns of Learning Disabilities," *Annals of Dyslexia*, 42, 1992, 143–158. (Quotation on p. 152.)
    This conclusion is contradicted by Coles, *The Learning Mystique*, Chapter 6.

31. Coles, *The Learning Mystique*. (See pp. 115–117.)

32. J. C. DeFries, Jacquelyn J. Gillis, and Sally J. Wadsworth, "Genes and Genders: A Twin Study of Reading Disability," in Albert M. Galaburda (ed.), *Dyslexia and Development: Neurobiological Aspects of Extra-ordinary Brains* (Cambridge, Mass.: Harvard University Press, 1993), pp. 187–204.

33. Lon R. Cardon, Shelley D. Smith, David W. Fulker, William J. Kimberling, Bruce F. Pennington, and John C. DeFries, "Quantitative Trait Locus for Reading Disability on Chromosome 6," *Science*, 268, June 1995, 276–279.

34. Billy Tashman, "Misreading Dyslexia," *Scientific American*, 273, August 1995, 14–15. (Quotation on p. 14.)

35. Shaywitz, "Dyslexia." (Quotation on p. 104.)

36. Dorothy Nelkin and Susan Lindee observe that explanations of inherent problems in individuals justify social policy predicated on the view that changing "social environment" and government resources can "only do so much." (Dorothy Nelkin and M. Susan Lindee, *The DNA Mystique: The Gene as a Cultural Icon* (New York: W. H. Freeman, 1995). (Quotation on p. 129.)

8. MONEY, POLITICS, AND LEARNING TO READ

1. John H. Franklin, *From Slavery to Freedom: A History of Negro Americans* (New York: Random House, 1969).

2. David B. Tyack, *The One Best System: A History of American Urban Education* (Cambridge, Mass.: Harvard University Press, 1974). (See pp. 228–229.)

3. Carl F. Kaestle, *Pillars of the Republic: Common School and American Society, 1780–1860* (New York: Hill and Wang, 1983). (Quotation on p. 107.) Also see Lawrence A. Cremin, *The American Common School* (New York: Knopf, 1951); Merle Curti, *The Social Ideas of American Educators* (New York: Charles Scribner's Sons, 1935), Chapter 3.

4. Ira Katznelson and Margaret Weir, *Schooling for All: Class, Race, and the Decline of the Democratic Ideal* (Berkeley: University of California Press, 1985). (Quotation on p. 70.)

5. Frank T. Carlton, *Economic Influences upon Educational Progress in the United States, 1820–1850* (New York: Teachers College Press, 1965), pp. 93–94. (Quotation on pp. 93–94.)

6. Classroom teachers had to deal not only with large numbers of students but with a diversity of ages and educational abilities, an insufficient array of instructional materials, and a high portion of youngsters who were bored and/or irritable. In the words of one former teacher, children were "roguish," "restless," and "turbulent." Under these conditions, poorly prepared and poorly paid teachers were faced with the challenge of keeping order and at the same time teaching something. Barbara Finkelstein, *Governing the Young: Teacher Behavior in Popular Primary Schools in 19th Century United States* (New York: Falmer Press, 1989). (See Chapters 1, 3, 5.)

7. Michael B. Katz, "The 'New Departure' in Quincy, 1873–1881: The Nature of Nineteenth Century Educational Reform," *New England Quarterly*, 40, March 1967, 3–30. (Quotation on p. 11.)

8. Katz, "The 'New Departure.'" (Quotation on p. 1.)

9. Approximately 39 percent of teachers were women in 1840; the figure was 46 percent by 1850, and approximately 60 percent by 1870. See Michael W. Apple, *Teachers and Texts: A Political Economy of Class and Gender Relations in Education* (New York: Routledge and Kegan Paul, 1986), pp. 60–61.

10. "Females are not only adapted, but carefully trained, to fill such positions, as well, or better than men, excepting the master's place, which sometimes requires a man's force; and the competition is so great, that their services command less than one-half the wages of male teachers." Report of the School Committee of the Town of Quincy for the School Year 1872–73 (Boston, 1873), pp. 5–6. (Quoted in Katz, "The 'New Departure,'" p. 12.)

11. Katz, "The 'New Departure.'" (Quotation on p. 25.)

12. The board was ruled by business leaders, even though the growing community of quarry workers (mostly Irish) was vying for representation on the board.

13. Katz, "The 'New Departure.'" (Quotation on p. 14.)

14. Jack K. Campbell, *Colonel Francis W. Parker: The Children's Crusader* (New York: Teachers College Press, 1965). (Quotation on p. 91.)

15. "School Spending, Performance Not Linked, Report Concludes," *Education Week*, September 15, 1993.

16. Eric A. Hanushek, *Making Schools Work: Improving Performance and Controlling Costs* (Washington, D.C.: Brookings Institution, 1994). (Quotation on p. 25.)

17. Eric A. Hanushek, "School Resources and Student Performance," in Gary Burtless (ed.), *Does Money Matter?: The Effect of School Resources on Student Achievement and Adult Success* (Washington, D.C.: Brookings Institution, 1996). (Quotation on p. 68.)

18. "Saving Our Schools," *Business Week*, September 14, 1992, pp. 70–78.

19. Jeanne Allen (ed.), *Can Business Save Education?: Strategies for the 1990s* (Washington, D.C.: Heritage Foundation, 1989).

20. Larry V. Hedges, Richard D. Laine, and Rob Greenwald, "Does Money Matter? A Meta-analysis of Studies of the Effects of Differential School Inputs on Student Outcomes," *Educational Researcher*, 23, April 1994, 5–14; Rob Greenwald, Larry V. Hedges, and Richard D. Laine, "The Effect of School

Resources on Student Achievement," *Review of Educational Research*, 66, Fall 1996, 361–396; Larry V. Hedges and Rob Greenwald, "Have Times Changed the Relation Between School Resources and Student Performance?" in Burtless (ed.), *Does Money Matter?*, pp. 43–92.

21. Hedges and Greenwald, "Have Times Changed . . . ?" (Quotation on p. 90.)
22. Hedges, Laine and Greenwald, "Does Money Matter?" (Quotation on pp. 10–11.)
23. Hedges and Greenwald, "Have Times Changed . . . ?" (Quotation on p. 80.)
24. Ronald F. Ferguson, "Paying for Public Education: New Evidence on How and Why Money Matters," *Harvard Journal on Legislation*, 28, 1991, pp. 465–498.
25. Ferguson, "Paying for Public Education." (Quotation on p. 488.)

Additional evidence that spending money contributes to academic achievement comes from an analysis of the connection between per-pupil expenditures and scores on the National Assessment of Educational Progress (NAEP). Examining the state test score rankings from the "worst-ranking state" to the "best-ranking state," Howard Wainer showed that a "state's NAEP ranking improves two places for every thousand dollars spent on students." Howard Wainer, "Does Spending Money on Education Help?: A Reaction to the Heritage Foundation and the *Wall Street Journal*," *Educational Researcher*, 22, 1993, 20–24.

The view that school spending influences academic achievement is indirectly reinforced by the correlation of a person's financial "rate of return" with school quality. Using a large sample available from the 1980 census, David Card and Alan Krueger found the earnings of men born between 1930 and 1949 were associated with measures of school quality, including pupil/teacher ratios and teachers' wages. They found that "rates of return are higher for individuals who attended schools with lower pupil/teacher ratios and higher relative teacher salaries." One might assume that the association is illusory, that "family background" actually affected both school quality and earnings. However, by "holding constant school quality measures," the researchers found "no evidence that parental income or education affects" rates of return. Their extensive review of the literature revealed "a high degree of consistency across studies regarding the effect of school quality on students' subsequent earnings." Although rate of return is not identical with measures of academic achievement, financial earnings and academic test scores have been correlated, suggesting that the former achievement is some kind of marker of the latter. "At a minimum," the researchers concluded, "our finding of a positive link between school quality and the economic return to education should give pause to those who argue that investments in the public school system have no benefits for students." David Card and Alan B. Krueger, "Does School Quality Matter? Returns to Education and the Characteristics of Public Schools in the United States," *Journal of Political Economy*, 100, 1992, 1–40; David Card and Alan B. Krueger, "Labor Market Effects of School Quality," in Burtless (ed.), *Does Money Matter?*, pp. 97–140.

26. Richard Rothstein and Karen Hawley Miles, *Where's the Money Gone?: Changes in the Level and Composition of Education Spending* (Washington, D.C.: Economic Policy Institute, 1995).

27. The effect of teacher compensation on student achievement must be considered within the job market for professional work. A comparison of compensation in comparable fields for new college graduates and more experienced teachers shows that "in both 1967 and 1991 teacher entry-level salaries were less than 85% of those for males in comparable professions." For females "the attractiveness of entry-level salaries as teachers has actually diminished because entry-level salaries in other professions for women with a college education have increased more rapidly than those for men since 1967." Thus, if higher salaries attracted more highly qualified graduates to teaching, greater academic gains might be expected. But if other professional salaries grew more, even higher teacher pay would not necessarily be sufficient for hiring high-quality graduates. Rothstein and Miles, *Where's the Money Gone?* (Quotation on pp. 44–45.)

28. Richard Rothstein, "The Myth of Public School Failure," *American Prospect*, Spring 1993, pp. 20–34. (Quotation on p. 240.)

29. Allan Odden, "Class Size and Student Achievement: Research-Based Policy Alternatives," *Educational Evaluation and Policy Analysis*, 12, 1990, 213–227; Ernest L. Boyer, "Early Schooling and the Nation's Future," *Educational Leadership*, 44, 1987, 4–6.

30. Jeremy D. Finn and Charles M. Achilles, "Answers and Questions about Class Size: A Statewide Experiment," *American Educational Research Journal* 27, Fall 1990, 557–577; C. M. Achilles, *Summary of Recent Class-Size Research with an Emphasis on Tennessee's Project STAR and Its Derivative Research Studies* (Nashville, Tenn.: Center of Excellence for Research and Policy on Basic Skills, Tennessee State University, 1995); Helen Pate Bain and C. M. Achilles, "Interesting Developments on Class Size," *Phi Delta Kappan* 67, 1986, 662–665; Elizabeth Ward, Charles M. Achilles, Helen Bain, John Folger, John Johnston, and Nan Lintz, "Project STAR Final Executive Summary, Kindergarten Through Third Grade Results (1985–89)," *Contemporary Education*, 62, 1990, 13–16.

31. Finn and Achilles, "Answers and Questions." (Quotation on p. 574.)

32. Barbara A. Nye, Jayne B. Zaharias, B. DeWayne Fulton, Van A. Cain, C. M. Achilles, and Dana A. Tollett, *The Lasting Benefits Study: Grade 8 Technical Report* (Nashville, Tenn.: Center of Excellence for Research and Policy on Basic Skills, Tennessee State University, 1995). (Quotation on p. 1.)

33. Achilles, *Summary of Recent Class-Size Research.* (Quotation on p. 21.)

34. Barbara A. Nye, Jayne B. Zaharias, Van A. Cain, B. DeWayne Fulton, C. M. Achilles, and Dana A. Tollett, *Project Challenge: Fourth-Year Summary Report* (Nashville, Tenn.: Center of Excellence for Research and Policy on Basic Skills, Tennessee State University, 1994).

35. Helen Bain, Nan Lintz, Elizabeth Word, "A Study of Fifty Effective Teachers Whose Class Average Gain Scores Ranked in the Top 15% of Each of Four School Types in Project STAR," unpublished manuscript.

36. Theodore A. Chandler, "Here's What to Try When You Can't Shrink Class Size Enough to Matter," *American School Board Journal*, 175, 1988, pp. 33–51. (Quotation on p. 33.)

37. Frances B. Cacha, "The Class Size and Achievement Controversy," *Contemporary Education*, 54, 1982, 13–17. (Quotation on p. 16.)

38. Heather Harder, "A Critical Look at Reduced Class Size," *Contemporary Education*, 62, 1990, 28–30. (Quotation on p. 29.)

39. Jonathan Kozol, *Savage Inequalities* (New York: Crown, 1991). (Quotation on p. 78.)

40. Tommy M. Tomlinson, "Class Size and Public Policy: The Plot Thickens," *Contemporary Education*, 62, 1990, 17–23. (Quotation on p. 17.)

41. U.S. Department of Education, *Class Size and Public Policy: Politics and Panaceas* (Washington, D.C.: Office of Education Research and Improvement, 1988). (Quotation on p. 11.)

42. Mark Pitsch, "Education Spending Declined During 80's, Report Says," *Education Week*, June 5, 1991.

43. M. Edith Rasell and Lawrence Mishel, *Shortchanging Education: How U.S. Spending on Grades K–12 Lags Behind Other Industrial Nations* (Washington, D.C.: Economic Policy Institute, 1990); Robert Rothman, "U.S. Not Biggest Spender on Education, Study Finds," *Education Week*, September 30, 1992, pp. 14–15.

44. Drew Lindsay, "States Do Not Spend Enough to Fix, Build Schools, Report Says," *Education Week*, January 10, 1996; Bob Peterson, "School Facilities at Crisis Level," *Rethinking Schools*, Spring 1996, pp. 3–4.

45. Lonnie Harp, "School-Finance Suits Look Beyond Money to Issues of Quality," *Education Week*, June 17, 1992.

46. Iver Peterson, "Whitman Puts Standards above Money for Schools," *New York Times*, January 12, 1996.

47. Peterson, "Whitman Puts Standards above Money for Schools." (Quotation on p. B5.)

48. Caroline Hendrie, "N.J. Finance Law Ties Funding and Standards," *Education Week*, January 15, 1997.

49. Marc L. Miringoff, *Index of Social Health, 1995: Monitoring the Social Well-Being of the Nation* (Tarrytown, N.Y.: Fordham Institute for Innovation in Social Policy, Fordham Graduate Center, 1995).

50. The indifference to millions of children begins before birth: lack of prenatal care for many women results in disabling conditions for 100,000 newborns each year. "Failure to Meet Goals on Infant Health Is Masked by Drop in Mortality Rate," *New York Times*, September 2, 1991.

Around birth, the U.S. infant mortality rate is higher than that of all Western industrialized nations. If the trends in children's health continue on their present paths, the nation will not meet six of the U.S. Surgeon General's eight major goals for maternal and infant health for the year 2000. *The State of America's Children Yearbook, 1996* (Washington, D.C.: Children's Defense Fund, 1996).

51. "U.S. Panel Warns on Child Poverty," *New York Times*, April 27, 1990.

52. "Conditions 'Bleak' for Rural Children, C.D.F. Finds," *Education Week*, January 8, 1992. Rural earnings are three-fourths of urban levels, but welfare payments to rural families under the Aid for Families with Dependent Children program are about half the urban levels.

53. *State of America's Children, 1996.* (Quotation on p. 2.)

54. *State of America's Children, 1996.*

55. Deborah L. Cohen, "Preschool Access Linked to Where a Family Lives," *Education Week*, September 15, 1993.

56. U.S. Department of Education, National Center for Educational Statistics, *Digest of Educational Statistics, 1989* (Washington, D.C.: U.S. Government Printing Office, 1989). (See p. 118.)

57. Poverty increases the likelihood of poor nutrition and ill health. One in eight children in the United States does not obtain enough food due to insufficient economic, family, or community resources. "Hungry households" have insufficient amounts of food about one week a month, and nearly one-third of the households have these shortages every month. Learning is apt to be affected because hungry children are "much more likely" than other children "to suffer from fatigue, frequent headaches, colds, and ear infections, and to need medical attention." "One in Eight Children in Households with Insufficient Food, Study Finds," *Education Week*, April 3, 1991.

In addition to the children classified as "hungry," an "additional one child in eight was found to be 'at risk' of developing a hunger problem." This translates into nearly 5.5 million "hungry" children and about 6 million more at risk of becoming hungry. The health of about 12 million American children is further jeopardized because they have no health insurance and, therefore, do not have decent health care. Lacking health care, these children's health increasingly is in "double jeopardy" because they develop the most health problems. T. Berry Brazelton, "Why Is America Failing Its Children?" *New York Times Magazine*, September 9, 1990.

58. Children's Defense Fund, *Wasting America's Future: The Children's Defense Fund Report on the Costs of Child Poverty* (Boston: Beacon Press, 1994).

The National Association of Education of Young Children (NAEYC, pronounced "nay-see") proposes using money to ensure that all young children have "growth-enhancing environments" that promote literacy. NAEYC advocates policies that will "provide the comprehensive health, education, and social services that families need to support children's development and learning, beginning with prenatal care. Recognizing the need for a comprehensive response to conditions that promote an array of literacy abilities and children's overall development, NAEYC's emphasis is not just on the poor, not only a call for ameliorating some of the worst conditions of poverty. Instead, NAEYC advocates "public policies [that ensure that all] families with young children enjoy economic security and access to basic health care" and "comprehensive social and educational services." Barbara Willer and Sue Bredekamp, "Redefining Readiness: An Essential Requisite for Educational Reform," *Young Children*, 46, July 1990, 22–24.

59. Harvey Kaye attributes the term to Ralph Miliband. Harvey J. Kaye, *Why Do Ruling Classes Fear History?* (New York: St. Martin's Press, 1996). (Quotation on p. 20.)

60. Alonzo B. Anderson and Shelley J. Stokes, "Social and Institutional Influences on the Development and Practice of Literacy," in Hillel Goelman, Antoinette Oberg, and Frank Smith (eds.), *Awakening to Literacy* (Portsmouth, N.H.: Heinemann, 1984), pp. 24–37.

61. Denny Taylor and Catherine Dorsey-Gaines, *Growing Up Literate: Learning from Inner-City Families* (Portsmouth, N.H.: Heinemann, 1988). (Quotation on p. 198.)

62. Taylor and Dorsey-Gaines, *Growing Up Literate*. (Quotation on p. 81.)

63. Marie M. Clay, *Becoming Literate: The Construction of Inner Control* (Portsmouth, N.H.: Heinemann, 1991). (Quotation on p. 93.)

64. Catherine E. Snow, Wendy S. Barnes, Jean Chandler, Irene F. Goodman, and Lowry Hemphill, *Unfulfilled Expectations: Home and School Influences on Literacy* (Cambridge, Mass.: Harvard University Press, 1991). (Quotation on pp. 2–4.)

65. Reginald M. Clark, *Family Life and School Achievement: Why Poor Black Children Succeed or Fail* (Chicago: University of Chicago Press, 1983). (Quotation on p. 144.)

66. Keith Bradsher, "Gap in Wealth in U.S. Called Widest in West," *New York Times*, April 17, 1995.

67. Louis Uchitelle, "Trapped in the Impoverished Middle Class," *New York Times*, November 17, 1991.

68. Donald L. Bartlett and James Steele, *America: What Went Wrong?* (Kansas City: Andrews & McMeel, 1992), Chapter 1.

The ascending shift of money has been helped by a sharp increase in recent years — 50 percent since the early 1980s — "in the percentage of people who work full-time but cannot by themselves lift a family out of poverty." Even a college education did not necessarily prevent falling into these circumstances: although those without a college degree were more likely to be earning less than the poverty level for a family of four, 3 percent of those with bachelor's degrees or more were at a below-poverty level in 1979, and the figure rose to 6 percent in 1994. Jason DeParle, "Sharp Increase Along the Borders of Poverty," *New York Times*, March 31, 1994.

Deteriorating conditions for working Americans have also been propelled by an erosion of the full-time (forty-hour) workweek, as more companies increase their profits by building their workforce around part-time workers who are paid less and get fewer (if any) benefits than do full-time employees. In the last twenty years, the number of involuntary part-timers — those who want full-time work but cannot get it—rose 121 percent to 4.9 million. "Part-Time Hirings Bring Deep Change in U.S. Workplaces," *New York Times*, June 17, 1991.

69. Lawrence Mishel and Jared Bernstein, *The State of Working America, 1994–1995* (Armonk, N.Y.: Economic Policy Institute, M. E. Sharpe, 1994). (Quotation on p. 2.)

    The lowest-earning 20 percent of Americans earned only 5.7 percent of income paid to individuals.

70. Lester C. Thurow, "Companies Merge; Families Break Up," *New York Times*, September 3, 1995.

71. "The Tax Swindle," *1199 News*, January–February 1991, p. 8.

72. "The Uses of Crisis," *Left Business Observer*, June 3, 1991, pp. 1–7. (Quotation on p. 7.)

73. Daniel D. Huff and David A. Johnson, "Phantom Welfare: Public Relief for Corporate America," *Social Work*, 38, 1993, 311–316.

74. "The 1997 Military Budget: A Ticking Time Bomb," *Defense Monitor*, 25, April–May 1996.

    When considering what portion of the federal budget should be designated military spending, Social Security should not be considered part of the income tax budget (and only in recent years has it been) because it is a disbursement fund that simply returns funds paid in. Thus, military spending, said to be approximately 30 percent of the federal budget, should more accurately be put at about 63 percent.

75. Seymour Melman, *The Permanent War Economy* (New York: Simon & Schuster, 1985).

76. "U.S. Survey Finds Serious Lack of Literacy Skills," *Reading Today*, 11, October–November 1993, 1–18. (Quotation on p. 1.)

77. National Center for Education Statistics, *Adult Literacy in America: A First Look at the Results of the National Adult Literacy Survey* (Washington, D.C.: U.S. Government Printing Office, 1993). (Quotation on p. 4.)

78. Bob Herbert, "A Job Myth Downsized," *New York Times*, March 8, 1996.

79. Mishel and Bernstein, *The State of Working America*. (Quotation on p. 5.)

80. Louis Uchitelel and N. R. Kleinfield, "The Price of Jobs Lost," in *New York Times, The Downsizing of America* (New York: Times Books, 1996). (Quotations on p. 4.)

    Although there has been a net increase of 27 million jobs since 1979, only about 35 percent of those who lose their jobs obtain jobs equally remunerative or better-paying.

81. Lawrence Mishel and Ruy A. Teixeira, *The Myth of the Coming Labor Shortage* (Washington, D.C.: Economic Policy Institute, 1991).

82. "Some Economists Challenge View that Schools Hurt Competitiveness," *Education Week*, November 13, 1991.

83. Peter T. Kilborn, "College Seniors Find More Jobs But Modest Pay," *New York Times*, May 1, 1994.

In 1991, 16 percent of male and 26 percent of female college graduates (those without postcollege degrees) between the ages of twenty-five and thirty-four worked at some time during the year but earned less than the poverty line for a family of four ($13,924). See Sheldon Danziger and Peter Gottschalk, *America Unequal* (Cambridge, Mass.: Harvard University Press, 1995).

84. From *Monthly Labor Review*, November 1995, cited in "Work and Its Future," *Left Business Observer*, April 3, 1996, pp. 1–2.

The divisions apparent in these top projected growth occupations coincide with an analysis that found that "low-level service industry work grew more quickly than high-skilled" jobs. The change from old to "new" jobs is evidence that the United States is becoming a country producing more jobs requiring fewer skills, and the employers of these jobs choose not to pay salaries that can support a family above the poverty level. William Serrin, "A Great American Job Machine?" *Nation*, September 18, 1991, pp. 269–272.

85. Scott Nearing and Joseph Freeman, *Dollar Diplomacy* (New York: Monthly Review Press, 1969 [1925]).

86. Robert Reich, *The Work of Nations* (New York: Knopf, 1991). (Quotation on p. 6.)

87. Louis Uchitelle, "U.S. Businesses Loosen Link to Mother Country," *New York Times*, May 21, 1991.

88. Robert Reich, "Who Champions the Working Class?" *New York Times*, May 26, 1991.

89. Arthur MacEwan, "Why the Emperor Can't Afford New Clothes: International Change and Fiscal Disorder in the United States," *Monthly Review*, July–August 1991, pp. 85–98. (Quotation on p. 85.)

90. Sidney M. Willhelm, *Who Needs the Negro?* (Cambridge, Mass.: Schenkman, 1970). (Quotation on p. 151.)

91. Uchitelle, "U.S. Businesses Loosen Link."

CONCLUSION: CHANGING THE LITERACY DEBATE

1. "Compelling Questions in Reading Education," *Reading Today*, 12, January 1995, 1–10.

2. James Collins, "How Johnny Should Read," *Time*, October 27, 1997, pp. 78–81. (Quotation on pp. 78, 81.)

3. Thomas Toch, "The Reading Wars Continue," *U.S. News & World Report*, October 27, 1997, p. 77.

4. Nicholas Lemann, "The Reading Wars," *Atlantic Monthly*, November 1997, pp. 128–134. (Quotation on p. 134.)

5. Pat Wingert and Barbara Kantrowitz, "Why Andy Couldn't Read," *Newsweek*, October 27, 1997, pp. 56–64. (Quotation on p. 60.)

6. The bill passed in the House by a voice vote on November 8, 1997.

7. Robert W. Sweet, Jr., "The Reading Excellence Act of 1997," *Right to Read Report*, 3, November 1997, 1–3. (Quotation on p. 1.)

8. See, for example, Jane Braunger and Jan P. Lewis, *Building a Knowledge Base in Reading* (Portland, Ore.: Northwest Regional Educational Laboratory, 1997).
9. Gerald Coles, *The Learning Mystique: A Critical Look at "Learning Disabilities"* (New York: Pantheon, 1987).
10. See Luis C. Moll (ed.), *Vygotsky and Education: Instructional Implications and Applications of Sociohistorical Psychology* (New York: Cambridge University Press, 1990).

INDEX

Printed in the USA
CPSIA information can be obtained
at www.ICGtesting.com
LVHW091132150724
785511LV00001B/102